Urban Transformations

Economic restructuring and demographic change have in recent years placed much strain on urban areas with the effects falling disproportionately on neighbourhoods that were previously underpinned by industry and manufacturing. This has presented policymakers and city planners with a binary choice: to resist change and stagnate or to change and attempt to keep up with the pace of global demand. This edited book tells the story of how urban transformation impacts on people's lives and everyday interactions – to question where and to whom benefit accrues from these changes.

Urban Transformations offers insight into both risk and reward as local communities and public authorities creatively address the challenge of building vital and sustainable urban environments. The authors in this edited collection argue that understanding the specifics of community, space and place is crucial to delivering insights into how, where, when, why and *for whom* urban areas might successfully transform. The chapters investigate urban change using a range of approaches and case studies – from the United States to Iran; from the United Kingdom to Canada. The varying scales at which governance or regeneration initiatives operate, the nature and composition of urban communities, and the local or global interests of different private sector actors all raise questions for urban policy and practice. It is important to not only consider the drivers of regeneration, but its beneficiaries need to be identified.

This edited volume addresses and elaborates on critical issues facing urban transformation and renewal as a basis for future discussion on strategies for 'successful' urban transformation.

Nicholas Wise is a Senior Lecturer in the Faculty of Education, Health and Community at Liverpool John Moores University, UK.

Julie Clark is a Lecturer in Sociology and Social Policy at the University of the West of Scotland, UK, specializing in urban policy.

Regions and Cities

Acting Series Editor in Chief
Ron Martin, *University of Cambridge, UK*

Editors
Maryann Feldman, *University of Georgia, USA*
Gernot Grabher, *HafenCity University Hamburg, Germany*
Kieran P. Donaghy, *Cornell University, USA*

In today's globalized, knowledge-driven and networked world, regions and cities have assumed heightened significance as the interconnected nodes of economic, social and cultural production, and as sites of new modes of economic and territorial governance and policy experimentation. This book series brings together incisive and critically engaged international and interdisciplinary research on this resurgence of regions and cities, and should be of interest to geographers, economists, sociologists, political scientists and cultural scholars, as well as to policymakers involved in regional and urban development.

For more information on the Regional Studies Association, visit www.regionalstudies.org

There is a **30% discount** available to RSA members on books in the *Regions and Cities* series, and other subject related Taylor and Francis books and e-books including Routledge titles. To order just e-mail Georg Wanek, Georg.Wanek@tandf.co.uk, or phone on +44 (0) 207 017 6364 and declare your RSA membership. You can also visit www.routledge.com and use the discount code: **RSA0901**

Urban Transformations

Geographies of Renewal and
Creative Change

**Edited by Nicholas Wise and
Julie Clark**

LONDON AND NEW YORK

First published 2017 by Routledge

2 Park Square, Milton Park, Abingdon, Oxfordshire OX14 4RN
52 Vanderbilt Avenue, New York, NY 10017

Routledge is an imprint of the Taylor & Francis Group, an informa business

First issued in paperback 2019

British Library Cataloguing in Publication Data
A catalogue record for this book is available from the British Library

Library of Congress Cataloging in Publication Data
Names: Wise, Nicholas, 1983- editor. | Clark, Julie, 1965- editor.
Title: Urban transformations : geographies of renewal and creative change /
    edited by Nicholas Wise and Julie Clark.
Description: Abingdon, Oxon ; New York, NY : Routledge, 2017. |
    Includes index.
Identifiers: LCCN 2016058392| ISBN 9781138652095 (hardback) |
    ISBN 9781315624457 (ebook)
Subjects: LCSH: Urban renewal—Social aspects. | City planning—
    Social aspects. | Public spaces. | Community development.
Classification: LCC HT170 .U73 2017 | DDC 307.3/416—dc23
LC record available at https://lccn.loc.gov/2016058392

ISBN: 978-1-138-65209-5 (hbk)
ISBN: 978-0-367-87792-7 (pbk)

Typeset in Times New Roman
by Swales & Willis Ltd, Exeter, Devon, UK

Contents

Figures

Tables

Contributors

Charles Barlow is Lecturer in Public Policy and Geography at the University of Chicago. His scholarly interests lie at the nexus of residential segregation, the politics of neighbourhood transformation, and financial innovation in the housing market.

Mark D. Bjelland is Professor of Geography at Calvin College in Grand Rapids, Michigan. His research focuses on the interrelationships between land use, environmental quality, and social justice. Prior to his academic career, he worked as an environmental consultant on numerous brownfield investigation and remediation projects.

Shauna Brail is Associate Professor, Teaching Stream at the University of Toronto, Urban Studies Program. Her research lies broadly in economic geography with a focus on the social, cultural and economic changes associated with the shifting strengths of cities.

Stephen T. Buckman is an Assistant Professor of Urban Planning in the School of Public Affairs at the University of South Florida. His research is concerned with issues of waterfront development and urban resiliency in relation to both the built form and socioeconomic dynamics.

Julie Clark is a Lecturer in Sociology and Social Policy at the University of the West of Scotland, UK, specializing in urban policy. Prior to her current post, she project managed the award-winning *GoWell East* research programme at the University of Glasgow, evaluating the impacts of regeneration and the Commonwealth Games.

David C. Folch is an Assistant Professor in the Department of Geography at Florida State University. David's research focuses on the data, measures and algorithms that support empirical research and public policy decisions. His work has involved developing improved spatial measures for residential segregation and social vulnerability.

Azadeh Hadizadeh Esfahani is a doctoral candidate in Geography at Clark University. Her interests include urbanization processes in neighbourhoods, place-making and participatory approaches. She has published and presented her work on urban renewal, and her current research focuses on the effects of different policies and activism in Tehran.

Jennifer L. Kitson is an Assistant Professor in the Department of Geography, Planning and Sustainability at Rowan University. She is an urban, cultural geographer interested in sustainable urbanism, historic preservation, the senses and the city, and the study of public life and space.

Rebecca Madgin is Senior Lecturer in Urban Development and Management at the University of Glasgow. Her published and current research explores the economic and emotional values of heritage and their role in urban redevelopment. She is the author of *Heritage, Culture and Conservation: Managing the Urban Renaissance* (2009).

Jennifer Mapes is Assistant Professor of Geography at Kent State University. Her research focuses on social, economic, and environmental change in American small towns.

Ekaterina Mizrokhi is a student at the University of Toronto in Urban Studies, Human Geography and Slavic Studies. Her research interests include combining the three aforementioned areas of study to explore the nature of post-socialist cities and urbanization in the Second World.

Ian Noyes is a graduate in Environmental Studies and Geography from Calvin College. He serves as director of the Big Laurel Learning Center in Kermit, West Virginia. Big Laurel is a non-profit organization that promotes the revitalization of the declining Appalachian Mountain coalfields through education, outreach and land restoration.

Marko Perić is Assistant Professor and Head of the Department of Management at the Faculty of Tourism and Hospitality Management, University of Rijeka. His fields of interest include strategic management, project management and sports management. He has co-authored four books and more than 35 papers on management issues.

Sonia Ralston is a student in the Daniels Faculty of Architecture, Landscape, Design at the University of Toronto majoring in the areas of Architectural and Urban Studies, and a minor in Geography. Her research interests include the architectural history of housing projects as they relate to political theory and activism.

Amie Thurber is currently a doctoral student, and she spent 15 years directing a non-profit training organization addressing racial and social disparities. Her research, practice and teaching interests involve transforming social inequality in neighbourhoods, amplifying resident-led resistance to gentrification, and developing best practices for community-engaged teaching and research.

Ian Riekes Trivers is a PhD candidate in Urban and Regional Planning at the University of Michigan in Ann Arbor. His current research focuses on the movement of ideas and policies in urban planning and design, with a particular interest in urban revitalization and postindustrial/shrinking cities.

Georgiana Varna works for the Scottish Cities Knowledge Centre based at the University of Glasgow and University of St Andrews. She focuses on urban regeneration and public space development in Northern European countries. She looks at urban development networks, urban design and university campuses as inclusive, livable urban quarters.

Nicholas Wise is a human geographer who focuses on sport, events and tourism, looking specifically at social regeneration, sense of place and community. He has conducted research in the Dominican Republic, Croatia and Serbia. His current research focuses on social regeneration linked to community change and local impacts in Croatia.

Zhixi Cecilia Zhuang is an Associate Professor at Ryerson University's School of Urban and Regional Planning. Her current research focuses on emerging suburban ethnic retail landscapes and aims to identify effective place-making practices for municipalities to tackle suburban retrofitting issues.

Foreword

This book presents a collection of papers drawn from four special sessions on urban renewal, which the editors hosted during the 2015 Association of American Geographers (AAG) Annual Meeting held in Chicago, Illinois. Our intention when we organized the sessions was to generate critical discussions by exploring a range of conceptual and methodological issues through the examination of different cases studies. The selection of cases in this edited collection is intended to illuminate the complexity of urban transformation. It includes 12 chapters, dealing with critical urban issues, including the tensions inherent in planning and managing urban change and how policy and practice can creatively contribute to new uses and meanings for communities in transformed spaces and places. The chapters are categorized under three themes, which are further outlined in the introduction: Place and Community; Policy, Practice and Approach; and Re-claiming, Re-using and Re-creating Space.

Urban-themed classes are highly interdisciplinary and widely taught in geography, sociology, planning, urban studies and architecture departments. Our aim in developing this book is to stimulate discussion and encourage debate within the fields of urban geography and urban studies about conditions that critically impact upon change in relation to policy, land use and economic development. Although particularly useful for undergraduate students and emerging scholars wishing to gain a wider understanding and appreciation of international cases and approaches, we believe that the focus on urban transformation, renewal and creative change will also be of interest to established academics writing in these fields. In addition, the range of cases explored will be relevant to those with an interest in the cognate domains of comparative policy and planning, as well as many policymakers and urban practitioners.

We would like to thank and acknowledge Sally Hardy and Daniela Carl from the Regional Studies Association for encouraging us to turn the organized sessions on urban renewal into an edited book collection. We are also grateful to recognize the Urban Geography Specialty Group from the AAG for sponsoring the sessions and the many enthusiastic participants who attended and contributed to discussions. We thank the 19 authors who have contributed to this edited collection for their commitment and dedication. A brief biography of each contributing author can be found at the beginning of the book.

Introduction

Geographies of renewal and creative change: assessing urban transformation

Nicholas Wise and Julie Clark

Critical directions

Processes of urban change are defined and understood differently across and within different geographies. In Europe, policymakers favour the term 'regeneration', whereas in North America, 'renewal', 'redevelopment' or 'revitalization' are commonly used. However, shifting economic conditions, demographic composition and environmental pressures mean that, for most long-established cities, managing urban change is a high-priority issue (Wang et al., 2014). In this book, we use the term 'transformation' in recognition of the agency underpinning urban change: whether driven by local situations, civic agendas, regional influences or national policy, the ongoing processes of unmaking and remaking in our cities necessarily serve or undermine different interest groups. Although economic growth, environmentally sustainable development and social justice might be broadly accepted as the ideal goals of urban planning (Bramley et al., 2004), there is no easy synergy between those objectives. As academics engaged with urban and social geography, it is our role to tell the story of how urban transformation impacts on people's lives and everyday interactions – to question where and to whom benefit accrues from these changes. The purpose of this book, therefore, is to critically assess the theory and practice of urban transformation in different geographic and socio-political contexts and, in doing so, offer insight into both risk and reward as local communities and public authorities creatively address the challenge of building vital and sustainable urban environments.

Contemporary interventions, designed to achieve urban transformation, can be considered as a subset within the long trajectory of forces driving urban morphology (see Bosselmann, 2009; Hénaff, 2016). The process of urbanization is accompanied by multiple political, economic and social drivers encouraging local government, private investors and reformers to promote and implement change in our cities (Harvey, 2000). Externally, wider economic trends, political shifts and cultural influences impact upon the structure and composition of urban areas (Lai, 2012; Leary-Owhin, 2016; MacLaran & Kelly, 2014) leaving a legacy unsuited to those who lack the economic means and purchasing power. Considering the North American and European context, the late 1960s were influenced by the Keynesian political economy, while deindustrialization and economic restructuring from the mid-1970s to the 1990s saw a turn to consumption-based economic strategy, with the proliferation of neoliberalism as the dominant paradigm (Bentley, 2002; Harvey, 2005; Leary-Owhin, 2016). Historically, physical renovation, particularly with regard to housing, has been the focus of urban renewal though economic restructuring, recession and, most recently, the global financial crisis, provide a critical impetus for wider action because 'corporations don't seem to need cities or particular communities any more' (Harvey, 2000, p. 13). Within this context, city planners, policymakers and government officials may perceive a binary choice: to change and attempt to keep up with the pace of global demand, or to resist change and stagnate (Richards & Palmer, 2010). However, this apparent dichotomy has been fractured as local communities, policymakers and scholars find new ways of understanding or effecting urban transformations.

Although this book functions as an exploration of creative change – innovative ways of managing or adapting to contemporary urban challenges – the term 'creative' does not necessarily imply a beneficial outcome for all concerned. Creative change can be perceived as tangible or conceptual. Cities continually seek creative alternatives in contemporary times, even if the proposed or ongoing change is similar to developments we have seen over the last several decades. Creative change can relate to community involvement in social housing projects, but this is contested, as we will see in the cases in this book. In times of recession, governments have invested in infrastructure and public realm projects as a means of regenerating urban areas and stimulating development (Altshuler & Luberoff, 2003). Against a backdrop of neoliberalism and market-led urban renewal (MacLaran & Kelly, 2014), more recent development strategies have extended to more creative or innovative investments, in areas such as leisure, culture, heritage and the knowledge economy (see Florida, 2002; Paddison & Miles, 2006; Brinkley, 2008; Hutton, 2009; Clark, 2011; Spirou, 2011; Smith, 2012; Beatley, 2013; Wise, 2016). Markusen (2014) looked at debates around the impacts of creative change, and while existing research and policymaking has focused on diversifying urban economies, more critical questions have been missed. For instance, location is at the forefront of such inquiry as well as how equitable new offerings are in the context of the social and economic fabric of the city. As scholars, we need to question and challenge the mission of change and interrogate how inclusive different actors are in supporting transformation and relevant supporting policies (Markusen, 2014). Such considerations help a wider audience better understand underlying missions and the need to be critical of the actual social and economic implications. Clark's (2011) edited collection examines the role of the entertainment industries, including sport and events, and how these industries are driving change and new developments in urban areas. However, whether for traditional investment projects or newer knowledge and creative economy initiatives, shrinking public sector budgets mean that the private sector has increasingly played a significant role in funding and subsidizing infrastructure and urban amenity development (see Cowan, 2016; Smith, 2012).

The imperative of attracting investment and people to troubled places has resulted in new power divisions, altered consumption patterns and a transformation of the meaning of those places for inhabitants and newcomers alike (Castells, 1996).

As cities around the world develop new spaces and redevelop others, Hénaff (2016) challenges us to better understand the act of building and changing the urban environment. Despite increasingly innovative approaches to place-making as a pathway to economic development and social sustainability (Porter & Shaw, 2009; Munzner & Shaw, 2015), issues of inclusion and exclusion persist, alongside the question of who the beneficiaries of neighbourhood and wider urban change will be. The pressure put on cities, regions and nations from economic shifts and urban change fall disproportionately on already struggling urban areas, particularly those where the social and economic fabric of the area has been previously underpinned by industry. While private investment in urban transformation projects can increase consumption, in many cases it has also resulted in greater economic disparities and increased levels of social exclusion (Mitchell, 2003).

Research into urban transformation has an essential role to play, developing our conceptual understanding of how people, place and policy interact, offering a critical perspective on the social, economic and environmental impacts of change. The work of Lefebvre (1991), exposing the social construction of space, has provided an invaluable framework to articulate and address inequitable power relations; processes of change can be unjust, and not all voices are heard or recognized as valid (Harvey, 2012; Klemek, 2008). Beyond the varied interests and policies that drive urban renewal initiatives, the will to understand the lived experience of urban change is exemplified in Heidegger's (1971) phenomenological approach to analysis. Heidegger (1971) goes beyond interrogating the physical aspects of change to consider who might be the focus of planning, policy and change, and who is overlooked. Leary-Owhin's (2016, p. 328) recent examination of the contribution of community actors and collective political action in the creation of public space offers a counter-strike against 'neoliberal provoked fatalistic pessimism' about the future of our cities. Likewise, the potential, as well as the challenge, of urban transformation has been illuminated by recent critical examinations of the trend of leveraging culture, heritage and the creative industries in service of urban regeneration (see Waitt & Gibson, 2009; Vivant, 2013; Markusen, 2014; Pappalepore et al., 2014; Munzner & Shaw, 2015; Cowan, 2016). Alongside conceptual and empirical analysis of the impacts of urban policy, there is also growing interest in and awareness of the scope of non-health policies to support communities and benefit the well-being of local residents (Hall & Hickman, 2002; Larsen & Hansen, 2008; Clark & Kearns, 2015; Clark et al., 2016; Wise, 2016).

In acknowledging some of the scholarship on which this volume aims to build, we recognize Paddison and Miles (2006) as providing a strong foundation of approaching creative and cultural-led regeneration approaches and strategies. This text contributes contemporary examples and cases, extending the knowledge base further. Tallon's (2013) work focuses on cases from the UK, whereas the edited collection by Madanipour et al. (2013) looks at a range of cases from across Europe. These books build on Bentley's (2002) volume that looked at urban renewal, regeneration and transformations just after the turn of the century, looking beyond physical infrastructural change and urban form to consider perspectives of experience and a range of critical approaches which relate culture, race, gender, socio-economic status and age to policy and politics. There are numerous books that address urban renewal and urban transformation, focusing on one to a few particular case(s) (e.g. Hyra, 2008; Hsing, 2012; MacLaran & Kelly, 2014; Leary-Owhin, 2016). The geographic and holistic focus of this book contributes further critical debates around policy, the changing meanings of urban spaces over time and the range of creative processes. As noted above, it is important to challenge and be critical of how renewal impacts or influences local populations.

The authors in this edited collection argue that understanding the specifics of community, space and place is crucial to delivering insights into how, where, when, why and *for whom* urban areas might successfully transform. Whether though formal administrative boundaries and governance systems or informal sorting mechanisms, which serve to either segregate different groups or bring them together through a shared sense of meaning or identity, spatial factors are at the core of urban life (Soja, 2010; Tuan, 1974). The varying scales at which governance or regeneration initiatives operate, the nature and composition of urban communities, and the local or global interests of different private sector actors all raise questions for urban policy and practice. Not only the drivers of regeneration but its beneficiaries need to be identified. The cost of change for local communities is seldom examined with sufficient rigour. To what extent can local people initiate and direct change within the context of new power structures? Changing urban space and amenities can change perceptions of the area for investors, visitors and, most importantly, for the people who live there. In times of often rapid change, sustaining community and social identities can be problematic. This edited volume is intended to address and elaborate on such questions, offering a base for future discussion of urban transformation. In seeking strategies for 'successful' urban transformation, the authors of this collection examine stories of change in the 12 chapters. The chapters investigate urban change using a range of approaches and conceptual stances related to critical challenges specific to each case, and consider the pressing issues facing place, policy and practice.

An outline of the book

Each chapter of the book explores the diverse ways in which urban transformation has impacted people and place within different contexts. The volume is organized in such a manner as to tell the story of urban transformation and renewal. Some chapters place greater weight on historical context in order to understand the dynamics drive contemporary, the demands, needs and rationales underlying change. Examinations of policy and community participation are used to question the extent to which renewal can be inclusive, as authors debate the impacts of neoliberalism and the creative destruction of capitalism. Within these chapters, a range of methods and conceptual approaches are used to explore issues including social activism, community engagement, the meaning of place, economic development, policy transfer, impacts of new housing, reclamation and adaptive reuse.

The first chapter, by **Julie Clark** and **Rebecca Madgin**, explores the involvement of artists and other creative actors in the intensive regeneration of Glasgow's post-industrial East End. An analysis of how artists envision their role within this contested process of transformation demonstrates the ways in which the work of an artist is conditioned by a variety of different pressures and urban agendas both *before* and *during* the delivery process. In so doing, the chapter explores how tensions within this process enshrine a particular view of an area's past and future heritages, revealing both successes and sanitization, as the artists seek to manage the tensions between the intrinsic and the instrumental functions of public art. The first two chapters take us from the past to the present. In Chapter 2, **Ian Trivers** discusses 'Regeneration in Motion', concerned with New York City's High Line as a travelling urban imaginary. This chapter connects impressions of re-claimed space across time, through which he refers to networks of discursive exchange. He notes that the project in New York City has inspired similar projects elsewhere around the world. **Mark D. Bjelland** and **Ian Noyes** investigate brownfield redevelopment in Michigan in Chapter 3, by analysing impacts using a neoliberal framework that emphasizes market-based solutions. This chapter continues the focus of the early chapters in this book by framing an industrial past alongside present renewal and redevelopment. Michigan is in the heart of the United States manufacturing belt and much of the focus on revitalization in the state's urban areas (such as Detroit and Flint) focuses on cleaning up former industrial 'brownfield' sites – which the state subsidizes. Because their study compares the projected need for brownfield site clean-ups to the actual distribution of public funds, **Bjelland** and **Noyes** argue that a neoliberal framework for brownfield redevelopment has not been successful in addressing the needs of the most distressed communities. Chapter 4 presents another case in the United States Midwest, and offers insight on downtown transformation, narrowing the scope and scale of research. **Jennifer Mapes** looks at planning, politics and change in Kent, Ohio's new downtown. The transformation of downtown Kent resulted in more than half of the city being renewed, and this chapter presents narratives of revitalization from the perspective of local politicians, city planners and Kent State University administrators.

Chapter 5 shifts the focus in this book towards more conceptual approaches to place. **Jennifer L. Kitson, Stephen T. Buckman** and **David C. Folch** look at amenity driven high density development. While **Bjelland** and **Noyes** in Chapter 3 and **Mapes** in Chapter 4 look at cases in Michigan and Ohio, respectively, both former production and manufacturing states that have seen significant decline in recent decades, **Kitson, Buckman** and **Folch** focus on greater Phoenix, Arizona, a city in a state that has seen much growth in recent decades. Their chapter proposes a conceptual framework for directing compact urban form in polycentric cities beyond the light rail station in Phoenix. They discuss amenity driven high density development, based on urban amenities, rather than transit, as the starting point for the pursuit of density. Moreover, the authors argue change is based on the importance of place as a critical component of the urban amenity concept, and draw on lessons learnt from three separate land-use zoning strategies in Phoenix.

The next two chapters delve into discussions of place-making. **Zhixi Cecilia Zhuang**, in her case on Toronto in Chapter 6, examines place-making and community from the perspective of ethnic retailing across five municipalities in Toronto's metropolitan area. She investigates over 100 suburban Chinese and South Asian retail clusters (which include around 3,800 businesses). Her work is concerned with the transformation of ethnic retail units over time and the analysis and images included show landscapes which reinforce a sense of place and expressions of community ethnicity. Continuing discussions of place-making, **Georgiana Varna** also offers subsequent critical insight by introducing discussions of place-breaking in Chapter 7. **Varna's** focus on community building is based on a consideration of the intentions of local planners followed by critique. Varna looks at three cases of waterfront regeneration in Glasgow (Pacific Quay, Glasgow Harbour and Broomielaw). She is also concerned with change over time, identifying key moments and decisions which have ultimately contributed to place-breaking in Glasgow, and offers a discussion on the city's desire to plan for an inclusive, vibrant and liveable city in communities along the waterfront (the River Clyde).

Chapter 8 acts as another transitional point in this book, with the following chapters focusing on public housing and residential redevelopment. **Azadeh Hadizadeh Esfahani** extends **Varna's** discussion of place-breaking from a different perspective. Her chapter on Tehran, Iran provides a typology of displacement, and the opportunities for identity-building, which is critiqued in her discussions of displacement. She discusses displacement as the spatial and physical relocation of residents, but is interested in uncovering the social dimensions of displacement relating to place, identity and community. **Hadizadeh Esfahani** employs an emergentist relational approach to argue that the renewal process should be intertwined with place-making which have potential to create new identities and stronger meanings pertinent to sense of place meanings. In Chapter 9, **Charles Barlow** looks at urban policy and the uneven geographies of housing in mixed-income neighbourhoods. Using an ethnographic approach in Chicago's Oakland community, **Barlow** is concerned with how struggles are manifested in public spaces, and how the right to the city is influenced by policy and practice that includes or excludes residents based on privileges that are usually only extended to the wealthy through innovation in the housing market. Chapter 10 continues this focus on public housing by looking at the case of Toronto's Regent Park, which received a $1 billion transformation in 2005. It is considered the largest public housing neighbourhood in Canada and its transformation changed the community from one that was once a lower-income community to a mixed-income community. From a community perspective, **Shauna Brail**,

Ekaterina Mizrokhi and **Sonia Ralston** discuss how transforming Regent Park focused on improving the quality of housing and quality of life for residents and reinforces the critical discussions of place in previous chapters.

Chapters 8, 9 and 10 focused on contested issues surrounding public housing and public spaces in three countries: **Amie Thurber** also looks at public housing and neighbourhood inequality, but takes a step back and reflects on the process of research in this area in Chapter 11. **Thurber's** work in Nashville, Tennessee raises critical and theoretical points that relate to a number of chapters in this collection. She discusses her engagement with theory to discuss urban change, policy and practice in her research on James Cayce Homes (a public housing project). Her chapter shares a narrative of urban transformation based on her role and experience conducting research. She reflects on her study by discussing how structural, social-process and post-structural approaches and understandings both reveal and obstruct people's lived experiences and offers insight on her fieldwork and involvement in research. Thurber's chapter on neighbourhood inequality puts emphasis on the need to address local and community impact in our research. The following chapter by **Nicholas Wise** and **Marko Perić**, Chapter 12, outlines a research agenda to assess social impacts of sports tourism regeneration in the Istria Region of Croatia. Chapters 11 and 12 conclude this collection by outlining approaches to process. **Wise** and **Perić** have identified a community in Croatia, which has seen extensive physical regeneration. They present a research approach that outlines a longitudinal study to look at social impacts of local community residents. This chapter is also concerned with place and community and identifies 14 social conditions from the social regeneration literature to inform better understanding of local perceptions of transformation. As with Barlow's study (Chapter 9), there is a need to understand how local residents are included or excluded, in this case as a result of sports tourism-led regeneration and upgraded amenities. A brief conclusion identifies some key themes and future directions of research on urban transformation, challenging us to focus on local impacts and local voices.

Urban transformation is fundamentally as much about people as about changing spaces and this edited collection seeks new understandings by incorporating knowledge from both similar and vastly different international cases. Geographers are especially concerned with understanding how processes are structured based on who is impacted and who benefits (Smith, 1990; Swyngedouw, 1997; Herod, 2011), addressing and critiquing political and economic complexities of power, control and hierarchy (see Delaney & Leitner, 1997; Gibson-Graham, 2002). This collection presents a number of debates concerning scale by highlighting how renewal results in noticeable spatial divisions. Smith (2000, p. 724) acknowledges scale as 'one or more levels of representation, experience, and organisation of geographical events and processes'. When we consider the geographies of urban renewal, we are looking how space and place are being transformed by the exercise of power, examining impacts sometimes on an entire city, an area of a city, or at the level of a particular neighbourhood.

This book now turns to the 12 cases which take us through reflections of the past to critical contemporary challenges and directions for future research. Each chapter investigates urban transformation and renewal, offering a different perspective on creative change; collectively, these represent some of the most critical challenges confronting place, policy and practice.

References

Altshuler, A. A., & Luberoff, D. (2003). *Mega-projects: The changing politics of urban public investment.* Washington, DC: Brookings Institution Press.

Beatley, T. (2013). Planning for sustainability in European cities: A review of practice in leading cities. In M. Larice & E. Macdonald (Eds.), *The urban design reader* (pp. 558–568). London: Routledge.

Bentley, I. (2002). *Urban transformations: Power, people and urban design.* London: Routledge.

Bosselmann, P. (2009). *Urban transformation: Understanding city design and form.* Washington, DC: Island Press.

Bramley, G., Munro, M., & Pawson, H. (2004). *Key issues in housing: Markets and policies in 21st century Britain.* Basingstoke: Palgrave Macmillan.

Brinkley, I. (2008). *The knowledge economy: How knowledge is reshaping the economic life of nations.* London: The Work Foundation.

Castells, M. (1996). *The rise of the network society.* Oxford: Blackwell.

Clark, J., & Kearns, A. (2015). Pathways to physical activity legacy: Assessing the regeneration potential of multi-sport events using a prospective approach. *Local Economy, 30,* 888–909.

Clark, J., Kearns, A., & Cleland, C. (2016). Spatial scale, time and process in mega-events: The complexity of host community perspectives on neighbourhood change. *Cities, 53,* 87–97.

Clark, T. N. (Ed.). (2011). *The city as an entertainment machine.* New York: Rowman & Littlefield.

Cowan, A. (2016). *A nice place to visit: Tourism and urban revitalization in the postwar rustbelt.* Philadelphia, PA: Temple University Press.

Delaney, D., & Leitner, H. (1997). The political construction of scale. *Political Geography, 16,* 93–97.

Florida, R. (2002). *The rise of the creative class: And how it's transforming work, leisure and everyday life.* New York: Basic Books.

Gibson-Graham, J. K. (2002). Beyond global vs. local: Economic politics outside the binary frame. In A. Herod & M. Wright (Eds.), *Geographies of power: Placing scale* (pp. 25–60). Oxford: Blackwell.

Hall, S., & Hickman, P. (2002). Neighbourhood renewal and urban policy: A comparison of new approaches in England and France. *Regional Studies, 36,* 691–696.

Harvey, D. (2000). *Megacities lecture 4: Possible urban worlds.* Amersfoort, The Netherlands: Twynstra Gudde Management Consultants.

Harvey, D. (2005). *A brief history of neoliberalism.* Oxford: Oxford University Press.

Harvey, D. (2012). *Rebel cities: From the right to the city to the urban revolution.* New York: Verso Books.

Heidegger, M. (1971). Building, dwelling and thinking. In *Poetry, language, thought* (trans. Albert Hofstadter). New York: Harper Colophon Books.

Hénaff, M. (2016). *The city in the making* (trans. Anne-Marie Feenberg-Dibon). London: Rowan and Littlefield International.

Herod, A. (2011). *Scale*. London: Routledge.

Hsing, Y-T. (2012). *The great urban transformation: Politics of land and property in China*. Oxford: Oxford University Press.

Hutton, T. A. (2009). *The new economy of the inner city: Restructuring, regeneration and dislocation in the 21st century metropolis*. London: Routledge.

Hyra, D. S. (2008). *The new urban renewal: The economic transformation of Harlem and Bronzeville*. Chicago, IL: University of Chicago Press.

Klemek, C. (2008). From political outsider to power broker in two 'Great American Cities': Jane Jacobs and the fall of the urban renewal order in New York and Toronto. *Journal of Urban History*, *34*, 309–332.

Lai, C. (2012). The racial triangulation of space: The case of urban renewal in San Francisco's Fillmore District. *Annals of the Association of American Geographers*, *102*, 151–170.

Larsen, H. G., & Hansen, A. L. (2008). Gentrification – gentle or traumatic? Urban renewal policies and socioeconomic transformations in Copenhagen. *Urban Studies*, *45*, 2429–2448.

Leary-Owhin, M. E. (2016). *Exploring the production of urban space: Differential space in three post-industrial cities*. Bristol: Policy Press.

Lefebvre, H. (1991). *The production of space* (trans. Donald Nicholson-Smith). Oxford: Blackwell.

MacLaran, A., & Kelly, S. (2014). *Neoliberal urban policy and the transformation of the city: Reshaping Dublin*. Basingstoke: Palgrave Macmillan.

Madanipour, A., Knierbein, S., & Degros, A. (Eds.). (2013). *Public space and the challenges of urban transformation in Europe*. London: Routledge.

Markusen, A. (2014). Creative cities: A 10-year research agenda. *Journal of Urban Affairs*, *36*, 567–589.

Mitchell, D. (2003). *The right to the city: Social justice and the fight for public space*. New York: Guilford Press.

Munzner, K., & Shaw, K. (2015). Renew who? Benefits and beneficiaries of *Renew Newcastle*. *Urban Policy and Research*, *33*, 17–36.

Paddison, R., & Miles, S. (2006). *Culture-led urban regeneration*. London: Routledge.

Pappalepore, I., Maitland, R., & Smith, A. (2014). Prosuming creative urban areas: Evidence from East London. *Annals of Tourism Research*, *44*, 227–240.

Porter, L., & Shaw, K. (2009). *Whose urban renaissance? An international comparison of urban regeneration strategies*. London: Routledge.

Richards, G., & Palmer, R. (2010). *Eventful cities: Cultural management and urban revitalisation*. London: Elsevier.

Smith, A. (2012). *Events and urban regeneration: The strategic use of events to revitalise cities*. London: Routledge.

Smith, N. (1990). *Uneven development: Nature, capital and the production of space*. Oxford: Blackwell.

Smith, N. (2000). Scale. In R. Johnston, D. Gregory, G. Pratt, & M. Watts (Eds.), *The dictionary of human geography* (pp. 724–727). Oxford: Blackwell.

Soja, E. (2010). *Seeking spatial justice*. Minneapolis: University of Minnesota Press.

Spirou, C. (2011). *Urban tourism and urban change: Cities in a global economy*. London: Routledge.

Swyngedouw, E. (1997). Excluding the other: The production of scale and scaled politics. In R. Lee & J. Wills (Eds.), *Geographies of economies* (pp. 167–176). London: Arnold.

Tallon, A. (2013). *Urban regeneration in the UK*. London: Routledge.

Tuan, Y. (1974). Space and place: Humanistic perspective. *Progress in Geography, 6*, 211–252.

Vivant, E. (2013). Creatives in the city: Urban contradictions of the creative city. *City, Culture and Society, 4*, 57–63.

Waitt, G., & Gibson, C. (2009). Creative small cities: Rethinking the creative economy in place. *Urban Studies, 46*, 1223–1246.

Wang, H., Shen, Q., Tang, B-S., Lu, C., Peng, Y., & Tang, L. (2004). A framework of decision-making factors and supporting information for facilitating sustainable site planning in urban renewal projects. *Cities, 40*, 44–55.

Wise, N. (2016). Outlining triple bottom line contexts in urban tourism regeneration. *Cities, 53*, 30–34.

1 Writing the past into the fabric of the present

Urban regeneration in Glasgow's East End

Julie Clark and Rebecca Madgin

Introduction

According to Butler (2003, p. 83):

> Developers to park wardens are turning to the arts for new ideas, regeneration, problem solving and community bridge building. The employment of artists in these (traditionally non-cultural) fields, where there are non-art issues and agendas at stake, is becoming the norm.

It has become a truism that urban regeneration should be a holistic practice, going beyond the demolition and rebuilding of the fabric of the city to incorporate at least an awareness of soft infrastructure – attending to the human dimensions of social, economic and environmental conditions (Landry & Bianchini, 1995; Urban Task Force, 2005). The patterning of deprivation at neighbourhood level is often a product of housing markets and employment opportunities, reinforced by years of disinvestment and stigma. Area-based interventions, designed to transform disadvantaged neighbourhoods into thriving communities, are a well-established policy approach, intended to alleviate poor conditions and compensate for market failures, with government support (Adair et al., 2000; DCLG, 2008). However, in the globalizing world, attracting international capital, and more affluent, tax-paying residents have become increasingly important in urban development strategy, as means of managing the challenge of economic austerity. As Butler (2003) shows, the arts are being used by a greater range of stakeholders to secure urban regeneration in deprived areas. Although the presence of public art in the city is not, of itself, a new phenomenon, it has become an established aspect of urban regeneration strategy. Whether commissioned alongside the planning of new towns or signifying the transformation of previously undesirable neighbourhoods, public art has been theorized as a mechanism for place-making, creating meaning and, in doing so, connecting people to urban space and supporting the development of community (Miles, 1997; Pollock & Paddison, 2014). This practice is often carried out in order to explicitly foreground elements of place identity while simultaneously improving the reputational aspects of place, attracting both human and capital investment to neighbourhoods undergoing transformation.

This chapter offers an exploration of how artists envision their role within this contested process of transformation in the East End of Glasgow. Drawing on an examination of the artists' commissions, design briefs, activities and art works, it outlines the ways in which the work of an artist is conditioned by a variety of different pressures and urban agendas both *before* and *during* the delivery process. We engage issues surrounding the temporality of public art, namely the different stages involved in formulating and implementing public art and how tensions within this process enshrine a particular view of an area's past and future heritages.

Product versus process

The relationship between art and urban regeneration has attracted attention from academics and policymakers alike. One of the major tensions within this literature is the ways in which the instrumental value of art, serving a function in terms of delivering a specific social, economic or political agenda, has been used to marginalize, and on some occasions, displace existing communities. The 'product' (i.e. the tangible public art installation) is often the focus of policymakers and practitioners whereas academics have sought to question the view of the Social Exclusion Unit that:

> Art [. . .] can not only make a valuable contribution to delivering key outcomes of lower long-term unemployment, less crime, better health and better qualifications, but can also help to develop the individual pride, community spirit and capacity for responsibility that enable communities to run regeneration programmes themselves.
>
> (Holden, 2004, p. 15)

Policy focus on examining the quantifiables tied to socio-economic indicators has foregrounded the *impact* of the *products* of public art (Ley, 2003; Cameron & Coaffee, 2005; Garcia, 2005; Kirchberg & Kagan, 2013; Chang, 2016). In contrast, this chapter instead focuses on the *process* of creating public art and how this is influenced by the competing agendas of the different stakeholders involved, with a particular focus on artists and creative individuals. We examine the complex territory of *process* by focusing on the ways in which artists are conditioned, through commissions and briefs, to think instrumentally about their creative practice. More specifically, the ways in which the creative mind of the artist is influenced by top-down pressures are explored, as are the impacts that this has on the narratives of an area's past, present and future. This engages with the view that while 'artists have a key role in the processes and practices of regeneration', there are 'few, if any studies of how artists actually "do" regeneration and inclusion in socially excluded urban communities' (Lees & Melhuish, 2015, p. 256).

The ways in which the process of co-creating public art reveals the constraints and tensions under which artists work is a neglected area of academic study with notable exceptions (see Pollock & Sharp, 2015). Markusen (2006) does, however, place emphasis on the role of artists within the process to state that commissioned artists are 'instrumentalized' to achieve other goals beyond artistic ones. Using four European case studies, Markusen (2006) demonstrates how artists can be parachuted into vacant brothels in Amsterdam to stimulate short, sharp shocks and re-create images, through to decisions to put art and artists at the centre of the redevelopment of historic industrial buildings in Helsinki. Here the emphasis is on both the instrumental use of artists to produce certain goals as well as the instrumental benefits of public art to the socio-economic diversity of an area. Existing analyses on the process of art and urban change are often framed as the distinction between participation and inclusion (Sharp et al., 2005; Pollock & Sharp, 2012; Lees & Melhuish, 2015). In particular, Pollock and Sharp (2012) called for a greater understanding of contestation and conflict within the process of community participation in public art commissions. Often this conflict comes from questioning whose voices are listened to within the participation process and how a singular view of place can be enshrined as a result of accessing the usual, rather than hidden voices. However, more recent work has demonstrated that shared spaces can be created through producing art in the city (Chakravarty & Chan, 2016). Furthermore, the process of creating the art works is the point at which tensions between the community are exposed, as certain narratives are privileged and others neglected in the final product (Madgin, 2013). Rather than focus on the means of participation and postulate on the extent to which this is representative of social exclusion or inclusion, this chapter instead examines how the process of creating public art is conditioned by a range of competing agendas which in turn condition both the physical legacy of the artwork and the symbolic meanings attributed to the past, present and future of the area.

Methods and case study

In order to examine the views of artists during the process of creating public art, the researchers adopted a qualitative methodology. This took the form of semi-structured interviews which lasted, on average, 1.5 hours. To inform both the interviews and the analysis, the researchers analysed a large body of extant archival material ranging from the briefs given to artists, planning documents, operational plans from the various creative organizations involved, and the annual reports and working documents produced by Clyde Gateway. Rather than stick to a narrow perspective on what might constitute a status of 'artist', the researchers adopted a wide definition and, as such, creatives from across the profession were interviewed. These included people employed by the public and private sectors, those who commissioned art, those who managed the delivery of public art as well as self-employed artists and writers. In total, eight interviews were carried out with creative actors who had a track record of working in both the case study area or who were influential in the development of public art as mechanism for urban regeneration.

The relatively impoverished East End of Glasgow in Scotland was used as the case study for exploration, focusing specifically on the neighbourhoods of Calton and Bridgeton. This area was chosen along pre-determined criteria, namely, that it had suffered from the cumulative effects of urban regeneration initiatives stretching back to the comprehensive redevelopment schemes of the 1960s. More recently, the area was also proximate to the Commonwealth Games, a major international sport event held in Glasgow in 2014. As such, the East End of Glasgow was the recipient of large funding schemes to deliver significant infrastructural, residential, commercial, cultural and sporting improvements (Clark & Kearns, 2016). Indeed, many of the public artworks in the area directly arose from the 'Cultural Olympiad' that supported the sporting activities at the Commonwealth Games. A large number of public art works are evident in the area, both inside buildings and in the public realm and were commissioned by a range of private and public sector organizations. In addition, Clyde Gateway, a quasi-autonomous delivery agency, designed to deliver a 25-year regeneration programme, including the Commonwealth Games and its socio-economic and environmental legacy, managed changes to the area. As such, the case study site enabled the research team to consider a range of different art works from pavement works, art mounted on walls and on development boards as well as written outputs through poems and songs inscribed within the built environment within the context of a long-term initiative to transform the East End of Glasgow.

Agency and the artist in regeneration

The remainder of this chapter investigates the reach and limitations of creative agency in relation to regeneration along different dimensions. First, the procedures behind the use of public art in regeneration are examined. Second, the interplay between process and outcomes is explored, specifically by focusing on the experience of creating public art from the perspective of creative workers. We conclude by considering the significance of creative input within regeneration practice.

Planning: public art for regeneration

In exploring the role of creative actors in urban regeneration, the period *before* it is agreed that work would begin formed a recurrent theme. From this perspective, the first point of intersection between commissioner and artist lies in the call for expressions of interest in delivering a project, where the client specifies what is required. The architect, James Wines, famously decried the vogue for finishing new housing developments by siting a monolithic sculpture in an area of public space with the question 'why do they always deposit that little turd in the plaza when they leave?' (cited in Wolfe, 2005, p. 12). As well as critiquing the aesthetic merit of the sculpture, Wines's dismissive quip highlights a further feature of this kind of public art: it is a decorative afterthought, which could be sited anywhere, being devoid of meaning in relation to place. Rejecting the idea of public art as a post-hoc decorative frill, Clyde Gateway, the urban regeneration partnership responsible for driving the East End renewal, issued a publication outlining its organizational *Character and values* (Clyde Gateway, 2009). Drawing on joint community and professional workshops, this document was created to act as a design statement for artists and developers engaged in the regeneration of the area. Notably, the workshops identified and included young adults living in the neighbourhood as a key demographic, with a vital contribution to make in imagining the future of the area. While the Clyde Gateway agenda is explicit about the imperative of attracting more people to the area to ensure a sustainable community, unlike approaches which emphasize the iconic building (see Varna, Chapter 7 in this volume), the *Character and values* statement underlines a focus on place-making and community opinions as integral to regeneration, in both aspiration and practice.

The Clyde Gateway approach, which underpins their remit to creative engagement while renewing the public realm, might be considered congruent with the principles of *new genre* public art. Rooted in social activist movements in the United States, new genre practice reconceptualizes the word 'public' in greater depth, to mean art which is socially engaged and strives to be in the public interest, rather than simply referring to work which is situated in the public realm (see Lacy, 1995). Commissioning public art for the new-build Eastgate project, home to 500 staff working in Community and Safety Services, the brief specifies that the artist will 'be involved in the construction phase of Eastgate from the start, as they will be appointed before one brick has been laid' (Clyde Gateway, 2011, p. 2). Within the *new genre* conceptual framework, the specifics of place are valued as an important aspect of the creative process, generating artwork that recognizes (at least selective aspects of) local heritage. In the case of recent regeneration-related art projects in east Glasgow, contrasting Wines's turds, local context has been recognized as a vital aspect of the work (Figure 1.1). Development proposals for the area are required to 'acknowledge this [industrial] history and reinvent the area creatively and *subtly* to rebuild a distinct and beautiful part of metropolitan Glasgow' (Clyde Gateway, 2009, p. 6, emphasis in original).

Nevertheless, a core concern of critical geography, in analysing design-led regeneration practice, is that development serves as an alibi for gentrification,

Figure 1.1 Details from the Eastgate Boundary Fence (authors' photographs).

constituting 'a speculative investment in a demographic not yet residing in the city' (Granger, 2010, p. 11). There is a functional duality in inviting artists to draw on the area's 'particularly rich heritage, well documented, with strong historical and cultural symbolism' (Clyde Gateway, 2011, p. 4) when they tender a design bid, in that improving the environment *for* local people also involves making it both attractive and saleable to new interests from beyond the local area (Jacobs, 1961; Florida, 2002). The brief issued to artists hoping to work in the area includes an overt direction towards the historical and social context of Glasgow's East End. Some suggestions point artists towards more predictable and 'gentrification friendly' aspects of the area's social history, including the Bridgeton Burns Club, a local society founded in 1870 to celebrate the work of Scotland's most famous poet, as well as the historic Carnegie-funded library, and natural features, such as a small river. Other suggestions more clearly emphasize the working-class roots of the area, such as the Bridgeton Umbrella (Figure 1.2), an elaborate, painted cast iron shelter or a now demolished Working Men's Club, which boasted the motto 'learn from the past; use well the future'. The brief does not romanticize the challenges working people faced, noting that the Umbrella acted as a shelter for the unemployed and the Club 'latterly became mainly drinking quarters'.

Figure 1.2 The Bridgeton Cross Umbrella (authors' photograph).

In practice, while artists were encouraged to think about heritage and distinctive features of place, the briefs seemed to function, predominantly, as a stimulus rather than a constraint, insofar the area as a highly diverse range of creative activity is now evident. Two aspects of the regeneration practice in particular are likely to have fostered this diversity. Alongside context, a second signature feature of new genre public art prompted by the brief for commissions and evident in the delivery of projects was a requirement that the production be in some way participatory. As with awareness of and sensitivity to context, we found evidence that, at least in principle, there was a trend towards fostering inclusive practice in relation to regeneration in east Glasgow. Velocity, the main commissioning partnership representing Clyde Gateway, Creative Scotland, Glasgow City Council and Glasgow Life, stipulated that their projects must 'positively and imaginatively interact with the public during the development of artwork proposals', as well as produce engagement and communications strategies (Velocity, 2012a). Added to this requirement, artists were selected through an open call. The call for expressions of interest is a key point of control for project commissioners; a wide range of responses offers the opportunity to 'narrow down what you want through the submissions you get in' (Creative A). From the perspective of would-be bidders, the open call approach might also be considered relatively inclusive. The impacts of this go beyond insuring that new artists have the opportunity to engage in public art. Rather than directly requesting a tender from someone who is either known to the funder or who has an established reputation for a particular kind of work, an open call offers scope for new and unanticipated approaches to the commission. As one interviewee described:

> If I had gone out to say we want stone sculptures in granite, it would have really limited the kind of ideas that we got. So the nature of proposals that came forward were, you know, yes there was one stone sculpture, but there were people who were very process based, there were people using plants and, you know for me, it was the favourite one, was we ended up actually using growing material, somebody putting up big iron sculptures, you know?
> (Creative C)

The combination of open calls and community collaboration has resulted in a range of both more and less traditional imaginings of the area's social and cultural heritage being written on and into the fabric of the environment. The largest and perhaps the highest profile commission was to 'realise a new permanent artwork on the approaches to, or in the vicinity of, the Emirates Arena and Sir Chris Hoy Velodrome' (Velocity, 2012b). The call ultimately resulted in the building of the Baltic Street Adventure Playground (Figure 1.3), designed by ASSEMBLE, a Turner prize-winning collective of architects, in conjunction with Create, a London-based organization which aims to connect artists with economically deprived communities.

The winning collective describe the project as referencing the post-war adventure play movement, in contrast to contemporary 'risk-averse' attitudes to play,

Figure 1.3 Baltic Street Adventure Playground (authors' photograph).

and providing space for children to engage in the artistic process of discovering and creating using found materials (Create London, 2014). Considered in isolation, this could be considered indicative of relatively high levels of artistic agency in this case, where the planning phase supports a framework that, at least alongside more instrumental functions, accommodates art as an intrinsically valuable activity.

Process and outcomes: creating public art

The regeneration partnership is explicit about the instrumental function of art. Commissioning public art serves an instrumental function for the urban regeneration partnership. It provides 'an approach that puts local people at the heart of its plans', acting as a mechanism for engaging with communities; the remit for the artist encompasses both reflecting the cultural and historic character of Glasgow's East End as well as, more vaguely, the 'area's future aspirations' (Clyde Gateway, 2011, p. 3). The transformation of social and physical space may, in the longer term, initiate gentrifying processes, which ultimately undermine local community and a sense of belonging to the neighbourhood (Kohn, 2013). However, practice to date suggests that the participatory dimension has been more than tokenistic, with community priorities as a significant influence, driving regeneration priorities.

Figure 1.4 Detail from Tullis Street Memorial Gardens (authors' photograph).

In particular, the early focus on Tullis Street Memorial Gardens (Figure 1.4), the public realm at Bridgeton Cross, and the acquisition and adaptive reuse of the derelict Olympia variety theatre came as a result of public consultation.

The interviews also included one participant who had insisted on community participation as a precondition of working on a local authority project, believing artistic involvement can change the way urban projects are shaped for the better:

> [. . .] actually doing workshops, drawings, model making, ripping up magazines and sticking things on walls kind of projections on the site you know at night time in January/February, worst weather but brilliant because it was dark and that actually changed the proposal! But it was that thing of kind of going if you are asking people what they want you have to listen to them and do something differently.
>
> (Creative A)

For all that public involvement in creative regeneration was valued as an enriching and inspiring process for the creative workers interviewed, in comparison with working as a gallery artist there are multiple practical, conceptual and strategic challenges. Although some interviewees spoke of 'best practice' as shortlisting potential candidates and offering a small fee in acknowledgement of the effort of developing a proposal, this is far from the norm and often artists are paid nothing. Bidding to work on one of the projects was seen as particularly onerous. Preparing even a preliminary expression of interest involved opportunity cost as well as intellectual capital. From a practical perspective, the requirements of a call for expressions of interest in a commission can, simultaneously, be unhelpfully demanding and impossibly general:

> Whenever you see a brief, it's got to do everything: everyone's got to *like* it, it's got to be brilliant, it's not allowed to go out of fashion, it's got to last forever, there's got to be no maintenance – that's almost, like, taken as read!
>
> (Creative F)

For larger projects, there can also be substantial direct costs, comprising weeks or even months of work. These include a need to secure and budget for cooperation from additional artistic collaborators, and from contractors supplying other skills, labour and materials. Applicants might be individual or form a creative team, potentially including designers, architects and landscape architects, as well as a project manager. The brief for the artwork that eventually became the Baltic Street Adventure Playground (Velocity, 2012a), stipulated that the project must:

- Bring multiple stakeholders together in a single vision.
- Positively and imaginatively interact with the public during the development of artwork proposals.
- Evidence how practice is informed by environmental concerns and how this impacts upon the work, particularly though the logistics of production and the use of materials and resources.
- Develop engagement, documentation plan, communication and evaluation strategies.

Beyond practical considerations, the conceptual challenge of responding to a brief can be complicated by divergent perceptions of what might constitute the cultural and historic character of the area and who, ultimately, will be the audience for the work. Writing about art and intention, Lacy describes the artist Jo Hanson as distinguishing art for the affluent – a 'private indulgence' – from public art, considered, by its nature, to be a 'social intervention' (Hanson, in Lacy, 1995). In what can be seen as a logical corollary, the production of the work should be participatory, involving the people of the place and, as a normative stance; the 'social intervention' dimension endorsed by advocates of new genre public art should be empowering to local people, expressing something of value and importance for, or at least about, the people and place where the work is sited. However, it is worth recalling that there is also a long and not particularly benign tradition of public art functioning as a social intervention; historically, it has predominantly served a political function, with statues of conquerors or leaders symbolically overlooking the subject population to establish status and reaffirm territorial ownership (Chakravarty & Chan, 2016). The selection of different aspects of place, people and history, around which the public art project will be designed and delivered, is, in itself, an act of conferring value. In some cases, that value may be commercial – one participant half-joked that he believed the reason he secured the commission was that his method of working would deliver twice the 'product' for the same amount of money. Frequently, artists and the people they worked with drew on the industrial past of the area, using stone and steel to capture the ephemeral: ways of life that are long gone. For better or worse, there may be an element of romanticism in carving images of industrial tools into granite or making wallpaper and decals out of old maps. However, connection with the past as an important aspect of community formed a strong theme in the interviews:

> I remember an early lesson I learned when I was a student asking people who lived in really deprived communities you know what do you think of your area and expecting them to say 'I can't wait to get out of it' and them telling me they don't want to live anywhere else. That was a shock to me as a student because I didn't understand that connection that people have with a community and the fact that they have always lived there, all their relatives are there, all their friends are there they couldn't imagine living anywhere else even if it didn't appear to be the greatest area in the world.
>
> (Creative B)

On occasion, the creative decision-making process was predominantly top-down, driven by the curiosity, aesthetic or convictions of the individual creative producer. One participant spoke about searching council buildings and archives as a starting point towards gaining a fuller picture social history; while shipbuilding has been widely recognized as part of the city's past, the Templeton carpet factory was a pivotal international centre for innovation, design and production: 'really skilled people who made these carpets and particularly who drew the designs and maybe that hasn't been celebrated' (Creative C). The outcome of this research was the Carpet Garden, an outdoor seating area with recovered designs inscribed on both paving and benches (Figure 1.5).

However, most often, participative practice was at the core of the conceptual approach, bringing varied understandings of what culture and heritage mean in relation to place. Formally, this might mean that initial ideas from the artist's proposal were then 'shaped by workshops with the community' (Creative D). Another approach was to design a system where people from the area decide which submissions to shortlist for interview and, ultimately, which artist they will work with:

> [. . .] you get all that artists' imagination and you put them on a table and say to the community 'well, which way do you want to go?'
>
> (Creative A)

Some artists emphasized informal approaches to community engagement, which were less likely to be signalled as part of the project concept. These might range

Figure 1.5 Detail from the Carpet Garden (authors' photograph).

from living, embedded, as part of the community to casually spending time with people from the area, eating in local cafes and chatting with strangers when outside for a smoke. This more ethnographic concept of engaging with heritage may be a long way from archival research but is no less valid. It will, however, generate ideas with a different focus:

> Why commission an artwork if it's not going to address something to do with the history of the locality? Then you might as well 1) get something out of a catalogue or 2) end up with a kind of signature piece by somebody really famous which could be plonked anywhere.
>
> (Creative G)

From the artists' perspective, securing the participation of active and engaged community organizations during the process of creation, yields a dynamic relationship, involving mutual learning. Artworks included a 100 m-long coloured mural, made from graphic panels and poetry, co-created by artists and local schoolchildren in place of the usual builders' boards, as well as a permanent installation referencing different contemporary and historical creative arts, including poetry, song, weaving and comedy. Perceptions of a lost or hidden past formed another theme within the interviews, with both artists and co-creators valuing the experience of sharing stories about the neighbourhood, within wider narratives of the city and a changing social and economic environment:

The people I spoke to thought that the story Bridgeton was a hidden story within the city because lots of industry was based here had gone, tenement clearances of the 60s and 70s has decimated or all but decimated the local population, that local people felt Bridgeton had been forgotten about.

(Creative E)

In one case, a research participant spoke of historical images and maps as a means by which migrants or others new to the community could build a connection with the area. Two more discussed the importance of *not* working with what might be termed the usual suspects, preferring the freshness and creativity of young people who have had more challenging lives. In other examples of sharing knowledge, local children taught the artists about micro-territories in the neighbourhood and vernacular language which then became part of public art works:

I need [the children] to own [their words] and let them mess around a little bit and – also, to correct me! I do love that, because we're always correcting their grammar, so they'll correct my grammar. Of theirs, they'll say, 'That's not how you say it, pal.' They don't say 'pal', they say, 'that's not how you say it, big man, uh, and ye dinnae spell it that way. Ye spell it this way.' You know? Which I think is phenomenal, you know? A grammar lesson in reverse, you know [. . .]?

(Creative F)

With conceptual approaches that encompass less formal or traditional interpretations of what social and cultural heritage might mean, come additional strategic challenges for the artist: publicly funded bodies are obliged to be risk-averse; it is also part of their remit to generate interest from private markets. In combination, these factors mean that even working with relatively progressive organizations will generate a wide range of tensions. This can include reporting to a committee of stakeholders with restrictive priorities and conceptions of what art is and should achieve. There is a caveat here that instrumental perspectives on the value of art were not the province of only the policy stakeholders. Participants expressed delight that some school pupils they worked with had gone on to art school or the pride people take in having distinctive artwork: 'I think it gives people swagger, a confident swagger' (Creative H). The superficial idea that 'it has to have a heritage feel to it' (Creative D) can result in the project commissioners pushing an agenda that is no longer meaningful to the artist's co-creators:

I mean this is where the kind of sadness comes in. 'Cause like, you know, that industry has gone [. . .] So you think, if I've got to do something there, why can't I just do something completely new? You know, of the kids now. You know sometimes you want to just say, let's ignore it. Heritage has been done to death in some places. How can we come up with something that's a celebration [. . .] just pretty much a celebration of the creativity of kids now?

(Creative C)

One artist also described criticism when, following a cooperative process, people from the local area community favoured abstract sculpture:

> Getting criticism because it is abstract, from people saying 'well, we want something that refers to the local area', such as references to the steamie [communal laundry] or the brickworks that was there.
>
> (Creative A)

The solution proposed was a briefing session with the local housing sales team, to help them explain how to translate the work to prospective buyers in the area. Preoccupation with saleability and ideas of what representations might be 'appropriate' can cause considerable tension. Community narratives which honour local participation in the Spanish Civil War, the political activism of the Calton martyrs, or the tragic loss of 29 young women crushed in a factory disaster, raised concerns about a focus on perceived negative images of place. Policy actors can show extreme sensitivity around anything perceived to be political, even drawn from a historic context or artistic source, or potentially referencing violence. For one of the artists, the frustration of dealing with commissioners was so great that, although he found the community engagement aspect deeply rewarding, he no longer worked on public art projects: 'I don't do it anymore. That's the last public art project I did. I can't bear it' (Creative G).

Conclusion: creativity in regeneration practice

> [Community members] talk as much about *now* and the *future* of Bridgeton as they do the past so [. . .] I think bringing the art aspect into it [heritage] allows a really creative approach, so you are starting off with stories about buildings and people and areas in the past but then using arts and engagement to then unlock some creativity about it. So people were creating stories, young people were creating stories, people were creating films based on old photographs and photographs they had taken of the reconstruction of the building and imagining what it is going to be like [. . .] speculating where it is going to go and [. . .] so I think the arts bit allows you to unlock a lot more if that makes any sense at all?
>
> (Creative E)

Investigating discourses of public participation within regeneration, Pollock and Sharp (2012, p. 3063) argue 'contestation and conflict should be recognised as appropriate reflections of community'. Addressing a deficit of knowledge in relation to policy claims about the arts as a pathway for realizing social and economic democratic change (Lees & Melhuish, 2015), this chapter advances the literature on the contested role of the arts within regeneration practice by exposing some of the mechanisms through which the terms of any co-creation are set and exploring the challenges that creative workers face in their practice.

As one of the research participants pointed out, constraint is an irreducible part of life; nevertheless, disentangling both overt and more subtle constraints bound up in commission and delivery offers a means of understanding how public art, as both process and product, is mediated by different visions of what a regeneration process can or should achieve. In this case, policy stakeholders managing the commissions demonstrated early awareness of and support for public participation when incorporating a creative dimension into regeneration projects. Glasgow's East End regeneration has embraced a relatively liberal understanding of what constitutes valid art and heritage, including play space and popular contemporary references, which will be more easily understood by long-time residents than newcomers. However, documentary analysis and the narratives of the artists participating in the research highlight a residual conservatism, which may be inescapable in a publicly responsible body and, in other hands, both process and outcomes could have been less imaginative and inclusive. Even where the commissioning body is supportive of co-creation which engages with participant meanings and priorities, understandings of heritage that are simple, saleable and sanitized, which conjure a romantic past, and don't involve too many dead people, are most likely to be attractive to the managers of regeneration.

Concomitantly, however, the future heritage of the area becomes reductionist and safe. The complexity of plural narratives is filtered out by the process of producing public art, which, as this chapter has demonstrated is on the one hand inclusive in terms of participation, but can be exclusive in terms of its execution. Participative artistic practice has the opportunity to enable inclusivity in terms of both people and narratives, yet is constrained at all stages by the Janus-faced process of participation. Text and images in the built environment can, however, be both attractive and interesting, as well as using references which may be uncomfortable but promote curiosity and discovery, to ensure that future heritages and future narratives engage not just with hidden and sanitized stories but authentic and complex narratives of an area and its changes over time.

Bibliography

Adair, A., Berry, J., McGreal, S., Deddis, B., & Hirst, S. (2000). The financing of urban regeneration. *Land Use Policy, 17*, 147–156.

Butler, D. (2003). *Changing people's lives – art and social inclusion*. Interrupt Artists in Socially Engaged Practice, Arts Council England, London.

Cameron, S., & Coaffee, J. (2005). Art, gentrification and regeneration: From artist as pioneer to public arts. *European Journal of Housing Policy, 5*, 39–58.

Chakravarty, S., & Chan, F. H. (2016). Imagining shared space: Multivalent murals in new ethnic '-towns' of Los Angeles. *Space and Culture, 19*, 406–420.

Chang, T. C. (2016). 'New uses need old buildings': Gentrification aesthetics and the arts in Singapore. *Urban Studies, 53*, 524–539.

Clark, J., & Kearns, A. (2016). Going for gold: A prospective assessment of the economic impacts of the Commonwealth Games 2014 on the East End of Glasgow. *Environment and Planning C: Government and Policy,* DOI:10.1177/0263774X15624923

Clark, J., Kearns, A., & Cleland, C. (2016). Spatial scale, time and process in mega-events: The complexity of host community perspectives on neighbourhood change. *Cities, 53*, 87–97.

Clyde Gateway. (2009). *Character and values.* Glasgow: Clyde Gateway.

Clyde Gateway. (2011). *Artist's brief: Eastgate Atrium Public Art Project.* Glasgow: Clyde Gateway.

Create London. (2014). Create London commissioned to deliver new adventure playground for the Commonwealth Games. Retrieved from http://createlondon.org/wpcontent/uploads/2014/05/BalticStr eet AdventurePlayground_PressRelease_2014.pdf

DCLG. (2008). *Public attitudes to housing in England.* Report based on results from the British Social Attitudes Survey. London: DCLG Publications.

DCMS. (2010). *Understanding the drivers, impact and value of engagement in culture and sport: An over-arching summary of the research/* CASE: Culture and Sport Evidence Programme (EPPI-Centre/ Matrix Knowledge Group).

Florida, R. (2002). *The rise of the creative class and how it's transforming work, life, community and everyday life.* New York: Basic Books.

Garcia, B. (2005). Deconstructing the City of Culture: The long-term cultural legacies of Glasgow 1990. *Urban Studies, 42*, 841–868.

Granger, R. (2010). What now for urban regeneration? *Proceedings of the Institution of Civil Engineers – Urban Design and Planning, 163*, 9–16.

Holden, J. (2004). *Capturing cultural value: How culture has become a tool of government policy.* London: Demos.

Holden, J. (2006). *Cultural value and the crisis of legitimacy: Why culture needs a democratic mandate.* London: Demos.

Jacobs, J. (1961). *The death and life of great American cities.* New York: Random House.

Kirchberg, V., & Kagan, S. (2013). The roles of artists in the emergence of creative sustainable cities: Theoretical clues and empirical illustrations. *City, Culture and Society, 4*, 137–152.

Kohn, M. (2013). What is wrong with gentrification? *Urban Research and Practice, 6*, 297–310.

Lacy, S. (Ed.). (1995). *Mapping the terrain: New genre public art.* Seattle, WA: Bay Press.

Landry, C., & Bianchini, F. (1995). *The creative city.* London: Demos.

Lees, L., & Melhuish C. (2015). Arts-led regeneration in the UK: The rhetoric and the evidence on urban social inclusion. *European Urban and Regional Studies, 22*, 242–260.

Ley, D. (2003). Artists, aestheticisation and the field of gentrification. *Urban Studies, 40*, 2527–2544.

Madgin, R. (2013). A town without memory? Inferring the industrial past: Clydebank re-built, 1941–2013. In C. Zimmerman (Ed.), *Industrial cities: History and future.* Frankfurt am Main: Campus Verlag.

Markusen, A. (2006). Urban development and the politics of a creative class: Evidence from a study of artists. *Environment and Planning A, 38*, 1921–1940.

Miles, M. (1997). *Art, space and the city: Public art and urban futures.* London: Routledge.

Pollock, V. L., & Paddison, R. (2014). On place-making, participation and public art: The Gorbals, Glasgow. *Journal of Urbanism: International Research on Placemaking and Urban Sustainability, 7*, 85–105.

Pollock, V. L., & Sharp, J. (2012). Real participation or the tyranny of participatory practice? Public art and community involvement in the regeneration of the Raploch, Scotland. *Urban Studies, 49*, 3063–3079.

Sharp, J., Pollock, V. L., & Paddison, R. (2005). Just art for a just city: Public art and social inclusion in urban regeneration. *Urban Studies, 42*, 1001–1023.

Urban Task Force. (2005). *Towards a strong urban renaissance: The urban renaissance six years on.* London: Urban Task Force.

Velocity. (2012a). *ABC commission: Brief for artists.* Glasgow: Velocity.

Velocity. (2012b). *East End Public Artwork Commission: Summary of artist's brief.* Glasgow: Velocity.

Wines, J. N. (2005). *Site: Identity in density.* Mulgrave, Victoria: Images Publishing Group.

Wolfe, T. (2005). Foreword. In *Site: Identity in density. Essays by Michael J. Crosbie, Michael McDonough and James Wines* (Ed. S. Womersley, pp. 12–15). Mulgrave, Vic: The Images Publishing Group.

2 Urban regeneration *in motion*

The High Line as a travelling urban imaginary

Ian Riekes Trivers

Introduction

New York City's High Line, a long-disused rail viaduct transformed into a high-design linear park, is arguably among the foremost contemporary urban revitalization icons. From what many considered a 'long shot' idea, it has become an inspiration and justification for a wide range of urban regeneration efforts in cities across the globe. This circulation of ideas and practices in urban planning and revitalization is far from new, though the focus on how it functions, particularly in an increasingly globalized and interconnected world, has become an important focus of contemporary study. Investigating urban revitalization and planning ideas or practices that 'travel' or are 'in motion', numerous metaphors for what exactly what is mobilized have been developed. Most, like 'policy transfer' and 'best practices' put the emphasis on organized networks, rational policy actors and clearly delineated models, policies and ideas.

However, technological change in the production and distribution of media and discourse, as well as a contemporary political context that valorizes ideas that come from the community over those that come from government, experts and formal networks, has meant that these notions of what travel may miss key shifts in the processes at work. The High Line, as a storied revitalization project in a city that is arguably one of the world's most important producers of aspirational urbanism today, provides a helpful case for examining this contemporary process. What travels of the High Line is more than a model, practice or idea that is transferred by experts and formal networks. Building upon the plentiful work around travelling and mobility, this chapter argues that the High Line that travels is best understood as a 'travelling urban imaginary'.

Looking at the High Line as a travelling urban imaginary puts the focus on how an accretive narrative incorporates a particular site's history, redevelopment process, urban context and global aspirations of urban experience. These are all put in motion through popular discourses that shape the revitalization phenomenon in the public imagination. Examining the above elements, this chapter will trace how the High Line was formed into an urban imaginary. Seeing the High Line through this lens invites more understanding about why these types of projects are powerful motivators of revitalization practices in other contexts. Emphasis is put on the narratives, meanings and aspirations embodied in the imaginary, which in turn de-emphasizes the role of formal networks and related technical-rational positioning as policy interventions. Such perspectives allow for critical examination of not only how these imaginaries motivate urban revitalization projects, but how well they actually fit the contexts and needs of the places where they are transferred.

Mobility and travelling: the High Line *in motion*

New York City's High Line is 'one of the world's best-known urban-renewal projects' (Kwaak, 2014). A high-design linear park built atop a 1.5-mile elevated former railway in the Lower West Side of Manhattan, its first phase opened in 2009, second in 2011 and final phase in late 2014. It is hard to overstate the excitement and attention the High Line has provoked in the press and wider public discourse. Even the casual observer of urbanism and urban revitalization will likely be familiar with the project. Few urban revitalization projects have made for debate in the Opinion section of *The New York Times* on multiple occasions (Rybczynski, 2011; Moss, 2012). Various media outlets have heralded the High Line as an innovation, a masterpiece of design, a redevelopment catalyst, a new form of public space and so much more. The park is celebrated as a truly enjoyable physical experience and a major investment in public space. Moreover, proximate areas have seen surging property values and increased tax receipts through new consumer oriented investments. The High Line has also sparked the imagination of people around the world regarding potential revitalization interventions in their urban fabric.

As the prescient architecture critic of the *Philadelphia Enquirer* called it soon after the completion of the project's first phase, the High Line 'may turn out to be the most influential work of architecture completed during the boom years, the Guggenheim Bilbao of its decade. Every city wants one' (Saffron, 2011, p. E1). From early on the High Line has been 'in motion' as an idea and practice. Even before completion of its redevelopment from abandoned relic to linear park, other cities have been inspired by the High Line. Initially, cities with similar post-industrial infrastructure adopted the concept or otherwise used the High Line to gain traction for their own revitalization plans (Taylor, 2010; Jaffe, 2011). These projects mostly include repurposing similar abandoned elevated urban rail viaducts as greenways or parks. Over time, more, and more loosely related typologically, projects around the world have adopted the mantle of 'a High Line' or otherwise associated themselves with the highly successful site. For example, projects inspired or otherwise associated with the High Line now include everything from obsolete vehicular bridges and tunnels to proposed new-built linear structures (CityMetric Staff, 2015). The research project that this chapter comes out of has identified 183 proposed, underway or completed schemes from around the world that have been linked to the High Line – either by their promoters and/or in the media and public discourse. With such wide influence, particularly as it moves beyond the realm of reusing urban rail infrastructure into seemingly unrelated types, it become clear that what transfers about the High Line is clearly not so much a well delineated idea, policy or practice to be adopted elsewhere but to be something more.

Understanding mobilized revitalization practices and ideas has become an important part of contemporary urban research in the era of hyper-globalization. It is the hallmark of globalization that goods, ideas, power and capital are mobilized and 'move'. Ideas about urban form and management have circulated since ancient times through trade, travel and empire. Eras of colonialism introduced new and altered systems of policy and idea transfer, particular in relation to power (King, 1980; Ward, 2000). A number of well-known works have tackled the spread of planning ideas in the modern era (see Sutcliffe, 1981; Rodgers, 1998; Hall, 2002). While the circulation of ideas and polices are far from new, it has intensified and accelerated with the forces of globalization (McCann & Ward, 2010). A 'turn toward mobilities' (Cresswell, 2011) in urban geography, policy and planning has resulted in increased interest in the contemporary process and impact of interconnected ideas and polices that 'move'. A number of different terms used to describe this notion of 'move', for instance: 'travelling', 'diffusion', 'policy-transfer' or 'best practices'. While the use of different terms indicates important differences in perspective, fundamentally what is being described is a process of moving something pertaining to practices and ideas by some means to some place. This always requires the identification of what is being moved, a mode of transfer and process of landing (how it is then situated or implemented in the receiving site).

When discussing urban revitalization aligned with the focus of this chapter, the first step is converting a real, physical place and outcome into a form that can travel. As Czarniawaska and Sevon (2005, p. 9) describe, things being moved:

> Must be simplified and abstracted into an idea, or at least approximated in a narrative permitting a vicarious experience, and therefore converted into words or images. Neither can words nor images travel until they have materialized, until they are embodied, inscribed or objectified.

This process of inscription is important and not neutral. It requires a process of 'editing' and 'flattening'. The metaphor editing points to the fact that the thing being mobilized is purposefully changed. Hedmo et al. (2005, p. 195) argue:

> The process of inscribing a real thing into an idea or an account of practice may be formulated more clearly and made more explicit; however, the editing process may also change not only the form of the idea or account but also its focus, content, and meaning.

Likewise, the metaphor of 'flattening' points to the way that real places and practices must be reduced to be mobilized and communicated. As such, this process relies on the construction of abstract models of urbanism, successful cites, lauded projects or policies as exemplars and guides. In the creation of cities as models, where individual, real, complex assemblages are flattened with 'the figurative uprooting and making mobile of certain places as referential components of particular models' (McCann & Ward, 2012, p. 329). The process of editing and flattening means 'the thing moved from one place to another cannot emerge unchanged' (Czarniawska & Sevon, 2005, p. 8). These models which can be put in motion are in fact socially constructed, always mediated in some way and shaped by the choice of agents, narratives, metaphors, symbols and mediums. This in turn 'problematizes politics of knowledge and practice' (Peck, 2011, p. 775).

The mediums, as well as the actors involved, in mobilization and transfers have been significantly expanded and sped up by internet technology and globalization. Much attention has been given to the role of frameworks such as 'policy networks' (see Dowding, 1995) and similar, more formalized structures and actors in them. However, it is increasingly recognized that places are 'unbounded' in their relations and interact at multiple levels and through a wide array of channels (McCann & Ward, 2012). While 'policy tourists', or policy professionals who visit other sites to seek solutions (Gonzalez, 2010), NGOs, think tanks and similar exchange organizing structures still matter greatly, the ever quickening transfer of images, media and other forms of communication between all places at all levels means that ideas and practices travel through a dizzying array of channels and mediums outside these networks. Furthermore, the current political environment valorizes community-led revitalization ideas or practices that originate from outside formal government and, to a lesser degree, expert networks. Ideas or practices generated or located and adopted by 'the community' have more political weight and authenticity. Therefore, it is increasingly necessary to look beyond more official networks, processes and actors (McCann, 2008). Understanding this expanded process is not a simple task, as the potential connections, sources, actors and the weights of each one are vast and complicated. However, as a wildly popular urban regeneration idea and practice, the High Line project provides a wealth of information to help reveal how it is transferred outside formal policy networks and other more formal channels (which also still contribute to its mobility). To do this it is helpful to think of the High Line as more than a model or practice but an urban imaginary that is constructed and narrated.

The urban imaginary

As described above, making revitalization mobile requires flattening, narration and change. In doing so, revitalization practices and ideas are no longer 'real', but rather constructed narratives influenced by history, actors, power and experiences. This particular perspective tends to fall outside of typical analysis of urban revitalization and policy. Urban planning and revitalization as professional and scholarly pursuits are most often aligned with the policy perspective of undertaking a rational exercise and, in doing so, attempt to 'reduce the city to an abstract, rational order' (Chambers, 1986, p. 183). But, as Chambers (1986, p. 183) argues, 'the city exists as a series of doubles: it has official and hidden cultures, it is a real place and a site of the imagination'. Here the concept of the 'urban imaginary' provides a helpful addition to the investigation of mobilized urban revitalization practices and ideas. As a concept, it stems from the underlying notions of the city as not only a place of imagination, but a place of such complexity that it can only be understood through imaginaries. This is particularly important when looking beyond more formal urban revitalization networks and actors that do not necessarily use a technical-rational perspective. As Donald (1992, p. 452) argues, 'metaphors, analogies and images are the means by which we make that historically produced and increasingly unrepresentable urban space intelligible and psychically negotiable'. From this basic but important observation flows a number of ways of describing and negotiating how people construct the city through imagination and practice. This is conceptually parallel to the notion of flattening a city into a model.

The concept of the urban imaginary comes out of multiple sources and perspectives. *Imagined communities* refers to the modern notion of the nation-state or, more importantly how 'nation-ness' represents a 'cultural artifact' opposed to material reality (see Anderson, 2006). The spread of the nation-state was a phenomenon of language, models, colonialism and capitalism. People could begin to imagine themselves as part of larger 'communities' of people with whom they had no direct connection but were united by a shared language and common cultural symbols. Anderson (2006) suggests the production of early nations emerged through the development of a shared vernacular, and 'print capitalism' created a visible model. Visible models and cultural artifacts spread throughout the world to foster nation-states. Anderson's (2006) compellingly argument is that nation-states were not necessarily natural historical-political progressions, but imagined aspirations developed in specific historical circumstances of one place that then spread throughout the world as an idea enabled by new technologies and globalization.

Building upon Anderson's (2006) concept, Çinar and Bender's (2007) perspective of the imaginary refers to the production of urban culture and experiences. Çinar and Bender (2007) emphasize more modern, or varied, forms of communication and discourse that shape contemporary urban imaginaries:

> The collective imagination operates not only through the written text [. . .] but also through a variety of different media in daily life, which is a cast field of collective experience. The urban experiences involve travels, interactions, and communicative practices of people within a city, which function to weave a sense of connectedness in space and in turn serve to imagine the city as a single place. The sorts of daily practices that [. . .] include popular media, film, art, and radio and market relations of personal networks that function similar as tools for the building of a collective imagination.
>
> (Çinar & Bender, 2007, p. xiv)

The quote above refers to the production of a local urban imaginary for a city. The same applies to how individual neighbourhoods or parts of that city become imagined (Çinar & Bender, 2007). Every urban neighbourhood, or site, becomes one interpreted through the imagination as a 'cool' place, 'poor' place, 'backward' place or 'black' place. These internal urban imaginaries also become external ones – ones ever more present in lives outside the city in a world where images and narratives travel so easily and quickly.

The external urban imaginary is of particular importance in the framing of iconic world cities. As Bender writes: 'the case of global cities like Los Angeles, images or representations tend to precede experience, and they contribute to the constitution of experience or, better, the interpretation or meaning given to experience' (Bender, 2007, p. 269). The urban imaginary creates a lens through which places are interpreted from the outside. As well, the development of this external imaginary cannot be separated from many of the acts of urban branding (Klingmann, 2007; Wilson, 2011; Zukin, 2014). The urban imaginary (broadly and specifically considered) becomes intertwined with the process of producing and transferring mobilized urban regeneration polices. The production of these urban imaginaries is 'a conscious act' worthy of attention (Donald, 1992).

The High Line: history and early imaginings

To understand the production of the High Line as a travelling urban imaginary it helps to understand its history. As a project based on industrial heritage and preservation, the High Line's imaginary builds on its past. The High Line was originally a component of the larger and ambitious Westside Improvement Project of the 1930s that, among other infrastructure improvements, removed 105 hazardous at grade crossings on key freight lines serving the warehouses of the west side of Manhattan with 13 miles of dedicated rail right of way. The High Line portion replaced an at grade railway running mostly down 10th Avenue, often called 'Death Avenue' for its repeated incidents between trains and vehicles and pedestrians. Prior to the High Line, 'Westside Cowboys' would, with limited success, ride ahead of already slow moving trains with flags and lanterns to warn vehicles and pedestrians. When opened in 1934 to freight traffic the High Line stretched over twice as far as what remains of it today. The High Line serviced warehouses and processing facilities, primarily for fresh fruits, vegetables and meatpacking. Of particular engineering pride, it used direct connections above grade to warehouses, separate from traffic and pedestrians below. Called by its creators 'one of the greatest projects ever undertaken [. . .] on Manhattan Island' (New York Central Railroad Company, 1934), the High Line was an important modernization project and played a role in a wider circulation of symbols and imaginaries from its beginning. Elevated railways were 'props in a world-historical drama', representing modernity and progress to the world (Scobey, 2002, p. 160). Not globally iconic itself, the High Line was a latecomer to the field of elevated rail infrastructure which dates back to the 1860s in New York and the early-1800s worldwide. Nonetheless, it fits firmly into the tail end of an important urban imaginary of progress and modernity of the time.

Initially a major improvement in the safety and traffic flow for the area, the High Line had a relatively short useful life. Like many of these types of structures, particularly in the United States, changes in technology and distribution systems cumulating in the middle of the twentieth century led to their obsolescence and eventual abandonment. In the 1960s, barely 30 years after its completion, a portion of the southern end of the structure was demolished due to diminishing demand for rail freight service. It is often told that the final train ran down the remaining northern section of the High Line in 1980 carrying frozen Thanksgiving turkeys, though the veracity of this story is unconfirmed. As recently as 1991, portions of the structure were demolished for infrastructure improvements and to open up valuable real estate. The remaining High Line was graffiti-covered, weed-choked and slowly rusting, and many considered the structure 'an awful blight' and impediment to the revitalization of the surrounding neighbourhood (Gray, 1988). Once a key image of progress, modernity and the smooth functioning industrial city, it became a symbol of the obsolescence and decay of the post-industrial city.

With its post-industrial decline the High Line and the area around it was 'off the map' for most New Yorkers. It transitioned into a mix of light industrial uses, with the longstanding meatpacking industry that partially remained being joined by auto repair and general warehousing. The area also developed a strong LGBT presence, home to a number of gay bars and dance clubs (Patrick, 2013). Due in part to its longstanding industrial uses and relatively poor public transportation links, the area was a notable laggard in the rocketing Manhattan real estate market of the late 1980s and early 1990s. As New York City's economy rebounded, industrial uses increasingly gave way to an emerging cultural scene with new galleries and artist lofts. With land becoming more valuable, the High Line, crossing over the middle of blocks instead of running over the street like most elevated railways in Manhattan did, covered large chunks of potentially valuable real estate. Regardless of the High Line's redevelopment, it was inevitable that the surrounding area would eventually be subsumed into the bigger Manhattan real-estate game and new housing production began to take off in the 1990s. Still, the surprisingly long tenure of industrial uses in the area with the ups and down of the real-estate market scuttled past attempts by property interests to have the High Line torn down to develop the underlying land. Likewise, CSX, the eventual owner of the structure, resisted, having no desire to outlay the $50 million-plus it would cost for demolition. In the event of removal, the easements would be nullified and full use of the land returned to the underlying owners – CSX would be saddled with the cost of demolition and receive no income from tearing down the High Line. The High Line's unusual obduracy, particularly in the context of the unrelenting tide of 'creative destruction in Manhattan' (Page, 1999), turned out to be its saving grace.

New imaginaries: from 'an awful blight' to a 'site for everyone's fantasies'

Key to redeveloping the High Line was to build upon its past and imbue it with a new, exciting future. Inklings of this process started in the 1980s when architects

Steven Holl and John di Domenico first proposed reuse of the High Line as housing with a public promenade and park, respectively (di Domenico, 1983; Holl, 1991). Their work was mostly known among design circles, but it represents an important postmodern turn in thinking about obsolete urban infrastructure. Over time, others proposed additional forms of reuse, including a tourist railroad and light rail transit (Gottlieb, 1986; Obletz, 1988). Initially these proposals did not turn the public tide against demolition of the High Line and did little to convince the property development sector of its potential value. But the increasing residential population surrounding the High Line began to take an interest in the fabric of their neighbourhood and the fate of its unique historic features.

Locked in a political battle where they would be forced to subsume the cost of demolition, CSX hired the Regional Planning Association (RPA) to create and promote a plan for alternative uses that would preserve the High Line. In 1999, at a Community Board meeting where a representative of the RPA presented their alternative ideas, including the recommended alternative of preservation as a park and pedestrian promenade, two community members, Robert Hammond and Joshua David met. The two went on to form Friends of the High Line (FHL), the non-profit that organized the redevelopment of the structure, helped raise money for construction and manages the park today. The fact that the idea came from a more formal planning organization and process is often left out of the accounts of the redevelopment the High Line, but descriptions of Hammond and David as grassroots heroes are nearly universal (and they do deserve considerable credit for their astute efforts and dedication).

One of the first, and rather savvy, steps that FHL took was to reveal images of the little known and seemingly undiscovered wild spaces on top of the High Line to a wider audience. Before there was a High Line to act as a visual reference point for an urban imaginary of the now popular concept of the high-design linear urban park, one had to be created. The High Line 'has always been driven by images' (Friends of the High Line, & Diller Scofidio + Renfro, 2008) and a key first step was photography: 'The High Line's development has been constituted by photography since its inception, as the first push for its preservation was rhetorically organised by images of its ruin and rescue' (Cataldi et al., 2012, p. 360). Early on Friends of the High Line founders David and Hammond enlisted the help of landscape photographer Joel Sternfeld to document the disused High Line in all its wild glory, grasses, trees and other plants having taken over the deck of the structure over the course of 20 years. These pictures were put together as a book to help raise awareness and funds for the High Line (Sternfeld et al., 2001) and later reprinted in a popular major magazine article (Gopnik, 2001). These images of a little seen urban wild and their dissemination were a key step to building excitement about the High Line. Mostly cutting through blocks in a less travelled part of the city, the High Line was not well known to contemporary New Yorkers and easy to look past. While some, like nearby residents such as fashion designer Diane von Furstenberg, loft-dwelling artists, office workers and those brave enough to sneak up, could see the wild green landscape on the High Line, most knew it only as a rusting hulk from below, if they paid much attention to it at all. The pictures of this unknown green wild in an ever less wild Manhattan sparked the imagination about a new frontier among a wide public.

The public's interest was piqued by the publication of the photographs and FHL organized a design competition for ideas on how to redevelop the structure (Friends of the High Line, 2003). This step helped focus the enthusiasm about the new frontier into exciting possibilities. The competition was not about practicality. Designs were fanciful and included everything from dragons to rollercoasters. One top-rated design envisioned the High Line as a linear pool. The rendering included a nude male figure in the pool copied from a David Hockney painting, an allusion to the longstanding gay community of the area. With the designs displayed for throngs of visitors in the main hall of Grand Central Terminal, the public imagination was further piqued. The High Line sparked the imaginations of New Yorkers and, with coverage of it in New York papers that have a national and international reach, increasingly people outside of New York. As co-founder Hammond put it: 'The weird thing is that the High Line is just a structure, it's just metal in the air, but it becomes a site for everybody's fantasies and projections' (Gopnik, 2001, p. 47).

The High Line became a *cause célèbre*. Wealthy New Yorkers, such as Von Furstenberg and her media tycoon husband, provided substantial donations and threw lavish fundraisers. Celebrities became involved as well. The actor Edward Norton, whose father was a key author of the Rails-to-Trails legislation that played a policy role of the conversion of the High Line to a park, was an early supporter and spokesman. He showed megastar Brad Pitt the still abandoned structure, helping him shimmy under a gate for an unsanctioned tour. Actor Kevin Bacon also joined the effort, his father a famous planner, and a picture of him with Edward Norton at the opening of the first phase often comes up in online searches for the High Line.

Sparking the public imagination was key to turning the political tide in favour of the redevelopment of the High Line. Of course, sparking the public imagination was not enough. The High Line project eventually had to confirm to a neoliberal political economy and justify itself as a property development and tax revenue generation tool, not just a public amenity (David & Hammond, 2011). As well, the growing public excitement over the High Line was leveraged by Mayor Bloomberg's administration to get powerful political and development interests behind the project. The Bloomberg Administration linked its support for the High Line park to neighbourhood support for upzoning of parts of the neighbourhood and for a football stadium at Hudson Yards (at the northern terminus of the High Line). Still, it was the early ability to spark the public imagination for a new urban experience that ensured its place in the discourse over the politics of parks and redevelopment that previously had little traction with the powerful real-estate development community and its many allied politicians. As Hammond recognized, its new existence in the public mind was a reflection of the dreams and imaginations that filled it before it was ever opened to the public. The excitement around this potential dream world pulsed through the media and various internet outlets locally, nationally and internationally.

Mobilizing the High Line's urban imaginary

Once completed in 2009, the initial phase was a booming success in terms of visitors, property values and tax receipts. Unlike the early pop of many projects, the High Line's popularity has continued to increase, drawing almost six million visitors in 2014 (Pogrebin, 2015). From the heavy media coverage of its design competitions and the excitement about its much-anticipated construction in the *New York Times* and other international news outlets based in New York, the urban imaginary of High Line had already begun to spread over the world. Once opened, throngs of visitors, a great many who were tourists, began to pick up on this imaginary, mixing it with their own experience and transmitting it through multiple means, particularly social media and similar outlets. Here the widespread and multilayered pre-existing imaginary of New York comes into play (Lindner, 2015) and makes the High Line difficult to extricate from its urban context. The High Line's designers, taking advantage of the somewhat unique vantage point in New York City offered by being on top of a structure 30 feet in the air, accentuated the framing of the city as backdrop. Mini-plazas, like the 'Death Avenue' Amphitheater where a sunken deck with rows of benches facing a large glass window give a view down 10th Avenue, framing it like a television show, 'create a priceless "only in New York" moment' (La Farge, 2012, p. 99). This notion of 'only in New York' is key. The context of New York City plays an important role in the High Line as an actual experience. Towering, often iconic, buildings, straight boulevards and nearby open space of the river provide dramatic views of what is arguably the 'capital' of urban aspiration for the world today (Rykwert, 2000).

This dreamy imaginary, deeply rooted in that of Manhattan, is cultivated by the supporters of the High Line, needing to keep the project popular in order to raise the significant additional funds, well beyond what the city allocates, for maintaining the complicated park. Newsletters, events, art and images of the High Line are all carefully curated and accentuated by the FHL. For example, an iteration of the Von Furstenberg merchandise sold in the park gift shop in the summer of 2014 was covered with the slogan 'dreams come true on the High Line'. Other shirts for sale at the time read 'park in the sky' to emphasize its uniqueness and dream-like qualities. Still others use images of vintage locomotives or the Westside Cowboys to connect present with past. The many visitors, reporters and others that experience the High Line relay this dreamy image of the experience in media, blogs, travelogues, guides, message boards and more. Much of the recapping of the High Line by visitors to the folks back home in various online media takes on the air of early accounts of 'picturesque travel'. The accounts are too lengthy to recount here but easily obtained online from the travel sections of media outlets outside New York and the copious user-generated content of travel sites like Trip Advisor, Facebook and countless blogs. In these accounts the High Line becomes a 'star-gazing event' (Boyer, 1994, p. 238) for visitors who both relay the minute details of clever design as well as the picturesque framing of the iconic Manhattan background. The discourse created reflects what Boyer described as the picturesque sense of travel as 'a way to escape the tedium of everyday life, projecting oneself into an exotic milieu [. . .] as well as telescoping experience, drawing fara-way background as a place full of mystery and adventure into the foreground' (Boyer, 1994, p. 247). The High Line they narrate does not travel as a project per se, but as an urban imaginary of an iconic New York experience.

This notion of framing the High Line in these types of picturesque tab-leaus is important too because, unlike many mobilized redevelopment projects of the past, it is particularly hard to image as a single entity. For example, the Guggenheim Bilbao, the high-design, iconic museum that anchored the renowned regeneration of the Bilbao, Spain waterfront, acts as a clear symbol of that practice and idea. While the use of it as a symbol of the Bilbao model flat-tens the wider context of regeneration, which was much more comprehensive and complicated than the museum itself, it in some ways rightly communicates the idea of the Bilbao effect that it sparked – a high-design museum as a catalyst for the regeneration of an urban neighbourhood. An image of the High Line with the same condensed message, however, is quite difficult. Borrowing from Lynch, it is not 'imagable' as one site (Lynch, 1960). A long, skinny, snaking structure, the only way to capture it all is a distant aerial photograph. Such photographs background much detail and are unsatisfying, yet images of the on-the-ground experience will cut out most of the park and are unable to cap-ture the experience of moving through it, which is key. As a result, despite the image-heavy discourse that circulates of the High Line, aerial photographs of the entire structure are not widely used. Instead, the High Line travels in framed images, snippets, each one carrying a specific message but unable to represent a whole, consistent image. Add to this the reports and tales of the High Line, imbued with the 'residue of a dream world' that envelops the actual experience (Cataldi et al., 2012) and that is what really travels of the High Line.

Feeding this lofty imaginary of the High Line, it has been lauded by critics as an innovation, a masterpiece of design, a new form of public space and much more. It has taken on a larger image than even that of a park or redevelopment project: 'New York's High Line, a public park elevated over the streets of Manhattan's west side, has helped to spark and urban revolution' (Fedele, 2014). Not a park, it has morphed into a symbol of a type of urbanism, an imagined place of the urban future, a place that transforms the old city into the future one. It fits into a larger context of what Short (2012) has called a 'global city imaginary', where the peo-ple of various cities embrace the production of symbols that connect them to an imagery of being a modern, global city.

Concluding discussion

While urban transformation ideas and policies are transferred through a variety of channels and by a range of actors – and certainly formal networks and actors remain a key part of that process – the High Line provides an example of a different and potentially overlooked contemporary mobilization process. Through media, discourse and imagery, mixed with a political environment that lauds ideas generated or adopted by the community, what is in motion of the High Line is produced, aspirational imaginary. The High Line's uniquely iconic status in an iconic city may make its transfer a potentially extreme example of a travelling urban imaginary. However, given the ever quickening transfer of ideas, images and discourse in a rapidly connected world, as well as the intensification of a narrow band of global cities as sites of perceived success, it is likely not an outlier.

Why should we care what travels of the High Line? The concept of a travelling urban imaginary puts the emphasis on how many urban revitalization ideas and practices *really* travel, at least in the case of large and symbolic schemes like the High Line. This is not to discount the still important role of experts, government and formal networks, which still play key roles and are undoubtedly still part of the process. But the way the High Line has been put in motion does not necessarily incorporate the technical-rational formalism that experts, policy professionals and other traditional actors would, at least putatively, imbue into a process of policy transfer. Instead, spread largely through discourse media on the internet across an enormous range of people and places, the High Line's mobilized urban imaginary invites the probing of the conceptions and aspirations of urbanism that are being widely sought in cities across the world. While certainly a bit of hyperbole, the notion that the High Line has 'sparked an urban revolution' is also certainly true. It has invigorated support and excitement for existing projects, focused attention on sites and structures formerly thought of as impediments to revitalization and generally shaped perspectives on urban revitalization priorities and actions around the world. The dreams and aspirations that flow with the imaginary around this 'revolution' play a role in planning and political processes that produce the built environment and allocate resources. In an era of 'austerity urbanism' (Peck, 2012) what garners public investment, or at least public excitement for it, is an important object of study.

Furthermore, honing this analysis should prove useful for the critical examination of mobilized ideas and policies, current and future. The concept of a travelling urban imaginary puts emphasis on the notion that they are not neutral and rational, but are constructed narratives and aspirations. The content of the imaginary should be deeply interrogated as a way of understanding what captures attention and shapes support. It also should encourage clearer thinking about how such an imaginary fits local needs. How do we know if a High Line is the right urban revitalization intervention for another place or how much mutation (adaptation of the idea or practice to a new context) should justify its implementation? There is no clear way to know and this inevitably must be worked through project by project. But demystifying the allure of such travelling imaginariness like the High Line should go a long way to helping clarify these conversations.

References

Anderson, B. (2006). *Imagined communities*. New York: Verso.

Bender, T. (2007). Conclusion: Reflections on the culture of urban modernity. In A. Çinar & T. Bender (Eds.), *Urban imaginaries: Locating the modern city* (pp. 267–277). Minneapolis: University of Minnesota Press.

Boyer, M. C. (1994). *The city of collective memory: Its historical imagery and architectural entertainments*. Cambridge, MA: MIT Press.

Cataldi, M., Kelley, D., Kuzmich, H., Maier-Rothe, J., & Tang, J. (2012). Residues of a dream world: The High Line, 2011. *Theory, Culture & Society, 28*, 358–389.

Chambers, I. (1986). *No popular culture: The metropolitan experience*. New York: Methuen.

Çinar, A., & Bender, T. (Eds.). (2007). *Urban imaginaries: Locating the modern city*. Minneapolis: University of Minnesota Press.

CityMetric Staff. (2015). Here are all the city parks attempting to copy New York's High Line. *CityMetric*, 29 January, London. Retrieved from www.citymetric.com/skylines/here-are-all-city-parks-attempting-copy-new-yorks-high-line-695.

Cresswell, T. (2011). Mobilities I: Catching up. *Progress in Human Geography, 35*, 550–558.

Czarniawska, B., & Sevon, G. (2005). Translation is a vehicle, imitation its motor, and fashion sits at the wheel. In B. Czarniawska & G. Sevon (Eds.), *Global ideas: How ideas, objects and practices travel in a global economy* (pp. 7–12). Malmo, Sweden: Liber & Copenhagen Business School Press.

David, J., & Hammond, R. (2011). *High Line: The inside story of New York City's park in the sky*. New York: Farrar, Straus and Giroux.

di Domenico, J. A. (1983). *The re-use of urban rail infrastructure*. New York.

Donald, J. (1992). Metropolis: The city as text. In R. Bobcock & K. Thompson (Eds.), *Social and cultural forms of modernity* (pp. 417–461). Cambridge: Polity Press.

Dowding, K. (1995). Model or metaphor? A critical review of the policy network approach. *Political Studies, 45*, 136–158.

Fedele, A. (2014). How public spaces make cities work. Retrieved from http://sourceable.net/how-public-spaces-make-cities-work/.

Friends of the High Line. (2003). *Designing the High Line: Ideas for reclaiming 1.5 miles of Manhattan: Winners and selected entries*. New York: Friends of the High Line.

Friends of the High Line, & Diller Scofidio + Renfro. (2008). *Designing the High Line: Gansevoort Street to 30th Street*. New York: Friends of the High Line.

Gonzalez, S. (2010). Bilbao and Barcelona "in motion." How urban regeneration "models" travel and mutate in the global flows of policy tourism. *Urban Studies, 48*, 1397–1418.

Gopnik, A. (2001). A walk on the High Line. *The New Yorker*, May, 44–49.

Gottlieb, M. (1986). West siders may get a reprieve from the IRT. *The New York Times*, 23 March, E7.

Gray, C. (1988). Streetscapes: The west side improvement; On the Lower West Side, fate of old rail line is undecided. *The New York Times*, 3 January.

Hall, P. (2002). *Cities of tomorrow: An intellectual history of urban planning and design in the twentieth century*. Oxford: Blackwell.

Hedmo, T., Shalin-Andersson, K., & Wedlin, L. (2005). Fields of imitation: The global expansion of management education. In B. Czarniawska-Joerges & G. Sevón (Eds.), *Global ideas: How ideas, objects and practices travel in a global economy* (pp. 190–212). Malmö, Sweden: Liber & Copenhagen Business School Press.

Holl, S. (1991). *Anchoring: Selected projects, 1975–1991*. New York: Princeton Architectural Press.

Jaffe, E. (2011). Descendants of the High Line. Retrieved from www.theatlanticcities.com/design/2011/09/what-high-line-hath-wrought/196/.

King, A. D. (1980). Exporting planning: The colonial and neo-colonial experience. In G. E. Cherry (Ed.), *Shaping an urban world* (pp. 203–226). London: Mansell.

Klingmann, A. (2007). *Brandscapes: Architecture in the experience economy*. Cambridge, MA: MIT Press.

Kwaak, J. S. (2014). Seoul plans High Line style elevated park. *The Wall Street Journal*, 1 September.

La Farge, A. (2012). *On the High Line: Exploring America's most original urban park*. New York: Thames & Hudson.

Lindner, C. (2015). *Imagining New York City: Literature, urbanism, and the visual arts, 1890–1940*. Cambridge, MA: Oxford University Press.

Lynch, K. (1960). *The image of the city*. Cambridge, MA: MIT Press.

McCann, E. J. (2008). Expertise, truth, and urban policy mobilities: Global circuits of knowledge in the development of Vancouver, Canada's 'four pillar' drug strategy. *Environment and Planning A*, *40*, 885–904.

McCann, E., & Ward, K. (2010). Relationality/territoriality: Toward a conceptualization of cities in the world. *Geoforum*, *41*, 175–184.

McCann, E., & Ward, K. (2012). Policy assemblages, mobilities and mutations: Toward a multidisciplinary conversation. *Political Studies Review*, *10*, 325–332.

Moss, J. (2012). Disney World on the Hudson. *The New York Times*, 22 August, A.25.

New York Central Railroad Company. (1934). *West Side improvement: Initial stage dedicated June 28, 1934*. New York. Retrieved from www.flickriver.com/photos/davidelevine/sets/72157622952611535/.

Obletz, P. (1988). Abandoned El takes U turn. *New York Newsday*, 2 May, 54.

Page, M. (1999). *The creative destruction of Manhattan, 1900–1940*. Chicago, IL: University of Chicago Press.

Patrick, D. J. (2013). The matter of displacement: A queer urban ecology of New York City's High Line. *Social & Cultural Geography*, *15*, 920–941.

Peck, J. (2011). Geographies of policy: From transfer-diffusion to mobility-mutation. *Progress in Human Geography*, *35*, 773–797.

Peck, J. (2012). Austerity urbanism. *City: Analysis of Urban Trends, Culture, Theory, Policy, Action*, *16*, 626–655.

Pogrebin, R. (2015). Whitney Museum contemplates a bigger future, with bigger expenses. *The New York Times*, 1 April, C1.

Rodgers, D. T. (1998). *Atlantic crossings: Social politics in the progressive age*. Cambridge, MA: The Belknap Press of Harvard University Press.

Rybczynski, W. (2011). Bringing the High Line back to earth. *The New York Times*, 15 May.

Rykwert, J. (2000). *The seduction of place: The city in the twenty-first century*. New York: Pantheon Books.

Saffron, I. (2011). A park on high: The extension of New York's vibrant High Line sparks excitement for our own Reading Viaduct – what could be a linear version of Rittenhouse Square. *Philadelphia Inquirer*, 17 June, E1.

Scobey, D. M. (2002). *Empire city: The making and meaning of the New York City landscape*. Philadelphia, PA: Temple University Press.

Short, J. R. (2012). *Globalization, modernity and the city*. New York: Routledge.

Sternfeld, J., Gopnik, A., & Stilgoe, J. R. (2001). *Walking the High Line*. Göttingen and New York: Steidl Pace/MacGill Gallery.

Sutcliffe, A. (1981). *Towards the planned city: Germany, Britain, the United States, and France, 1780–1914*. New York: St Martin's Press.

Taylor, K. (2010). After High Line's success, other cities look up. *The New York Times*, 14 July.

Ward, S. V. (2000). Re-examining the international diffusion of planning. In R. Freestone (Ed.), *Urban planning in a changing world: The twentieth century experience* (pp. 40–60). New York: Routledge.

Wilson, M. (2011). Sex and the city: Another urban imaginary. *Frontiers: A Journal of Women Studies*, *32*, 5–8.

Zukin, S. (2014). Postcard-perfect: The big business of city branding. *The Guardian*, 6 May.

3   Urban revitalization in a neoliberal key

Brownfield redevelopment in Michigan

Mark D. Bjelland and Ian Noyes

Introduction

Recent urban renaissance projects have seen cities reimagine their skylines, waterfronts, waterways and inner-city districts by clearing, cleaning and redeveloping former industrial sites. Former industrial lands that have undergone or are currently undergoing environmental clean-up and redevelopment include, for example: London's Olympic Park, Toronto's waterfront, Melbourne's Docklands, Sydney's Darling Harbour, Brooklyn's Flushing riverfront and Gowanus Canal, Vancouver's False Creek, Portland's Pearl District and Minneapolis's Mill District. Derelict former urban industrial sites are often prime candidates for urban revitalization projects in both developed and developing countries (Wu & Chen, 2012). However, the redevelopment of under-utilized industrial properties, referred to as brownfield sites, is complicated by environmental contamination, clean-up costs and legal liability concerns. This chapter argues, in the United States the reuse of brownfield sites has been addressed within a neoliberal framework that values market solutions, private sector initiatives, public–private partnerships and entrepreneurial urban governance. In Michigan, as in most other states, legal and financial concerns in redeveloping brownfield sites have been addressed by streamlining environmental regulations, reducing technical and legal uncertainties and supporting private sector redevelopment initiatives with generous public subsidies. As with other government programmes, tensions exist between equity and efficiency. The environmental justice movement, which helped identify the brownfields issue in the United States, called for targeting public subsidies to distressed communities. On the other hand, the reality of fiscal retrenchment at state and federal levels and the neoliberal framework for brownfield policy prioritizes efficiency. This study explores that tension between efficiency and equity by looking at where public subsidies have been directed within a state marked by an extensive legacy of both industrial activity and highly uneven spatial development.

Brownfields and urban revitalization

The term 'brownfield' emerged in different contexts, and thus is approached differently by North America and European scholars (Adams & De Sousa, 2007).

In the United States, concern with brownfields emerged in response to legal and technical challenges of redeveloping potentially contaminated industrial sites. Thus, brownfield sites are defined in the United States as vacant or under-utilized industrial or commercial properties with potential environmental contamination. In the UK, for example, concern with reducing urban sprawl led to numerical targets for the percentage of new housing located on brownfield sites which were defined as previously developed land, regardless of the potential for environmental contamination (Ganser & Williams, 2007). Regardless of the definition considered, the existence of brownfield sites raises important questions about the effects of uneven urban economic development and land-use systems. Moreover, in the absence of public intervention, developers tend to pass over brownfield sites in favour of greenfield sites.

Abandoned contaminated sites raise legal and ethical questions concerning responsibility for cleaning up the toxic legacies and obsolete structures of the industrial past. The Comprehensive Environmental Restoration, Compensation, and Liability Act (CERCLA) of 1980 and the Superfund Amendments and Reauthorization Act of 1986 (SARA) were original legal frameworks for addressing site contamination stemming from past activities in the United States. CERCLA, nicknamed Superfund for its revolving clean-up trust fund, intended to make polluting industries responsible for site clean-up costs. The CERCLA trust fund was funded by special taxes on the chemical and petroleum industries which were used to clean up abandoned or uncontrolled hazardous waste sites. CERCLA applied strict, joint, several and retroactive liability clauses so that any party associated with a site, regardless of fault, could be held fully responsible for all site investigation and remediation costs. In practice, large corporations with deep pockets were initially held responsible by the United States Environmental Protection Agency (EPA). Likewise, SARA applied stringent clean-up standards for contaminated soils and water, forcing clean-ups to meet any applicable, relevant or appropriate requirements.

Together, CERCLA's liability structure and SARA's stringent standards cast a foreboding shadow over urban industrial and commercial property markets and was largely responsible for the brownfields crisis that emerged in the 1990s. In addition to the Superfund sites which posed immediate risks to human health or the environment, older cities contained large numbers of old industrial sites with less severe contamination than Superfund sites – brownfields – where environmental liability concerns and clean-up costs posed barriers to economically beneficial reuse projects, provoking a crisis for older cities in the United States (Glaser, 1994; Platt, 1998). Surveys in the 1990s revealed that significant numbers of banks had altered their lending patterns to avoid potential liability for past contamination at industrial sites, effectively 'brownlining' much older, industrial land (Swartz, 1994; Yount & Meyer, 1994; Meyer & Reaves, 1997). Lost jobs, a lost tax base and blight associated with brownfield sites created a significant burden for older industrial cities. Inventories of brownfield sites estimated as much as 15 per cent of the land area in Detroit, Michigan and 10 per cent in Chicago, Illinois consisted of brownfield sites (Simons & Iannone, 1996).

Neoliberal consensus and brownfield redevelopment

Neoliberal assumptions undergird contemporary urban development processes in North America and Europe (Brenner & Theodore, 2005). Within a neoliberal framework, cities must adopt an entrepreneurial stance marked by fiscal discipline, market-led urban renewal projects and public–private partnerships (see Harvey, 1989). As federal and state funding for local governments has declined and responsibility has been devolved to local units of government, cities have been forced to rely more on local property taxes. This neoliberal turn has increased the importance of private sector investors and developers and spurred the entrepreneurial city's increased use of tax increment financing (TIF) in hopes of increasing future property values (Weber, 2006). Contradicting its outward presentation, neoliberalism does not mean reduced state spending. Rather, governments are expected to provide strong financial incentives in order to leverage private sector investment in inner-city urban renewal areas (Adair et al., 2003). Neoliberalism has proved to be highly adaptable and has shown itself compatible with the shift to sustainability discourses in urban governance (Gibbs et al., 2013). Thus, within neoliberal cities, place promotion, economic development, livability and sustainable development are often conflated in quests to green the entrepreneurial city (Jonas & While, 2007).

Existing arguments pertinent to brownfield redevelopment highlight efficient use of existing infrastructure, elimination of blight in impoverished communities, creation of jobs in areas of high unemployment, increased densities in areas served by public transit, reduced pressure for greenfield development and the opportunity for a bold new urban imaginary on the *tabula rasa* of brownfield sites. The proliferation of brownfield sites was also framed as an environmental justice issue as sites were geographically concentrated in minority and low-income communities (Eckerd & Keeler, 2012). Infill reuse and redevelopment of brownfield sites came to be seen as the ultimate form of recycling by reusing derelict land and promoting a more sustainable, compact urban form. Given limited public sector resources, promotion of private sector redevelopment of brownfield sites was seen as the ideal fusion of urban entrepreneurialism and sustainable development. Convinced of the importance of reducing sprawl and concerns about environmental justice, environmental regulators at the United States EPA and at the state level partnered with developers and local government officials to develop streamlined brownfield programmes that would lure investment to neglected locations. This green urban entrepreneurialism was led by coalitions of planners, developers and environmental regulators, all working to lure mobile capital to sullied urban spaces. The different arguments marshalled in support of brownfield redevelopment meant that the neoliberal consensus emerged alongside undercurrents of sustainable development and environmental justice. This gave the brownfield movement greater coalition-building power, but also left unresolved tensions between economic efficiency, equity and sustainability.

Unlike Superfund sites which posed clear threats to human health and the environment, brownfield sites were framed primarily as legal or financial risks to potential developers. Where CERCLA had placed a heavy financial burden on industrial corporations and imposed stringent environmental regulations, the neoliberal brownfield consensus that emerged in the late 1990s called for a variety of policy instruments and reforms focused on removing barriers to private sector investment. Policy instruments including protections for lenders and developers against legal liability for past contamination. Regulatory reforms included relaxed risk-based clean-up standards and streamlined approvals. Furthermore, federal and state grants were combined with tax incentives for private sector investors tackling brownfield projects (Tansel et al., 1999). These reforms have helped to help make brownfield redevelopment a normal, albeit somewhat more complicated, part of the urban land development process (Wernstadt & Hersh, 2006). Still, in many locations, successful brownfield redevelopment relies upon public subsidies for site investigation, clean-up and redevelopment work, so such sites can compete against greenfield sites (De Sousa, 2000; see also Kitson et al., Chapter 5 in this volume). For example, a United States Conference of Mayors (2006) study found that in 87 per cent of cities, the main barrier to brownfield site redevelopment was a lack of public clean-up subsidies. In addition to clean-up grants, tax incentives and relief from potential third party liability and clean-up liability, real-estate developers have called for reduced requirements for public hearings on redevelopment projects (Wernstadt et al., 2006). Additional public spending on infrastructure and transportation improvements in the surrounding area has also been justified to stimulate private real-estate investment in brownfield site redevelopments (Meyer & Lyons, 2000; Johnson et al., 2002; Amekudzi & Fomunung, 2004).

Given their neoliberal origins, state and local brownfield programmes have had a pragmatic economic development orientation, focused on completing construction projects and generating property taxes to recover the public investments. However, a number of authors have bemoaned the lack of objective evaluation of public investments in brownfield programmes (Amekudzi et al., 1997, Wernstadt & Hersh, 2006). Most evaluative studies have focused on economic efficiency criteria such as job creation, private investment levels and financial returns on public investment (Gilliland, 1999; Hamm & Walzer, 2007; Howland, 2007). In their study of 55 state-funded brownfield clean-up and redevelopment projects across Michigan, Jones and Welsh (2012) judged the programmes very successful in promoting clean-up and redevelopment of brownfield sites. The criterion for success in Jones and Welsh's (2012) study, however, was the return on public investment, not equity or community benefits.

The United States EPA's criteria for evaluating brownfield assessment grant proposals go beyond economic efficiency criteria and reflect a concern with economic distress, social justice and sustainability. Their own project evaluations focus on project completion rates but do examine potential differences based on the demographics of the host communities (United States EPA, 2012). Solitaire and Greenberg used equity as their evaluation criteria, comparing the demographics and socio-economic status of communities receiving United States EPA's brownfield assessment pilot programme grants with similar-sized cities that did not receive grants. They concluded that the EPA's pilot programme grants were environmentally just because they successfully targeted cities that were relatively poor with high minority group populations (Solitaire & Greenberg, 2002). Lee and Mohai (2012) evaluated the environmental justice aspects of brownfield site clean-up in greater Detroit; they found that sites near low-income and minority communities were cleaned up faster than sites in other communities.

Michigan's brownfield approach

Michigan provides an important test of brownfield policies because of its central location within the United States manufacturing belt. Michigan also plays a leading role in supporting the redevelopment of brownfield sites. Spatial restructuring of core manufacturing activities such as automobiles, appliances and steel has left Michigan with one of the country's largest inventories of under-utilized industrial sites (National Association of Local Government Environmental Professionals, 2004). The Michigan Economic Development Corporation (2008) estimates there are 18,000 hectares of brownfields in Michigan, and the EPA estimated that Detroit alone has 45,000 tax-forfeited brownfield sites (United States Environmental Protection Agency, 2000). The loss of manufacturing firms in Michigan is rivalled by few other states. Detroit is by far the most distressed large city in the United States. When the city underwent bankruptcy in 2013 it was the largest municipality to ever do so in United States history. In addition to Detroit, other cities in Michigan such as Flint and Benton Harbor have been taken over by governor-appointed emergency managers as they faced impending bankruptcy.

Michigan governor Rick Snyder has worked vigorously to replace the state's Rust Belt image with a new moniker as the 'Comeback State'. Snyder's goals for reinventing Michigan include attempting to 'create more and better jobs, restore our cities, [and] protect our environment' (Snyder, 2012). As part of the reinvention campaign, Michigan has sought to make state government programmes more efficient and market-driven. 'Pure Michigan' is a $31 million advertising campaign to rebrand the state (Lane, 2014); advertisements began in 2006 and focus on the state's natural beauty and Great Lakes shoreline. As this chapter will argue, the challenge of reinventing Michigan, however, requires dealing with the state's legacy of under-utilized and environmentally contaminated brownfield sites.

Hula and Bromley-Trujillo (2010) identified two important innovations in Michigan's brownfield policies: 1) flexible clean-up standards, and 2) limited owner liability – each responding to inadequacies of the federal CERCLA legislation and creating a more conducive environment for private sector investment. Land owners in Michigan are not responsible for contamination they did not cause. To avoid liability, new owners are required to file a Baseline Environmental Assessment (BEA) with the Michigan Department of Environmental Quality (DEQ) within 45 days of acquiring a property and exercise due care. Due care involves preventing human exposure to contamination and preventing the spread of contamination. Clean-up standards in Michigan are based on planned land uses and a less stringent standard of 10^{-5} excess cancer risk rather than the EPA standard of 10⁻⁶. The Michigan DEQ permits the use of institutional controls to manage risk so that paving a parking lot over contaminated soils could be considered an acceptable remedy to minimize exposure. A review of BEA filings from 1995 to 2005 provided overwhelming evidence that there was an active market for brownfield properties in Michigan and that developers' and lenders' concerns were being addressed (Hula & Bromley-Trujillo, 2010).

Two other key policy innovations in Michigan's approach to brownfields were a primary reliance on voluntary, private sector actions to address brownfields and public sector subsidies that stand out for their wide scope and magnitude (Hula & Davis, 2004; Hula et al., 2009). Brownfield work by Michigan's local governments and their private sector partners has been funded through several state programmes including: $45 million in the 1988 Michigan Environmental Protection Bond, $77.2 million in the Cleanup and Redevelopment Fund and $335 million for Brownfield Redevelopment Grants through the voter-approved Clean Michigan Initiative (Michigan DEQ, 2015). In their 2014 report, the Michigan DEQ boasted that through these grant and loan programmes more than 500 sites have been prepared for redevelopment yet they warned that 'there are still thousands of sites to be addressed that need additional funding' (Michigan DEQ, 2015, p. 18). In addition to grants and loans, the Brownfield Redevelopment Financing Act (PA 381) of 1996 authorized local government units to create brownfield redevelopment authorities with the power to implement brownfield plans using tax increment financing to fund eligible activities. In 2000, the State of Michigan created special incentives for 144 designated core communities. Core communities could now use brownfield tools on a wider range of blighted and functionally obsolete property. Eligible activities include environmental response work, demolition, public infrastructure improvements, site preparation and lead and asbestos abatement. Brownfield tax increment financing is particularly attractive because it can be used for expenses such as demolition and public improvements such as parking facilities which are ineligible for conventional TIF programmes.

While environmental justice concerns have influenced the distribution of United States EPA brownfield grants, Michigan's brownfield investigation and clean-up grant and loan programmes operate within a neoliberal framework that emphasizes economic efficiency, entrepreneurial local government and public–private partnerships. Nomination of sites for the grant programmes depends on the initiative of local government actors who are strongly influenced by expressions of interest from the private sector real-estate developers. Brownfield sites lacking a viable redevelopment proposal are generally ineligible (Michigan DEQ, 2011). On the one hand, the legislation for Michigan's Cleanup and Redevelopment Fund establishes a wide range of goals including 'to address public health and environmental problems or to promote redevelopment' (Act 451, Section 324.19608). However, the legislation also specifies that the funds are to be used on properties with 'demonstrable economic development potential' (Act 451, Section 324.19508). Similarly, the Clean Michigan Initiative Brownfield Redevelopment Grants are to be used for 'identified economic redevelopment projects' (Michigan DEQ, 2016).

Methods

This study continues Solitaire and Greenberg's (2002) attention to equity in the distribution of brownfield subsidies with two significant differences. Where previous research focused on the rather modest EPA assessment grants, we focus on the much larger state and local subsidy programmes. Furthermore, where they defined equity as distributing funds to economically distressed communities, we define equity as distributing funds based on demonstrated need, which we take to be a community's estimated inventory of vacant former industrial sites. Our approach is to develop a predictive model for the spatial distribution of brownfield sites based on historic manufacturing activity and deindustrialization. Mapping historic industrial land uses has been shown to predict the locations of contaminated sites (Colten, 1990). Analysis of the spatial patterns of industrialization, deindustrialization and site clean-up activity in the Minneapolis-St Paul metropolitan region showed that the abundance of brownfield sites was highly correlated with indicators of historic industrial activity (Bjelland, 2004). Of particular importance in predicting a community's brownfield burden was the number of manufacturing establishments operating in the period prior to passage of key environmental regulations governing the handling and disposal of toxic substances such as the Resource Conservation and Recovery Act (RCRA) of 1976 and the CERCLA in 1980. By comparing the predicted geography of brownfield sites to the spatial distribution of public subsidies for brownfield work we can assess the extent to which Michigan's system of private initiative and public subsidies is working effectively throughout the state, that is, whether public funds are being allocated equitably to places based on their burden of brownfield sites.

This study's spatial analysis uses 84 areal units: the 83 counties in Michigan with Wayne County divided into two parts – Detroit and suburban Wayne County. Dividing Wayne County offers two advantages: it splits the state's most populous county into two areal units of comparable population size and it allows an analytical focus on the state's historically most important manufacturing centre. Data on brownfield grants, loans and tax increment financing awarded between 1992 and 2014 were obtained from the Michigan DEQ. The primary source of industrial data was the United States Census Bureau's *Census of Manufactures, Geographic Area Series* from 1939 to 2012, generally issued twice a decade. Unfortunately, no census of manufacturing was conducted between 1939 and 1947, thus our data misses the peak of wartime production activity.

Our predictive model assumes an area's share of the state's brownfield site inventory is proportional to its share of the state's pre-CERCLA manufacturing and deindustrialization legacy, hereafter referred to as the industrial legacy. It is reasonable to assume that any vacant, former manufacturing facility is a brownfield site. Furthermore, the probability that the site contains significant contamination goes up if it was in use prior to the passage of RCRA in 1976 and CERCLA in 1980. The local share of the state's industrial legacy was computed based on the average of its share of the state's totals for two variables measuring manufacturing activity prior to CERCLA and two measuring deindustrialization:

1) Maximum number of manufacturing establishments prior to 1980.
2) Loss of manufacturing establishments, peak to 2012.
3) Maximum number of manufacturing jobs prior to 1980.
4) Loss of manufacturing jobs, peak to 2012.

We combine the number of manufacturing establishments with data on manufacturing jobs because establishments vary widely in size, usage and degree of environmental clean-up required. The number of jobs offers a reasonable indicator of the magnitude of individual manufacturing operations and the likely costs in remediating such facilities. The measures of maximum numbers and losses are complementary since the maximum number of manufacturing establishments and jobs speaks to the magnitude of historic industrial legacy but not to the extent of deindustrialization. For each of the four measures, first the local share was computed by dividing the local value by the state-wide total. Then, the results for each of the four measures were averaged to compute each area's share of Michigan's industrial legacy. The expected brownfield subsidy allocated to each county was calculated as the county's share of Michigan's industrial legacy multiplied by the total amount of state subsidies. The differences between actual and expected subsidies were divided by the 2010 population to make the values comparable between regions.

Spatial distribution of public subsidies

The State of Michigan has disbursed $406 million in brownfield subsidies to communities across the state, $190 million in grants and loans for 381 projects and $217 million in tax increment financing for 401 different projects. Recipients include 67 of 83 counties, including all of the state's metropolitan regions and major cities. State funding of brownfield investigation and clean-up work totals $41 per Michigan resident. An initial examination of the spatial distribution reveals that Detroit received $58 per resident, which, if one ignores the industrial history of that city, suggests a reasonably fair distribution. However, that per capita calculation uses the 2010 population in the denominator rather than the 1950 population when Detroit was more than 2.5 times as populous. Suburban Wayne County received $74 per person and Schoolcraft County on Lake Michigan in the Upper Peninsula received $361 per person while Grand Traverse County on Lake Michigan in the northwest corner of the Lower Peninsula received $240 per person. For a more meaningful analysis of the geography of subsidies for brownfield work, we compare it to the region's industrial legacy.

Spatial restructuring of the manufacturing industry has resulted in waves of relocations and displacements, hitting Michigan particularly hard because of its location in the heart of the United States manufacturing belt and its central role in the automotive industry. First, in the middle of the twentieth century firms relocated within the state to suburban locations with ample greenfield land and highway access. In the 1980s, manufacturing operations began leaving the state for lower-wage regions elsewhere in the United States and in Mexico. The state peaked in manufacturing employment in 1967 and since has lost over half its manufacturing jobs with losses exceeding 500,000 jobs (Table 3.1). The loss in jobs has been, in part, due to the replacement of labour with capital. However, the number of manufacturing establishments in Michigan has also declined by 25 per cent from its peak in 1992. Thus, with heavy job losses in its manufacturing sector, Michigan was the only state in the United States to lose population during the period 2000–2010.

Michigan's industrial legacy was highly concentrated in Detroit, the Detroit suburbs and nearby Flint in Genesee County. Historic manufacturing activity and deindustrialization has been most pronounced across the highly urbanized southern tier of the state (Figure 3.1). On the other hand, industrial activities were relatively limited in the rural northern Lower Peninsula and Upper Peninsula of the state. Michigan's four largest cities at the time CERCLA was passed in 1980, Detroit, Grand Rapids, Flint and Warren, have all suffered extensive deindustrialization. Only Grand Rapids has avoided significant population loss. Deindustrialization has been most pronounced in Detroit, Grand Rapids and Flint since they have experienced all three waves of spatial restructuring. Warren, an industrial suburb of Detroit, appears to be following the same path of decline as the older central cities with a lag period of several decades. Most importantly, these industrial cities have had net losses of more than half their manufacturing establishments and manufacturing jobs. From its peak, Detroit has had net losses of 89 per cent of its manufacturing establishments and 95 per cent of its manufacturing jobs. Detroit's losses are likely underestimated since there was no census of manufacturing during its Second World War peak of production. Flint has had net losses of 58 per cent of its manufacturing establishments and 89 per cent of its manufacturing jobs. As a consequence, both Flint and Detroit have witnessed massive depopulation and fiscal distress.

While Detroit has been the state's historic centre of manufacturing, all Michigan counties had at least some industrial legacy that would predict the existence of brownfield sites. At the low end, 11 counties, all located in northern Michigan or the Upper Peninsula, had a local share of the state-wide industrial legacy of less than 0.10 per cent. At the high end, Detroit was calculated to have 29.9 per cent of the state's industrial legacy, followed by 10.6 per cent in suburban Wayne County. For the 83 Michigan counties plus the city of Detroit, the local share of the state's industrial legacy predicts the local share of state brownfield subsidies reasonably well, explaining about 40 per cent of the variation between areas (r-squared = 0.403). For example, Kent County, home to the state's second largest city Grand Rapids, was calculated to have 3.8 per cent of the state's industrial legacy and thus was predicted to receive 3.8 per cent of the state's brownfield site funding or $15.5 million. Instead, Kent County received $20.7 million or 5.1 per cent of the state's brownfield subsidies, $5.2 million or 33 per cent more than predicted. The ordinary least squares best-fit line has a slope of 0.83 indicating that

Table 3.1 Profile of population and manufacturing activity in Michigan and most populous cities in 1980

	Detroit (Wayne)	Flint (Genessee)	Grand Rapids (Kent)	Warren (McComb)	Michigan
Year of peak population	1950	1960	2000	1970	2000
Peak population	1,850,000	197,000	198,000	179,000	9,922,000
Population, 2010	714,000	102,000	188,000	134,000	9,884,000
Population decline from peak to 2010	61%	48%	5%	25%	0.4%
Year of peak manufacturing establishments	1954	1967	1958	1977	1992
Peak no. of manufacturing establishments	3,543	168	613	713	16,531
Manufacturing establishments, 2012	382	70	293	320	12,444
Decline in manufacturing establishments	89%	58%	52%	55%	25%
Year of peak manufacturing employment	1947	1954	1947	1972	1967
Peak manufacturing employment	338,400	59,900	44,200	60,000	1,045,000
Manufacturing employment, 2012	17,600	6,400	18,000	13,600	514,000
Decline in manufacturing employment	95%	89%	59%	77%	51%

Data Sources: United States Census Bureau, Census of Manufactures, Geographic Area Series: Michigan, 1947–2012. United States Census Bureau, Census of Population, 1940–2010.

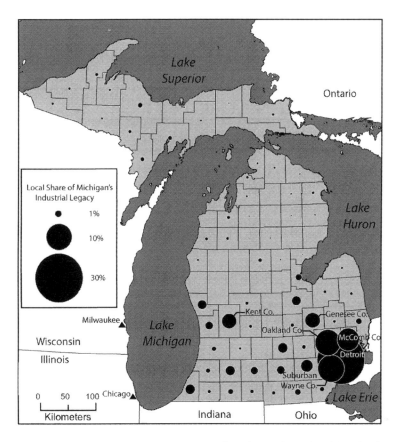

Figure 3.1 Local share of Michigan's manufacturing and deindustrialization legacy for Detroit and Michigan counties, calculations by authors (data: United States Census Bureau, Census of Manufacturers, series 1947–2012).

a 1.0 per cent increase in a county's share of the state's industrial legacy would result in a 0.83 per cent increase in that county's share of state-wide brownfield spending. While our model to predict a local area's share of brownfield subsidies based on its industrial legacy works reasonably well, a case by case examination of the relationship between predicted and actual brownfield subsidies reveals several geographic areas with significant deviations.

Favoured locations

Receiving substantially more in state brownfield subsidies than predicted was suburban Wayne County just west of Detroit and a number of counties bordering the Great Lakes (Figure 3.2). The additional subsidies received by suburban Wayne County were relatively modest on a per capita basis. That was not the case in Monroe County on Lake Erie, Grand Traverse, Berrien and Muskegon counties

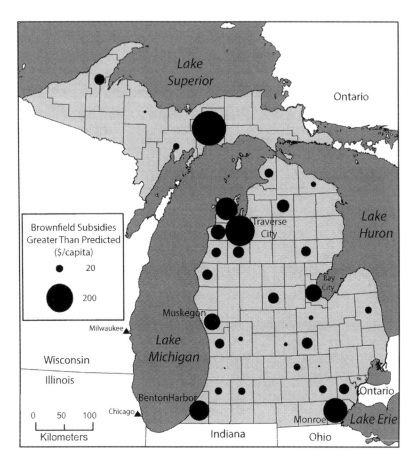

Figure 3.2 Michigan counties receiving disproportionately large brownfield subsidies.

on Lake Michigan or Bay County on Lake Huron. Here, the subsidies per capita ranged from $79 to $225 per capita greater than predicted.

The role of amenities in drawing real-estate investment and spurring financially viable brownfield site redevelopment projects is apparent in comparisons between groups of counties. The 14 Lower Peninsula counties bordering Lake Michigan attracted more than three times the predicted amount of brownfield grants, loans and TIF, garnering 24.0 per cent of the state's brownfield subsidies despite having just 10.8 per cent of the state's population and 7.7 per cent of the state's industrial legacy (Table 3.2). The recreational counties as classified by the United States Department of Agriculture (USDA) are also over-represented in brownfield subsidies. The four retirement destination counties as designated by the USDA did even better, receiving more than 12 times their predicted share.

Traverse City in Grand Traverse County, a Lake Michigan resort and retirement destination, has been among the greatest recipients of state subsidies for

Table 3.2 Brownfield subsidies for amenity regions of Michigan

Category	Number of counties	Population, 2010	Share of Michigan's industrial legacy	Predicted brownfield subsidies	Actual share of state subsidies	Actual state subsidies	Difference per capita
Lower Peninsula counties on Lake Michigan	14	1,069,000	7.7%	$31,600,000	24.0%	$97,500,000	$62
Recreational counties	36	839,000	5.8%	$23,400,000	11.2%	$45,500,000	$26
Retirement destination counties	4	138,000	0.5%	$2,000,000	6.3%	$25,500,000	$170
Michigan, statewide	83	9,884,000	100.0%	NA	100.0%	$406,000,000	NA

brownfield work relative to its industrial legacy. Traverse City is a playground for the winners in Michigan's new post-industrial economy and the polar opposite of southeast Michigan's Rust Belt decay. Traverse City borders two narrow peninsulas filled with resorts, marinas, wineries and fruit orchards. Traverse City is also a gateway to Sleeping Bear Dunes National Lakeshore. While Traverse City's industrial legacy is relatively minor, its environmental contamination issues were not insignificant. Brownfield projects have addressed a heavily contaminated former manufactured gas plant site and a cyanide plume beneath portions of the city. In Traverse City, brownfield projects have focused on converting lake and riverfront properties to mixed-use commercial and residential buildings, many of them second homes promoted to buyers in cities such as Chicago and Toronto (see Jones & Welsh, 2012).

Bypassed places

Receiving substantially less in state brownfield subsidies than predicted are areas in southeast Michigan that have struggled with deindustrialization and the consequences of concentrated poverty and fiscal distress (Table 3.3). Detroit had 29.9 per cent of Michigan's industrial legacy and yet received only 10.2 per cent of the state's brownfield subsidies. This represents a loss of $80 million or $112 per capita in Detroit when compared to the predicted quantity. McComb County and Oakland County, both north of Detroit, have both received less than expected in brownfield subsidies. McComb County had 7.7 per cent of the state's industrial legacy and yet received just 0.6 per cent of the state's brownfield subsidies. Other jurisdictions that received substantially less in subsidies than predicted were Detroit area suburban counties Lenawee and St Clair, and Genesee County, home to Flint, Michigan. In Flint, the use of county-scale analysis undoubtedly obscures the depth of deindustrialization and distress in the central city, masking its decline with averages that include its relatively prosperous suburbs.

In-between places

Benton Harbor captures both extremes: it is a distressed manufacturing community in a popular tourist and second home area located along Lake Michigan 145 kilometres from Chicago. While Benton Harbor was an industrial centre, its twin city Saint Joseph, Michigan, on the opposite bank of the St Joseph River, is the primary tourist centre. While Benton Harbor is 89 per cent African American and has a poverty rate of 47 per cent, Saint Joseph is 88 per cent white and has a poverty rate of 8 per cent. Benton Harbor is the headquarters of Whirlpool Corporation, the world's largest appliance manufacturer. The region retains the corporation's management and engineering functions but all local production facilities have been closed in favour of lower-wage production locations elsewhere in the United States, Mexico and abroad. Benton Harbor is the site of an immense brownfield redevelopment project spearheaded by Whirlpool Corporation's local foundation and community development arm. Approximately 230 hectares of riverfront land

Table 3.3 Areas receiving fewer state brownfield subsidies than predicted

Area	Metropolitan region	Share of Michigan's industrial legacy	Predicted brownfield subsidies	Actual share of state subsidies	Actual state subsidies	Difference	Difference per capita
Detroit, City	Detroit-Warren-Dearborn MSA	29.9%	$121,300,000	10.2%	$41,200,000	($80,100,000)	($112)
Macomb County	Detroit-Warren-Dearborn MSA	7.7%	$31,500,000	0.6%	$2,300,000	($29,200,000)	($35)
Oakland County	Detroit-Warren-Dearborn MSA	10.0%	$40,500,000	4.5%	$18,425,000	($22,100,000)	($18)
Genesee County	Flint MSA	3.8%	$15,600,000	0.7%	$2,761,000	($12,800,000)	($30)
Lenawee County	Detroit-Warren-Ann Arbor CSA	0.87%	$3,500,000	0.02%	$100,000	($3,400,000)	($34)
St Clair County	Detroit-Warren-Dearborn MSA	0.85%	$,3,500,000	0.03%	$140,000	($3,360,000)	($20)

near the Lake Michigan harbour has been converted from derelict factories to two hotels, four marinas and a golf course community with 850 upscale single family houses (Jones & Welsh, 2012). Benton Harbor's only lakefront park was partially sacrificed for part of the golf course, leading to two citizen lawsuits. Meanwhile the housing market in the nearby neighbourhoods of Benton Harbor suffers with extremely low values, high rates of foreclosures, abandoned housing and empty lots. The new golf course homes and marina hotels are aimed at a completely different market, primarily for second-home buyers and long-distance commuters from the Chicago area. The project is a bold departure from the community's industrial past. It does nothing to stem the deindustrialization and manufacturing job losses, but instead attempts to lure outside capital in search of amenities and leisure activities.

Conclusions

In practice, urban redevelopment in Michigan has become brownfield redevelopment. Michigan's brownfield programmes, while administered by the Remediation Division of the Department of Environmental Quality, have shifted closer to the UK definition of brownfields as previously developed land. In contrast to CERCLA's stringent environmental regulations and attempts to make polluting industries pay, Michigan's brownfield programmes have all the trademarks of neoliberal urban renewal: entrepreneurial urban governance, relaxed regulations, public–private partnerships and generous public subsidies for market-led real-estate developments. Legislative changes to public financing rules for brownfields have stretched the programme into an inclusive, all-purpose redevelopment financing tool offering special advantages over conventional urban redevelopment tools. In Michigan, environmental issues have broader political support than urban reforms. The legislature has been willing to allocate significant funds to address environmental contamination but less willing to address inequities in local government finances or implement regional growth management. However, the malleability of the concepts of 'contamination' and 'brownfield' have created an opening for funding green urban entrepreneurialism. In short, urban economic development practitioners and environmental regulators have adopted a strategic environmentalism, remaking CERCLA's stringent regulations and liability regime into an investment friendly, neoliberal brownfield redevelopment climate.

The irony of the neoliberal, market-led consensus for addressing brownfields is that brownfields themselves are prime manifestations of uneven urban development and the creative destruction of capitalism in its latest neoliberal incarnation. By regularly shifting production to new locations, capitalism engages in a spatial fix to postpone the crises posed by its internal contradictions (Harvey, 1985). Thus, the uneven landscape of brownfield sites is simply an inevitable by-product of a dynamic, competitive capitalist economy in which capital moves with speed while its imprint on the landscape remains relatively fixed in space. Brownfield redevelopment financing has often been geared to luring mobile capital into place through bold imaginaries, remaking former industrial lands into residential and recreational destinations attractive to newcomers and outside investment. Analysis confirms that public subsidies for brownfield work are reaching many of the areas with the greatest burden of sites, although the quantity of subsidies received by a community is influenced by other factors that influence the strength of the local property market. That places with a relatively minor industrial legacy such as the recreation and retirement destination counties in northern Michigan have garnered so much in brownfield funding suggests that the financial need and backlog of sites in other areas is quite significant.

The neoliberal approach to brownfield redevelopment has produced a geographically uneven distribution of public subsidies. Subsidies have flowed disproportionately to high amenity lakeshore, recreational and retirement destinations. Public subsidies have been less successful in reaching the distressed, deindustrialized spaces envisioned in the brownfield policy debates. In other words, the public subsidies have flowed most readily to places where problems of deindustrialization are least severe and have not served distressed communities such as Detroit and Flint nearly so well. Economic efficiency appears to have trumped environmental justice concerns.

References

Adair, A., Berry, J., & McGreal, S. (2003). Financing property's contribution to regeneration. *Urban Studies, 40*, 165–180.

Adams, D., & De Sousa, C. (2007). Brownfield development: A comparison of North American and British approaches. European Urban Research Association Conference, Glasgow, 12–14 September.

Amekudzi, A., Attoh-Okine, N., & Laha, S. (1997). Brownfields redevelopment issues at the federal, state, and local levels. *Journal of Environmental Systems, 25*, 97–121.

Amekudzi, A., & Fomunung, I. (2004). Integrating brownfields redevelopment with transportation planning. *Journal of Urban Planning and Development, 130*, 204–212.

Bjelland, M. (2004). Brownfield sites in Minneapolis-St. Paul: The interwoven geographies of industrial disinvestment and environmental contamination. *Urban Geography, 25*, 631–657.

Brenner, N., & Theodore, N. (2005). Neoliberalism and the urban condition. *City, 9*, 101–107.

Colten, C. (1990). Historical hazards: The geography of relict industrial wastes. *Professional Geographer, 42*, 143–156.

De Sousa, C. (2000). Brownfield redevelopment versus greenfield development: A private sector perspective on the costs and risks associated with brownfield redevelopment in the Greater Toronto area. *Journal of Environmental Planning and Management, 43*, 831–853.

Eckerd, A., & Keeler, A. (2012). Going green together? Brownfield remediation and environmental justice. *Policy Sciences, 45*, 293–314.

Ganser, R., & Williams, K. (2007). Brownfield development: Are we using the right targets? Evidence from England and Germany. *European Planning Studies, 15*, 603–622.

Gibbs, D., Krueger, R., & MacLeod, G. (2013). Grappling with smart city politics in an era of market triumphalism. *Urban Studies, 50*, 2151–2157.

Gilliland, E. (1999). *Brownfield redevelopment: Performance evaluation.* Washington, DC: Council for Urban Economic Development.

Glaser, M. (1994). Economic and environmental repair in the shadow of Superfund: Local government leadership in building strategic partnerships. *Economic Development Quarterly, 8*, 345–352.

Hamm, G., & Walzer, N. (2007). Returns from redeveloping brownfields: Preliminary estimates. *Community Development: Journal of the Community Development Society, 38*, 87–98.

Harvey, D. (1985). The geopolitics of capitalism. In D. Gregory & J. Urry (Eds.), *Social relations and spatial structures* (pp. 128–163). London: Macmillan.

Harvey, D. (1989). From managerialism to entrepreneurialism: The transformation in urban governance in late capitalism. *Geografiska Annaler. Series B. Human Geography, 71*, 3–17.

Howland, M. (2007). Employment effects of brownfield redevelopment: What do we know from the literature? *Journal of Planning Literature, 22*, 91–107.

Hula, R., & Davis, P. (2004). Michigan brownfield redevelopment efforts. In A. Donati, C. Rossi, & C. Brebbia (Eds.), *Brownfield sites II: Assessment, rehabilitation and development* (pp. 243–251). Southampton: WIT Press.

Hula, R., Bromley-Trujillo, R., & Hamlin, R. (2009). Bending priorities: A study in policy framing. State of Michigan's Brownfield Initiative. *Transylvanian Review of Administrative Sciences, 27*, 105–128.

Hula, R., & Bromley-Trujillo, R. (2010). Cleaning up the mess: Redevelopment of urban brownfields. *Economic Development Quarterly, 24*, 276–287.

Johnson, K., Dixson, C., & Tochterman, S. (2002). Brownfield redevelopment and transportation planning in the Philadelphia region. *Journal of the Institute of Transportation Engineers, 72*, 26–31.

Jonas, A., & While, A. (2007). Greening the entrepreneurial city? Looking for spaces of sustainability politics in the competitive city. In R. Krueger & D. Gibbs (Eds.), *The sustainable development paradox: Urban political economy in the United States and Europe* (pp. 123–159). London: Guilford.

Jones, R. A., & Welsh, W. (2012). Michigan brownfield redevelopment innovation: Two decades of success. In R. Hula, L. Reese, & C. Jackson-Elmoore (Eds.), *Reclaiming brownfields: A comparative analysis of adaptive reuse of contaminated properties* (pp. 341–382). Burlington, VT: Ashgate.

Lane, A. (2014). Pure Michigan attracted 4 million travelers spending $1.2 billion from outside state in 2013. *Crain's Detroit Business*, 11 March.

Lee, S., & Mohai, P. (2012). The socio-economic dimensions of brownfield cleanup in the Detroit Region. *Population & Environment, 34*, 420–429.

Meyer, P., & Lyons, T. (2000). Lessons from private sector brownfield developers: Planning public support for urban regeneration. *Journal of the American Planning Association, 66*, 46–57.

Meyer, P., & Reaves, C. (1997). Brownlining banks: The bank merger movement and urban redevelopment. *Journal of Economic Issues, 31*, 393–400.

Michigan Economic Development Corporation. (2008). *Brownfield redevelopment.* Cited in Adelaja, S., Shaw, J., Beyea, W., & McKeown, C., *Potential application of renewable energy on brownfield sites: A case study of Michigan.* Land Policy Institute Report LPR-2009-Renewable Energy-003.

Michigan Department of Environmental Quality (DEQ). (2011). *Fact sheet: Brownfield redevelopment grants and loans.* Retrieved from www.michiganbusiness.org/cm/Files/Brownfields/5-DEQ-Brownfield-Contacts-Map.pdf.

Michigan Department of Environmental Quality (DEQ). (2015). *A MDEQ report on the: Environmental Protection Bond Fund, Cleanup and Redevelopment Fund, Clean Michigan Initiative Bond Fund as of 30 September 2014*.

Michigan Department of Environmental Quality (DEQ). (2016). *CMI brownfield redevelopment grants*. Retrieved from www.michigan.gov/deq/0,4561,7-135-3311_4109_29262-151085--, 00.html.

National Association of Local Government Environmental Professionals. (2004). *Unlocking brownfields: Keys to community revitalization*. Northeast-Midwest Institute, Washington, DC.

Platt, R. (1998). Recycling brownfields. *Urban Land, 57*, 30–35.

Simons, R. A., & Iannone, D. (1996). *Brownfields supply and demand analysis for selected Great Lakes cities*. Cleveland, OH: Great Lakes Environmental Finance Center, Cleveland State University.

Snyder, R. 2012. *Reinventing Michigan*. Retrieved from www.michigan.gov/documents/ snyder/ReinventingMichiganCard_368353_7.pdf.

Solitaire, L., & Greenberg, M. (2002). Is the U.S. Environmental Protection Agency brownfields assessment pilot program environmentally just? *Environmental Health Perspectives, 110*, 249–257.

Swartz, R. (1994). Michigan's approach to urban redevelopment involving contaminated properties. *Economic Development Quarterly, 8*, 329–337.

Tansel, B., Hidalgo, R., & Curiel, J. (1999). Brownfields remediation and redevelopment policies, incentives, and pilot projects. *Journal of Environmental Systems, 27*, 15–31.

United States Census Bureau. (1947, 1954, 1958, 1967, 1972, 1977, 1982, 1987, 1992, 1997, 2002, 2003, 2007, 2011, 2012). *Census of Manufactures, Geographic Area Series: Michigan*.

United States Conference of Mayors. (2006). *Recycling America's land: A national report on brownfield redevelopment, volume 4*. Washington, DC: The United States Conference of Mayors.

United States Environmental Protection Agency (EPA). (2000). *EPA brownfields supplemental assistance*. Detroit, MI: EPA 500-F-00-0-013.

United States Environmental Protection Agency (EPA). (2012). *Evaluation of the Brownfields Program*.

Weber, R. (2006). Extracting value from the city: Neoliberalism and urban redevelopment. *Antipode, 34*, 519–540.

Wernstadt, K., & Hersh, R. (2006). Brownfields regulatory reform and policy innovation in practice. *Progress in Planning, 65*, 2–74.

Wernstadt, K., Meyer, P., Alberni, A., & Heberle, L. (2006). Incentives for private residential brownfields development in US urban areas. *Journal of Environmental Planning and Management, 49*, 101–119.

Wu, H., & Chen, C. (2012). Urban 'brownfields': An Australian perspective. 18th Annual Pacific-Rim Real Estate Society Conference, Adelaide, 15–18 January.

Yount, K. & Meyer, P. (1994). Bankers, developers, and new investment in brownfield sites: Environmental concerns and the social psychology of risk. *Economic Development Quarterly, 8*, 338–344.

4 The new main street

Planning, politics and change in downtown Kent, Ohio

Jennifer Mapes

Introduction

Residents of Kent, Ohio today talk about 'New Kent' and 'Old Kent'. Old Kent was a quirky but deteriorating small downtown in the 1980s and 1990s. As a college town, the economic state of the city was precariously balanced between dismal daytimes and a thriving nightlife of students visiting bars and restaurants. New Kent was built quickly between 2008 and 2012, with a few buildings still under construction in the years following. The redevelopment includes a revamped downtown infrastructure: new sidewalks, streetlights and roads, as well as new multi-storey brick buildings and 50 new businesses. More than $130 million was invested in the city, creating more than 700 new jobs (Kent State and the City of Kent Honored, 2015).

While this project of only 20 lots would have a small impact on the landscape of a larger city, in the small town of Kent (2013 population 32,345), its impact is dramatic. Half of the downtown business district was replaced, and the district itself expanded eastward to meet the edge of the Kent State University campus. The redevelopment received many accolades, was named 'Best Project' by the Ohio Economic Development Association (Milligan, 2012) highlighted in an article in the *New York Times* (Schneider, 2013) and served as a case study for the United States Department of Housing and Urban Development (Kent, Ohio and KSU, 2015). By 2014, the city was reporting a $2.2 million tax revenue increase and 85 per cent growth in Chamber of Commerce membership (Downtown Kent Revitalization, 2014; Kent, OH and KSU, 2015).

The changes in downtown Kent, Ohio raise (and answer) a number of questions about urban redevelopment at this scale. Why change? How do cities encourage and implement change? Who benefits? Who is harmed? The focus of this chapter is primarily on the 'how' question. Specifically, I analyse the steps leading up to what became a cascade of redevelopment in the city of Kent and compare my findings to the narrative the city and university offer about whom to credit. I conclude by considering the implications of a simple, versus complex, narrative of urban change.

Redevelopment of downtown districts

The phenomenon of cities undergoing transformation on a multi-block scale is described by several different terms including urban renewal, urban regeneration and urban revitalization. In this chapter, I use the term 'redevelopment' to refer to the purchase of existing buildings and empty lots by public and private entities, the demolition of these buildings and the construction of new buildings and city infrastructure in their place. The primary goal of this public–private partnership is economic development: a return on investment for the private entity and an increase in revenues (income, sales and property taxes) for the public entity.

Redevelopment in cities is not merely a twentieth- or twenty-first-century phenomenon, of course, nor is it limited to American soil. The great fires of London and Chicago produced wide-scale rebuilding. In his master city plans across the United States, Daniel Burnham proposed that cities 'make no small plans' and his designs recommended wide-scale replacement of older buildings with more a more modern, integrated, urban core. Likewise, architect Le Corbusier favoured a 'radiant city' built from scratch on a blank canvas. In some of the most controversial and broadly impactful examples of redevelopment, the United States government funded the transformation of multi-block areas in hundreds of cities through the practice of urban renewal. Born of 'technocratic optimism', the programme focused on rebuilding cities to improve social order (Klemek, 2011). The turning point for this history was the change in implementation of neighbourhood revitalization from grassroots to private, via a funding mechanism approved with the Housing Act of 1954 (von Hoffman, 2008). While nominally a housing provision, the funds were often rerouted into commercial development (Judd, 2002).

The goal of improving neighbourhoods, in the United States and Europe, is combined with changing tastes in architecture to create a powerful force in neighbourhood change. Additionally, these programmes came about during an era of heavy government intervention (and funding), and the rise of key figures like Robert Moses who pushed through local change (Klemek, 2011). Referring back to the introduction of this edited book, in the United States, the term 'urban renewal' is inseparable from the viewpoint that this type of transformation is unnecessarily destructive, unjust and undemocratic (Klemek, 2008). The power of the government to regulate land use is central to the ability to redevelop at the multi-block level. Redevelopment laws and actions rely upon the ability of the government to declare an area blighted, to rezone, and the compulsory purchase of a property under eminent domain (Sutton, 2008).

Urban renewal has transformed the landscapes of hundreds of cities large and small in the United States and has spurred a great deal of research focused on the social impacts of redevelopment (e.g. Pritchett, 2003; Zhang & Fang, 2004; Orueta & Fainstein, 2008). In particular, academics and activists alike blame urban redevelopment on the rise of gentrification in large cities. Lees et al. (2008, p. xv) define gentrification as 'the transformation of a working-class or vacant area of the central city into middle-class residential and/or commercial use'. Concerns about gentrification focus on the displacement of poor residents due to increased housing costs and investment in retail offerings and job opportunities that are aimed at wealthier citizens. Researchers have considered the neoliberal aspects of redevelopment and weighed the extent to which the state was *directing* or *aiding* gentrification (Lees, 2012).

The process of redevelopment is also examined with a focus on municipal actors who actively promote the city to the people Richard Florida calls 'creatives' (see Zimmerman, 2008). Questions arise about the tools used to transform these parts of the city and the extent to which the transformation is 'natural' or forced. While the impacts of urban renewal and shifts in political tastes have resulted in some increases in transparency and public participation, urban change remains heavily influenced by private developers and individual municipal actors. The *Susette Kelo et al. v. City of New London, Connecticut et al.* decision in 2005, that upheld the use of eminent domain, is just one example of the ongoing battle over large-scale transformation. In this case, the United States Supreme Court agreed that private redevelopment projects eventually benefit the public, and therefore allowed the taking of private property for these uses.

Despite the concerns inherent in the large-scale redevelopment of neighbour-hoods, there is also strong interest in supporting these projects. Cities and their residents depend on taxes generated by successful businesses, solid property values and employed citizens. Therefore, the concept of redevelopment is also used to describe the best practices in improving the economic status of communities (Burayidi, 2001; Faulk, 2006). These practices, often researched in the down-towns of large urban areas, are also a topic of interest for smaller cities (Paradis, 2000; Rhodes & Russo, 2013).

After years of sprawl being the accepted (albeit increasingly critiqued) *modus operandi* for cities and developers, by the early 2000s they began to recognize a renewed interest in city centres rather than edges. Ford (2003, p. 3) described this trend: 'Downtowns are a vital component in the quest to understand how we can modify our policies and procedures so as to encourage the preservation of older existing landscapes and to minimize unaesthetic, sprawling development.'

The redevelopment of downtown districts is important to city government and residents, but there are broader implications for the future of land use in urban areas. Attractive city centres, built at high density and with multiple transit options (including walking), are not only good for city finances, they also slow sprawl. Thus, the success of downtown business areas has broader implications.

A short history of Kent's city and campus

Kent, in northeast Ohio, is about 15 miles northeast of Akron (population 198,100) and 40 miles south of Cleveland (2013 population 390,113) (Figure 4.1) in Portage County. The United States Census considers Kent a suburb of Akron. Kent is in the Akron Metropolitan Statistical Area and the Cleveland-Akron-Canton Combined Statistical Area. The reality is a bit more complicated, since Kent is at the southern edge of Cleveland suburbs and also stands on its own, in terms of employment. In 2000, 38 per cent of residents of the Kent zip code also worked within the city's zip code or at the university (Kao, 2010). Kent's population is estimated at about 32,345 by the United States Census, a demo-graphic influenced by Kent State University's enrolment of 28,981 (Kent State University Facts & Figures, 2016), although only 28 per cent of these students live in college housing.

Before it was a college town, Kent was a mill town known as Franklin Mills. European settlers in the 1800s built factories along the Cuyahoga River, which

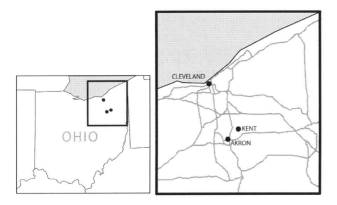

Figure 4.1 Kent's location in northeast Ohio.

runs through the centre of the city. Like many mill towns, Kent then became a railroad stop in the mid-1800s, part of a vast network that connected the cities of the Northeast to the agricultural output of the Midwest (Figure 4.2). The city was renamed in 1864 to honour influential businessman Marvin Kent, who helped make the town a key point on the Atlantic and Great Western Railroad. Manufacturing jobs dominated the economic landscape. Today, one of Kent's major landmarks is a grain mill that still operates 24 hours a day (DiPaolo, 2009).

The population of Kent remained small, however, until the 1910 state of Ohio decided to locate a new normal (teacher training) school at the edge of the small town. In 1935, the college was granted university status by the state (Hildebrand, 1998). The student population grew after the Second World War to 6,000 in 1955, then again during the Vietnam War as the population reached 21,000 in 1970 (Kent State University Historical Timeline, n.d.). As the university population grew, it eventually surpassed the city's total population and became a major employer. As the university size grew, the city's population grew: it more than doubled from 12,418 in 1950 to 28,183 in 1970.

The blue-collar Kent of the first half of the twentieth century was soon eclipsed by college town Kent, creating tensions between residents and campus, as described by long-time resident Don Schjeldhl in an interview. This divide was highlighted and cemented by the shooting in 1970 on campus by the Ohio National Guard following a protest against the invasion of Cambodia during the Vietnam War. Four students died in the shooting, which garnered the university unwanted international attention and a temporary decrease in enrolment (Porter, 2012).

Over the next few decades, downtown Kent declined. Much of this was less due to tensions between the campus and city, and instead to broader national trends. Traditional retailers moved to suburban locations where they could offer more parking and larger stores. Two state highways were built to create a bypass around Kent's downtown. While this may have eased traffic congestion, it also routed potential retail customers around the city's remaining downtown businesses, according to city engineer James Bowling.

Figure 4.2 People gather to watch July 4th fireworks behind the historic train station (now a restaurant), overlooking the city's railroad and the Cuyahoga River.

At the centre of downtown decline was the 95-year-old, six-storey Franklin Hotel at the city's main intersection. The residential floors of the hotel, which were converted to student apartments, were condemned in 1979 and never again inhabited (Smith, 1999). The ground floor was occupied by a variety of restaurants and bars, and closed permanently in 2000. In the years that followed, the city hounded the owner without success to sell the building or demolish it (Smith, 2002).

Meanwhile, city officials continued to lament the loss of downtown retail, but seemed uncertain what to do about it. Twice, developers nearly built a retail centre on the outskirts of town. In 1989, a mall was proposed, but eventually the developer abandoned these plans (Stoffel, 1990). Then in the 1990s, planning reports pushed for a revitalization of downtown Kent, and a reconnection between the campus and the city. One of goals in the 1993 'Visions of a New Era' report focused on re-establishing a link between the university and downtown via a pedestrian walkway (Goodman, 1993, pp. 41–45). The city's 2004 master plan reiterated the call for downtown renewal. This plan focused on sustainability and recognized the importance of a walkable urban centre. 'Kent residents desire their community to be walkable. Residents want intersections to be safe for pedestrians, and they want to be able to walk to activity centres within their respective neighbourhoods' (Bicentennial Plan, 2004, p. 96). The plan goes on to focus on the importance of a retail-oriented and walkable downtown. In particular, the plan calls for downtown to be the city's 'economic focal point' (Bicentennial Plan, 2004, p. 9).

The document named the neighbourhood between campus and downtown a special planning area, the 'Campus Link Neighborhood'. Research conducted for the plan found disconnect between town and gown, with faculty, staff and students not shopping or eating downtown. Several plans for the area were proposed to remedy this, with a focus on modifying the state-managed highway bypass that ran between the city and downtown. They described the addition of a university-oriented hotel and conference centre, as well as townhouses geared toward faculty, students and staff (Bicentennial Plan, 2004, p. 71).

Building a new downtown

In 2008, construction began on a small new retail venue in downtown Kent. By 2016, new development there grew to encompass more than half the downtown area, and expanded into residential areas between the city's business district and the Kent State campus. New development included multi-storey mixed-use buildings, apartments aimed at college students, a university-funded hotel, parking garage, new county courthouse, new police station and two new Kent State campus buildings (Figure 4.3). The new development replaced vacant lots, parking lots, some one-storey retail buildings and dozens of single-family homes, most of which were student rentals.

Like many small towns, Kent had already seen its share of small revitalization projects. In the 1990s, the city's historical society bought the old train station along the river and it was turned into a restaurant. The old silk mill along the river was restored into apartments and a yoga studio in 2001, and a few years later a new library and fire station were built. In 2004, a hard-fought negotiation with the Ohio EPA led to the restoration of the flow of the Cuyahoga River through downtown, but the city's historic dam was preserved (Cuyahoga River Restoration Project, n.d.).

The first real change, though, was right in the heart of downtown, at the city's main intersection. A local entrepreneur, Ron Burbick, bought the properties surrounding the old Franklin Hotel, demolished the less desirable buildings and restored the facades of historic brick buildings on Main Street. He funded the construction of an alley between Main Street and Erie Street that he called 'Acorn Alley', and populated it with businesses suggested by his research with Kent residents (a popcorn shop, shoe store and ice cream parlour). Acorn Alley opened in 2009. Burbick said in an interview that he was inspired by the storefronts in London to create the facades along the alley, which was then draped in strings of electric lights and lined with brick.

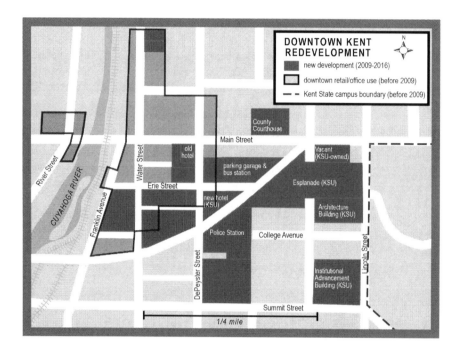

Figure 4.3 Map of development relative to downtown and the Kent State University campus.

By revitalizing the block surrounding the old hotel, Burbick gained leverage with the city, and worked out a deal to purchase the building. After decades of haggling, the city purchased the hotel from its owner for $735,000 (Noble, 2013). They then resold the hotel to Burbick for $400,000, and he spent $6.5 million restoring the long-vacant structure, assisted by $1.6 million in historic preservation tax credits. In 2013 the Buffalo Wild Wings chain moved from their much smaller location into the two-storey former lobby of the hotel. Burbick brought a speakeasy-style wine bar to the basement and luxury apartments to the upstairs (Watt, 2013).

Construction along Acorn Alley took place during the heart of the 2008–2009 recession. The recession also affected another major catalyst in Kent's downtown renewal: a large parking garage. For years, the county's transportation agency, PARTA, had planned to build their headquarters in downtown Kent. The building would combine a bus station with a parking garage (bicycle parking, retail and offices were also part of the plans). The project did not get off the ground, though, until the local agencies became eligible to apply for federal TIGER funds. These funds, for shovel-ready projects, were aimed at creating jobs during the recession (Federal Transit Administration Celebrates Opening of Kent Central Gateway Transit Center, 2013). This funding added one more large new building to downtown Kent.

As these projects were under way, the university finally got serious about a long-discussed downtown hotel and conference centre. The hotel would serve visiting sports teams, guest speakers and other university interests, for instance meeting rooms would allow for conferences within walking distance of campus (Schneider, 2013). Perhaps more importantly, the university decided to extend their pedestrian walkway (known as the 'Esplanade') from campus into downtown (Figure 4.4). Several academic buildings were built along the Esplanade as campus development moved toward campus for the first time, rather than away from it.

The city of Kent worked with Fairmount Properties to develop the key block downtown. These buildings, called 'College Town Kent', include 15 retail stores and restaurants at ground level and three major employers (Figure 4.5). Fairmount Properties was responsible for other college town developments (in Ames, Iowa; Rochester, New York; and Toledo, Ohio), as well as for a similar main street replica in nearby Hudson, Ohio. The Fairmount development also includes student apartments, and the company plans to next build a mixed-use block that will host a small grocery store (Howard, 2015).

Figure 4.4 Kent State's Lester Lefton Esplanade, looking west toward downtown Kent. On the right is the PARTA Central Gateway and left is the Kent State University Hotel & Conference Center.

Figure 4.5   College Town development by Fairmount Properties including Fresco
Mexican restaurant and Ametek offices. The flags represent countries where
Ametek now does business (outsources manufacturing labour).

The city contributed to the downtown redevelopment through infrastructure improvements. Two downtown alleys were paved with cobblestones and had utility lines buried. Sidewalks were reconstructed to encourage walking and pedestrian improvements were also added to intersections. The city invested in improved downtown signage, including way finding maps and banners. For landscaping purposes, colourful bike racks were added throughout downtown and parking was redone in an effort to improve overall appearance. Most of these improvements were financed by Tax Increment Financing (TIF), which provided funds based on a predicted increase in property taxes (Ruller, 2010).

Telling the story of the 'Kent Miracle'

Public and private investment between 2009 and 2014 implemented many new urbanist best practices and created an entirely new landscape in much of downtown Kent. A local newspaper editor has called this transformation 'the Kent Miracle' (DiPaolo, 2013). How and why did this happen? The city and university answer to this question credits two men, university president Lester Lefton and city manager Dave Ruller, for the bulk of the work that went into this transformation. According to this story, it took the arrival of Lefton (in 2006) and Ruller (in 2005) to turn the town around. 'It took two guys from someplace else who didn't know any better,' Ruller told the *New York Times* when the newspaper wrote about the redevelopment (Schneider, 2013). 'David and I just wanted it done,' Lefton said in an interview.

Local newspaper editor Roger DiPaolo, who literally wrote the book on the city's history, described in an interview a story of neglect by city and university officials until Lester and Ruller showed up:

> You got Lefton that comes in and you have Ruller that comes in, and they really liked each other. They could work with each other. They didn't have any baggage of, 'Oh, I can't do this,' or, 'This won't work.' They basically just decided, 'We're going to make it work, no matter what happens.'

The men themselves describe drawing out their plans for downtown on a napkin at the local deli (Winer, 2014). As Ruller remembers, 'We shared a bunch of "Why Not" Kent moments: why can't we have a hotel downtown, why can't there be more restaurants, why can't we be a destination for people that share our love for vibrant university cities?' (Ruller, 2011). In an interview, Lefton told a similar tale of the famous turkey sandwich that led to collaboration with Ruller on the transformation of downtown.

For Lefton, the entire downtown project turned on the construction of a hotel that could host university guests, conferences and also serve as amenity to companies with headquarters downtown. The hotel was a downtown catalyst that would provide patrons within close proximity of downtown shops and restaurants. He saw the hotel also as a faculty and student recruitment tool. Likening university politics to hand-to-hand combat in the Second World War, Lefton said municipal politics was more traditional in its deal-making and focus on mutual goals. He and Ruller had 'a lot of conversation about finding ways to get to "yes"'. The talks centred on buying land, swapping land, 'doing things that others have talked about for years,' Lefton explained (Wolff, 2014). Lefton said in an interview that there had been 50 years of talk about downtown but 'nobody was willing to put any of their skin in the game', which was where he and Ruller came in.

Lefton retired in 2013, but before he left the Board of Trustees voted to name the Esplanade walkway in his honour. Lefton was not in office during the planning and construction of the original Esplanade, which snakes through campus, providing a car-free pedestrian zone between the Student Center and many academic buildings. But he is credited with envisioning and implementing its last crucial piece: between campus and downtown. 'There could not be a more fitting tribute to President Lefton than naming the Esplanade, which now physically and symbolically connects town and gown, in his honour,' (Chair of the Kent State Board of Trustees Jane Murphy) Timken said. 'With a clear vision, a commitment to excellence and unshakable optimism, Dr. Lefton has led Kent State to new heights of achievement' (Myers, 2013). The university spent $2.6 million to extend the

Esplanade (and campus) through a residential neighbourhood (Furguson-Rich, 2013). A good portion of this cost came from purchasing homes and demolition.

Lefton is frequently paired with City Manager Dave Ruller as the second key player in the downtown project. Whereas Lefton often cited his years in Ann Arbor, Michigan as inspiration for redeveloping downtown, Ruller came to Kent from Charlottesville, Virginia, home of the University of Virginia. He frequently cites the past cities he lives as influencing his ideas for Kent. In the case of Charlottesville, he described a college town that capitalized on the city's downtown–campus connection. 'I saw Kent, fairly candidly, as a tremendous opportunity,' he told the (Cleveland, OH) *Plain Dealer*. 'It had all the right pieces. They just needed to be put together in the right order' (Nichols, 2009). Ruller's blog about his job and goals for Kent (Kent360.com) is a celebration of new urbanist principles and urban cheerleaders like Richard Florida (see Ruller, 2007a). During his first year on the job, the blog included links to articles about universities building hotels (Ruller, 2006a) and a link to a *New York Times* article about UConn's reconstruction of Mansfield, Connecticut's downtown (Gordon, 2006; Ruller, 2006b).

A third individual who appears in the story of Kent's redevelopment is Ron Burbick, the multimillionaire redeveloper who redeveloped properties along Main Street before any of the other projects were in motion. Burbick's investments came at the heart of the 2008–2009 recession:

> I always said, 'If you build it, they will come.' There had been so many blue-ribbon panels and they had all been a lot of talk – nothing ever came of it. I personally took it as a challenge to say, 'Something can be done,' and then kick-started it.
>
> (Nichols, 2009)

Having spent $18 million on his piece of downtown, Burbick is more than willing to take credit for jumpstarting redevelopment: 'I pulled the trigger and went, and now they're scrambling to catch up' (Magaw, 2012). Local banker Howard Boyle II even recommended renaming Kent in honour of Burbick, who many believe was a catalyst development with his investment in the city (Nichols, 2009).

Together, these narratives suggest what historians call a 'great man theory', or in this case, the great men theory. This theory argues that key events in history would not have occurred without the actions of a great man, who served as catalyst for some of the world's most important events (Harter, 2008). In Kent, much credit is given to Lefton, Ruller and Burbick – and much of this credit is earned; however, this is only one part of a more nuanced story of change in downtown Kent.

The role of time and neglect in the 'Kent Miracle'

The great man theory of urban transformation suggests overnight change that just needed a catalyst, or in this case, two (or three) catalysts. It is interesting to note that this narrative describes a less-than-democratic version of how downtown Kent was redeveloped. It is fortunate, then, that the reality is more complicated. A review of the events leading up to the redevelopment years suggests that time was not the enemy of downtown Kent, but its friend.

Public support was essential for the transformation of downtown

Change in Kent is a by-product of popular culture: malls are out; walkable downtowns are in. The language of Ruller and Lefton reflects an admiration for new urbanist principles. 'We are trying to create a pedestrian-oriented, people-scaled sense of place,' Lefton said to a crowd of businesses owners at an annual breakfast meeting. 'Place matters and Kent is going to be a place that matters' (Downtown Kent Revitalization Project, 2012). These words may warm the heart of a modern-day planner, but this sentiment was not nearly as popular during the shopping mall era of the 1980s and 1990s.

Had Lefton and Ruller pushed for a revival of downtown during this period, they would not have been likely to receive much support from their constituencies. 'Progress' at this time pushed for expansion into city margins: along interstates, in commercial strips with plenty of space and parking. In Kent, forward momentum was strongly dependent upon public support for redevelopment. Planning documents of the 1990s and early 2000s show an increase in support for city-led interventions that would bring businesses back downtown.

But even then, there was very little by way of planning terms like 'new urbanism' or 'pedestrian-friendly', 'mixed use' or 'walkable downtown'. Instead, public concerns were more immediate: to fill the storefronts; to restore dilapidated facades. Organizations like the Kent Environmental Council voiced opposition to proposals for a mall or big-box centre at the city's outskirts, but their focus was primarily opposition to development near environmentally sensitive lands (Stoffel, 1990; Smith, 2000).

Investment, both public and private, followed renewed interest in downtowns

Similarly, developers like Fairmount Properties (which developed about half of the downtown lots) have jumped on the new urbanist bandwagon. A Fairmont Properties developer agreed that downtowns were newly attractive for investment as they brought a diverse range of consumers to the table: 'there's this convergence occurring where what the Millennials are seeking is the same thing that the retiring boomers are seeking. It's all pointing back to the urban core. It's pointing back to cities.' He said that nurturing a high quality of life in a city is of particular advantage to the university as they seek to recruit faculty from across the country.

Ruller (2007b) wrote a blog post called 'Unmalling of America', in which he explained how Kent needed to keep pace with developers creating 'fake downtowns', and take advantage of the city's authentic main street to attract investment. Ruller (2007b) also notes:

Malls definitely had their heyday, but so did the horse and buggy, so it's good news for Kent that the retail world has turned once again and malls are out, while downtown shopping has made a serious comeback.

Similarly, state and federal funding sources, once only concerned with basic infrastructure, were increasingly willing to fund economic development and pedestrian-oriented projects. Whereas in the past, the Ohio Department of Transportation (ODOT) would have focused their funding efforts on automobiles, the state was now willing to help pay for projects like the Esplanade. In an interview, Ruller also noted that the state relinquished control over the bypass that divided the downtown from campus, allowing the city to create crosswalks that were previously not permitted.

Time heals all (or most) wounds

The pairing of Ruller and Lefton in the redevelopment narratives is no coincidence. The university and the city were both needed to enact change downtown. For this partnership to come about, time and distance from the 1970 shootings were needed. While the 1970 events are typically connected to the Kent State campus, a closer look at the period shows many protests before the shooting occurred downtown, including fires in the streets, sit-ins blocking the roadway and broken windows. After the shooting, many residents blamed the protesters for both the deaths and injuries as well as for the infamy that came to Kent. Students, meanwhile, resented the blame and harsh comments from the community about the shooting (Jennings, 1995; Lewis & Hensley, 1998).

Councilwoman Heidi Schaffer credits former Kent State President Carol Cartwright for re-establishing ties with the city. Cartwright preceded Lefton, who took over as university president in 2006. After arriving at Kent State in 1991 she began regular meetings with leaders of the two organizations, which she said in an interview gradually changed the outlook of people on both sides of town:

> We opened up a conversation [. . .] I think people gradually got more comfortable with each other, and started to trust one another more. When we had a 25th anniversary on May 4th, in 1995, we brought Peter, Paul and Mary to have a concert here. It was the first time that many townspeople had participated in any kind of commemorative activity. They were standing shoulder to shoulder with faculty and students in the MAC Center, at the concert. They talked about the fact this gap was being bridged, that things were changing.

It takes a village to change a city

Focusing on Kent's 'great men' may be an easy and engaging way to tell the story of downtown redevelopment but a complex story, told over decades, is more telling of how urban transformations occur – of course, Ruller and Lefton do acknowledge these complexities. Ruller gave credit to the committees, council people and others who pre-dated him: 'the early efforts didn't have the splash or wow factor, but they did help lay the foundation'.

A closer analysis of the actions leading to the 2008–2012 rebuilding speaks more broadly to the idea that political capital is needed for action. Politicians (be they a city manager or a university president) rarely act in a vacuum and neither do investors. Therefore, while the importance of great men (and women) remains, we also need to credit smaller actors: everyday players on the city scene. In Kent, this includes those who laboured on the 1993 visioning report and 2004 master plan; who pushed back against the mall and big box projects; who served on university-city committees month after month.

Councilwoman Heidi Shaffer, who sat on the council as it voted for the contracts and spending that would transform downtown Kent, credited a public that showed its willingness to support these decisions. 'To some degree,' she said in an interview, 'it came from the middle and it came from above. The middle had to convince the above. The middle, the people that would come into Kent that were fresh and new and some of the people that been here, so it joined forces.'

In granting credit to the 'little people', and to the long game of urban politics and planning, rather than a short-term focus on celebrity, citizens may become more empowered and emboldened to enact change within their own cities and neighbourhoods. An inclusive narrative is not only more accurate; it also recognizes that urban transformation can be a democratic process. In conclusion, to incorporate a decades-long history of urban change involves recognizing that a shift in landscape and economy takes both years of planning as well as key moments of action.

Acknowledgements

The interviews cited in this chapter were conducted in summer 2015, in collaboration with David Kaplan and Kelly Turner with support from Kent State University.

References

Bicentennial Plan. (2004). City of Kent. Retrieved from www.kentohio.org/reports/bicentennial.pdf.

Burayidi, M. A. (2001). *Downtowns: Revitalizing the centers of small urban communities.* New York: Routledge.

Cuyahoga River Restoration Project: Final Summary. n.d. City of Kent. Retrieved from www.kentohio.org/reports/dam.asp.

DiPaolo, R. (2009). *Rooted in Kent.* Kent, OH: Kent Historical Society.

Downtown Kent Revitalization. (2014). City of Kent Urban Land Institute Cleveland. Retrieved from http://cleveland.uli.org/wp-content/uploads/sites/18/2014/08/KentState 2014.pdf.

DiPaolo, R. (2013). Bowman breakfast. *Kent360.com*, 16 April. Retrieved from www.kent360.com/8353-50-years-of-town-gown.html.

Downtown Kent Revitalization Project Wins Best Project Award. (2012). Kent State University. Retrieved from www.kent.edu/kent/news/downtown-kent-revitalization-project-wins-best-project-award.

Faulk, D. (2006). The process and practice of downtown revitalization. *The Review of Policy Research, 23*, 625–645.

Federal Transit Administration Celebrates Opening of Kent Central Gateway Transit Center. (2013). U.S. Department of Transportation. Federal Transit Administration, 5 August. Retrieved from www.fta.dot.gov/newsroom/12286_15601.html.

Ford, L. R. (2003). *America's new downtowns: Revitalization or reinvention?* Baltimore, MD: Johns Hopkins University Press.

Furguson-Rich, M. (2013). KSU's esplanade to be named for Lefton. (Akron, OH) *Beacon Journal*, 5 October. Retrieved from www.ohio.com/news/local/ksu-s-esplanade-to-be-named-for-lefton-1.434575.

Goodman, L. (Ed.). (1993). *Visions of a new era*. Urban Design Center of Northeast Ohio.

Gordon, J. (2006). UConn decides to build its own college town. *New York Times*, 9 August. Retrieved from www.nytimes.com/2006/08/09/realestate/09storrs.html.

Harter, N. (2008). Great man theory. In A. Marturano & J. Gosling (Eds.), *Leadership: The key concepts* (pp. 67–71). London: Routledge.

Hildebrand, W. (1998). *A history of Kent State University*. Kent, OH: Kent State University.

Howard, C. (2015). Fairmount Properties, Newbrook Partners present plans for former Kent courthouse. (Ravenna, OH) *Record-Courier*, 4 June.

Jennings, T. (1995). Kent's psychic wounds have finally healed. *Los Angeles Times*, 4 May.

Judd, D. (2002). *City politics: Private power and public policy*. New York: Addison-Wesley Educational.

Kao, H. (2010). Commute map. Original data from the Census Transportation Planning Package (2000). Retrieved from http://hairycow.name/commute_map#from:44240.

Kent, Ohio and KSU: A Public Private Partnership Downtown. (2015). U.S. Department of Housing and Urban Development. Retrieved from www.huduser.gov/portal/casestudies/study_05222015_1.html.

Kent State and the City of Kent Honored with Catalytic Partnership Award. (2015). Kent State University, 22 June. Retrieved from www.kent.edu/kent/news/kent-state-and-city-kent-honored-catalytic-partnership-award.

Kent State University Facts & Figures. (2016). Kent State University. Retrieved from www.kent.edu/facts-figures.

Kent State University Timeline (n.d.). Kent State University. Retrieved from http://ucm.dreamhosters.com/timeline/ksutimeline.html.

Klemek, C. (2008). From political outsider to power broker in two 'Great American Cities': Jane Jacobs and the fall of the urban renewal order in New York and Toronto. *Journal of Urban History, 34*, 309–332.

Klemek, C. (2011). *The transatlantic collapse of urban renewal: Postwar urbanism from New York to Berlin*. Chicago, IL: The University of Chicago Press.

Lees, L. (2012). The geography of gentrification: Thinking through comparative urbanism. *Progress in Human Geography, 36*, 155–171.

Lees, L., Slater, T., & Wyly, E. (2008). *Gentrification*. New York: Routledge.

Lewis, J., & Hensley, T. (1998). The May 4 shootings at Kent State University: The search for historical accuracy. *Ohio Council for the Social Studies Review, 34*, 9–21.

Magaw, T. (2012). Longtime Kent businessman Ron Burbick primes the city's development pump. *Crain's Cleveland Business*, 9 April. Retrieved from www.crainscleveland.com/article/20120409/SUB1/304099986/longtime-kent-businessman-ron-burbick-primes-the-citys-development.

Milligan, J. (2012). Downtown Kent revitalization project named 'Best Project' in the state. *Kentwired*, 8 November. Retrieved from www.kentwired.com/latest_updates/article_8699dec1-1106-58cc-ac21-cef5a3c16a69.html.

Myers, J. (2013). Esplanade to honor departing KSU President Lester Lefton. *Kentwired*, 4 October. Retrieved from www.kentwired.com/latest_updates/article_e3989d91-1d3a-57f3-ba06-49f502ea0c00.html.

Nichols, J. (2009). Downtown Kent, Ohio, rising Phoenix-like as city, KSU and businesses coalesce. (Cleveland) *Plain Dealer*, 26 November.

Noble, J. (2013). Kent's Acorn Corner springs to life. (Ravenna) *Record-Courier*, 10 May.

Orueta, F., & Fainstein, S. (2008). The new mega-projects: Genesis and impacts. *International Journal of Urban and Regional Research, 32*, 759–767.

Paradis, T. (2000). Conceptualizing small towns as urban places: The process of downtown redevelopment in Galena, Ill. *Urban Geography, 21*, 61–82.

Porter, C. (2012). Four decades later, Kent State turns a page. *Wall Street Journal*, 24 November, A6.

Pritchett, W. (2003). The 'public menace' of blight: Urban renewal and the private uses of eminent domain. *Yale Law & Policy Review, 21*, 1–52.

Rhodes, J., & Russo, J. (2013). Shrinking 'smart'?: Urban redevelopment and shrinkage in Youngstown, Ohio. *Urban Geography, 34*, 305–326.

Ruller, D. (2006a). Universities building hotels. *Kent360.com*, 4 July. Retrieved from www.kent360.com/category/city-university-stuff/page/31.

Ruller, D. (2006b). University and city partnerships: No city gets left behind. *Kent360.com*, 3 September. Retrieved from www.kent360.com/220-university-and-city-partnerships-no-city-gets-left-behind.html.

Ruller, D. (2007a). Living downtown. *Kent360.com*, 9 August. Retrieved from www.kent360.com/672-living-downtown.html.

Ruller, D. (2007b). Unmalling of America. *Kent360.com*, 13 July. Retrieved from www.kent360.com/666-unmalling-of-america.html.

Ruller, D. (2010). Kent downtown redevelopment update. *Kent360.com*, 13 September. Retrieved from www.kent360.com/3400-kent-downtown-redevelopment-update.html.

Ruller, D. (2011). Bowman breakfast. *Kent360.com*, 30 September. Retrieved from www.kent360.com/6387-bowman-breakfast.html.

Schneider, K. (2013). A partnership seeks to transform Kent State and Kent. *New York Times*, 5 February. Retrieved from www.nytimes.com/2013/02/06/realestate/commercial/development-aims-to-bring-kent-state-and-its-city-closer.html?_r=0.

Smith, D. (1999). Old Kent hotel needs repairs. (Ravenna) *Record-Courier*, 14 April. Retrieved from www.recordpub.com/local%20news/1999/04/14/old-kent-hotel-needs-repairs.

Smith, D. (2000). Shopping center gets OK in Kent. (Ravenna, OH) *Record-Courier*, 20 September. Retrieved from https://recordpub.com/local%20news/2000/09/20/shopping-center-gets-ok-in-kent.

Smith, D. (2002). Kent hotel may get new life. (Ravenna, OH) *Record-Courier*, 3 February. Retrieved from www.recordpub.com/local%20news/2002/02/03/kent-hotel-may-get-new-life.

Stoffel, J. (1990). Notebook: Kent, Ohio: Opponents fail to stop mall. *New York Times*, 16 December. Retrieved from www.nytimes.com/1990/12/16/realestate/national-notebook-kent-ohio-opponents-fail-to-stop-mall.html.

Sutton, S. (2008). Urban revitalization in the United States: Policies and practices. United States Urban Revitalization Research Project, 25 June. Retrieved from www.columbia.edu/cu/c2arl/pdf_files/USURRP_Phase_I_Final_Report.pdf.

von Hoffman, A. (2008). The lost history of urban renewal. *Journal of Urbanism*, *1*, 281–301.

Watt, M. (2013). Kent landmark sprouts new life. *Properties Magazine*, June. Retrieved from www.metisconstruction.com/about/news/kent-landmark-sprouts-new-life/.

Winer, M. (2014). City credits Lefton with solidifying town-gown relations. Retrieved from www.kentwired.com/latest_updates/article_51a036f4-c9b1-11e3-acde-0017a43b2370.html.

Wolff, C. (2014). KSU president touts successes in farewell interview. *Cleveland Jewish News*, 12 June. Retrieved from www.clevelandjewishnews.com/news/local/ksu-president-touts-successes-in-farewell-interview/article_4d98ae92-f233-11e3-adcd-0019bb2963f4.html.

Zhang, Y., & Fang, K. (2004). Is history repeating itself? From urban renewal in the United States to inner-city redevelopment in China. *Journal of Planning Education and Research*, *23*, 286–298.

Zimmerman, J. (2008). From brew town to cool town: Neoliberalism and the creative city development strategy in Milwaukee. *Cities*, *25*, 230–242.

5 Beyond rail

Amenity driven high-density development for polycentric cities

Jennifer L. Kitson, Stephen T. Buckman and David C. Folch

Introduction

The 'century of the city' is marked by a fundamentally new set of environmental and urbanization trends that make the bundling of urban development and sustainability an imperative (Seto et al., 2010). This is especially the case for sprawling, auto-dependent polycentric cities that have seen rapid growth in the last few decades. Local governments in such places are striving to achieve the agglomeration benefits of increased density, such as greater efficiency and walkability, without incurring the negative effects of agglomeration (e.g. pollution, congestion and longer travel times). In polycentric cities where rapid suburban growth has been the standard for decades, high-density compact urban form is only achieved through municipal intervention in the form of public–private partnerships, development associated with new municipal infrastructure projects, or direct and indirect developer incentives. While uncertainties remain about the degree to which compact urban form is the silver bullet for all urban ailments, strong planning interventions to facilitate density garner widespread support (Ewing & Hamidi, 2015). In short, a critical aspiration of twenty-first-century polycentric cities is to increase high-density, mixed-use development, but the strategies for achieving such aims are limited in the face of ingrained greenfield, sprawl-oriented development paradigms (see also Bjelland & Noyes, Chapter 3 in this volume).

Transit-oriented development (TOD) has been widely heralded as the premier urban planning mechanism for twinning urban development and sustainability goals. By incentivizing high-density development at light rail transit stations (LRT), municipalities bank on TOD residents reducing auto-trips through transit ridership, which in turn generates the co-benefits of compact urban form: improved livability, walkability and economic vitality with decreased CO_2 emissions, air pollution and traffic congestion. Yet the premise of TOD, that urban dwellers want proximity to transit so that they can drive less, is increasingly dismantled. Recent research suggests that TOD does not actually need the 'T' (Chatman, 2013). People are residing near transit stations, but not using transit (or at least not rail). Given the high cost of transit infrastructure and the low rates of ridership among residents of TOD, a new strategy for achieving compact urban form is needed. Urban planners, Chatman (2013, p. 17, emphasis added) argues, must 'broaden their efforts to develop dense, mixed-use, low-parking housing *beyond rail station area*'.

In this chapter we propose a conceptual framework for achieving compact urban form in polycentric cities beyond the rail station. We take urban amenities, rather than transit, as the starting point for the pursuit of density. Urban amenities are increasingly found to be the basis for which the mobile, 'creative class' (Florida, 2002) makes location decisions, both regionally and within cities (Glaeser et al., 2001). We find the importance of place to be an undervalued yet critical component of human dwelling decisions and city-making. By building the concept of place into the urban amenity literature, we argue that nodal concentration of urban amenities, specifically those associated with memory and meaning (such as historic infrastructure), have tremendous potential to fulfill the urban development and sustainability aspirations of polycentric cities (high-density *and* high-amenity). We draw on the experience of Phoenix, Arizona, the quintessential post-Second World War sprawling metropolis, in outlining lessons learned from historic districts (HD), TOD and canal oriented development (COD) land-use zoning overlay strategies.

Our proposition, termed 'amenity driven *high-density* development' (ADHD), arises from the fact that cities and urban developments are increasingly fighting for attention amidst the cacophony of urban choices (Musterd & Murie, 2010). While it is not our aim to overstate the parallels between the medical and urban initialisms explored here, the loose association is, in many ways, conceptually apt. The increasingly frenetic, distracted sensibilities of both urban dwellers and the built environs necessitate new strategies that embrace, rather than criticize, this dynamism. To remain competitive, a polycentric city-region needs a variety of distinctive nodes that afford their diverse demography residential choice. Aside from the issues of ridership and cost, light rail infrastructure systems are linear and inflexible, posing significant limitations in cities without a singular urban core. The contours of the new urban era also demand municipal strategies that are achievable within the (short) lifespan of collective memory and the terms of elected officials. The post-recession economy is characterized as doing more with less; a frugal urban development approach is requisite to gain support from residents, developers and city governments. Because the correlation between compact urban and transportation use remains uncertain (Badoe & Miller, 2000), access to transit, we posit, should not be the only amenity afforded by compact urban form developments. Our goal is ultimately to strengthen all forms of compact urban development, including TOD, through emphasizing and maximizing place-based urban amenities.

We begin with an overview of the urban amenity concept, outlining the dimensions of leading and lagging amenities. While transit is billed as a leading amenity for TOD, recent research points towards the actual importance of lagging amenities for inhabitants of TOD. We couch this suite of difficult-to-quantify lagging amenities within the place literature, contextualizing the critical importance of the past in making meaningful places. In the following section, the role of zoning in polycentric city-regions is discussed using Phoenix, Arizona as a case study. We then compare and contrast the zoning affordances and limitations of historic preservation districts and transit-oriented development, for their abilities to facilitate place-making and density, respectively. Lastly, we offer the example of canal oriented development in Phoenix as a best-of-both worlds ADHD exemplar whereby place-making and density-making align in generative, amenity-rich ways.

Urban amenities

The urban amenity is a slippery concept to grasp. We all have conceptions of what we consider amenities, but a dispassionate perspective recognizes that one person's high valued amenity might have little value to someone else. Most people see good schools as an amenity but a retired couple will put far less value in this amenity when choosing a place to live than a couple with two young children. Therefore, when thinking about the urban landscape, it is impossible to attribute one amenity (or class of amenities) as the single driving force behind the variation in city form.

Urban amenities are 'location-specific goods' (see Diamond Jr & Tolley, 1982). More specifically, amenities are features of a place that make it a *desirable* location for commercial, residential or recreational development. This place-based understanding of amenities remains integral to the enduring value of the concept, especially for twenty-first-century considerations of density and sustainability. However, the vast array of amenities, their subjective nature and their varied ability to influence change make them difficult to systematically codify. For our purposes, amenities fit on a two-dimensional field ranging from 'leading' to 'lagging' on one dimension, and from 'weak' to 'strong' on the other (Figure 5.1). This flexible, conceptual framework captures amenities in a way that can inform our understanding of how they influence development. We note that most any disamenity (e.g. a landfill) could be characterized as an amenity if only through its lack of presence. As will become clear, there is some subjectivity on where a particular amenity in a particular city will be located in this field.

The leading-lagging dimension speaks to the dichotomy between the exogenous and endogenous nature of urban concentration and growth. Some amenities are clearly exogenous to the growth pattern and can be characterized as leading. For example, physical features, such as higher elevations or proximity to water (Hoyt, 1972), are locational amenities that have drawn human settlement since the earliest cities were formed. Lagging amenities are those that emerge endogenously from the urban landscape; for example, low crime rate, a clear amenity, evolves from the confluence of the built environment, the people that occupy that space and policing (Jacobs, 1961). While these two examples lie at extreme ends of the continuum, a freeway interchange lies more toward the middle. The construction of an interchange is a massive exogenous injection of infrastructure funding at a particular location; however, it is reasonable to assume that its construction is based on some existing or future traffic demand.

The weak–strong dimension implies that all amenities are not of equal magnitude in terms of their influence on urban development. This is clearest to see in

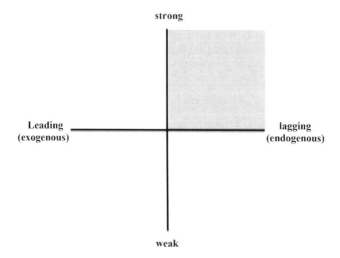

Figure 5.1 Amenity space.

attributes that may exist in all parts of the city, such as schools. In principle, any school performing above average could be considered an amenity, but parents do not typically evaluate schools in such a binary way; they ascribe higher value to those schools that are consistently the highest performers. Furthermore, the same amenity does not have the same importance in all urban areas. Connectivity is likely to be more valued in a city like San Diego, which is built around impassable hills and canyons, than in Oklahoma City, which has a grid layout allowing direct access between most places. Even within one city, we would expect a sports arena built near an area with an existing high concentration of activity to be a stronger amenity than one built in a suburban location.

This characterization of urban amenities implies that there are complicated feedback loops in the amenity landscape for any particular city. Amenities drive development, and development itself drives amenities. When looking at an urban area at one point in time, it is not difficult to identify the clusters of development, and then deduce the amenities *sustaining* each cluster. It is an entirely different challenge to disentangle the amenity timeline that drove the location to its current status quo. But this is the challenge faced by urban planners when developing zoning maps or deciding how to allocate incentives – they need to consider which amenities should be emphasized in future developments to replicate known success stories.

Research on TOD provides a glimpse into the differentiation between leading and lagging amenities, and their importance on the built environment. A survey of residents living in the immediate vicinity of rail transit stations in the San Francisco, Los Angeles and San Diego regions found that only one-third of residents say the presence of the rail station was one of their top three reasons for living there (Lund, 2006). Cervero and Landis (1997) find heterogeneity in the land-use impacts of transit stations in the San Francisco region, with some stations at the centre of employment and housing growth while others see little to no change. There is growing evidence that TOD is successful, not because of the transit amenity, but in spite of it. Lund (2006) finds that 'type or quality of housing', 'cost of housing', 'quality of neighborhood' and 'access to shops or services' on average rank higher than transit access. These results indicate that transit stations, a leading amenity, might not be the primary motivation for residents, but that the lagging amenities are the basis of residential location decision-making. This dissonance between the promised leading amenity TOD offers (transit access and ridership) and the actualized lagging amenities which residents desire, such as neighbourhood character and walkability, presents an opening for rethinking the value of amenity-driven development.

Importance of place in amenity driven high-density development (ADHD)

One of the earliest Victorian-era definitions of the amenity concept in British urban planning encompassed three qualities that still resonate today: environmental health, pleasantness and civic beauty and preservation (Smith, 1974). Such timeless, yet difficult to quantify features, resemble the desires of contemporary TOD residents for whom ambiance and character of place matter as much, or more than, transit access (Lund, 2006; Chatman, 2013). Throughout the evolution of the urban amenity concept, from Victorian Britain to modern-day Phoenix, one dimension is both critical, yet under-theorized – the importance of *place*. The notion of place refers to the meaningfulness of location in human experience (Relph, 1976; Tuan, 1990, 2001) and it presents opportunities for rethinking amenity-driven development in generative ways.

Cresswell (2015) articulates three fundamental aspects of place (following Agnew, 1997) that each have bearing for urban amenities: place as location, locale and sense of place. The most basic understanding of place as a physical location on the Earth's surface illustrates the obvious, but often overlooked consideration that urban amenities are site-specific, place-based features. This is not to say that urban amenities are not dynamic or subjective (the preference for dog parks can wax and wane), but urban amenities are necessarily embedded in the geographic experience of particular neighbourhoods and city-regions. This means that, in an era where city-regions are grappling with how to attract a mobile population amidst the homogenizing forces of a global economy, much opportunity exists to leverage distinctive place-based assets (Musterd & Murie, 2010).

The second meaning of place, as locale, refers to the material setting within which social relations occur. This idea is akin to what urban planners refer to as 'imageability', the unique assemblage of built environment, physical form and aesthetic qualities that make a place navigable, memorable and enjoyable (Lynch, 1960, 1995). In a post-industrial, global economy the manner in which the built environs of places are typecast – 'sprawling', 'historic', 'suburban' – matters greatly. Places today, posit Light et al. (1998, p. 6), 'are commodities in an international market and they must to an unprecedented degree sell themselves as tourist destinations, industrial sites or bundles of amenities suited to this or that class of prospective residents'. As we look forward, the need for firms and residents to locate in any particular city-region or neighbourhood may depend upon the fluctuating costs of transportation and communication technologies. When a firm or person can be equally productive in many locations, the deciding factor may pertain to the imageability of a particular place.

Sense of place, the third meaning of place, refers to the subjective, emotional attachment people have to place. Place-making efforts, those that intentionally generate place-identity and meaning, are increasingly perceived as critical in the making of good places, from the neighbourhood to regional level (Gehl, 2010). In a hyper-mobile modern global economy, where meaning, for many Americans, is not necessarily generated through long-term tenure in place, new types of place-based memory and meaning practices have emerged (Jivén & Larkham, 2003; Knox, 2005). The use of urban design, form and aesthetics to express a sense of *pastness* – a selective, simplified or imaginary sense of the past – has become a prevailing place-making strategy (Jackson, 1994; see also Clark & Madgin, Chapter 1 in this volume). The practice is commonplace in new residential subdivisions, commercial developments and cities largely constructed in the post-Second World War era. The nostalgic underpinning of such urban development schemes is an undeniably integral component of their popular appeal and success especially in terms of instantly making place meaningful via 'historic' charm, character and atmosphere. Thus, the burgeoning heritage industry and its nuanced integration into everyday life, from historic streetscapes to neotraditional architecture, attest to the use of nostalgia in place-making strategies.

Nowhere is the nostalgic impulse more evident and pervasive than our residential landscape. Successive waves of suburbanization have tapped the nostalgic desire for idyllic rural life replete with geographic stability. From the streetcar suburbs to the master-planned subdivision, residential developments incorporate agrarian fantasies in both urban form (the detached single-family dwelling with private yard) and urban design (an array of village-life inspired revival architectural styles). Recent movements toward re-urbanization, including historic districts, New Urbanism, Smart Growth and TOD, do not escape the nostalgic impulse – they simply deploy a different form of pastness, the desire for idyllic *urban* life. Such re-/new-urbanist agendas push neotraditional development in decidedly nostalgic ways; in both urban form (the traditional town centre, alleys, porches, urban streetscapes) and urban design (revival and regional architectural styles). Most of the New Urbanist adherents deny or dismiss the influence of nostalgia as a propulsive force. Yet, revival and 'historic' styles are employed, they conceded, because it is what buyers want (Duany et al., 2000).

But middle-class America is figuratively and literally *moved* by the nostalgic impulse. Urban dwellers continue to flock to historic neighbourhoods, neotraditional New Urbanist communities, and historicized master-planned subdivisions. Faux-traditional architectural styles embody what people want, the *idea* of history, of pastness (Levi, 2005). Dostrovsky and Harris (2008), for example, argue that the preference for historicist styles in domestic architecture since the 1960s is pervasive enough to evidence a widespread cultural shift or zeitgeist in the North American residential landscape. For some, the deployment of nostalgia as marketing ploy has rendered the expression a pejorative, synonymous with an imagined past and 'bad history' (Lowenthal, 1998, 1999). For others, the persistence and influence of nostalgic practice has warranted a more nuanced account of its generative potential in everyday life. 'Put to such uses,' says Cashman (2006, p. 154), 'nostalgia becomes a register for critical (that is, judicious) thought that may inspire critical (that is, vitally important) action.' In auto-centric city-regions lacking a dense urban core, the nostalgic impulse to revive a 'lost' urbanism is a generative force in meaningful place-making.

Density and zoning in a polycentric city: Phoenix, Arizona

Polycentric urban form refers to the existence of multiple urban centres in one area, region or geographical space (Kloosterman & Musterd, 2001). Decentralizing forces can lead to the creation of multiple centres that develop around, and often merge with, a single metropolis (Champion, 2001). As such, the core–periphery pattern is increasingly supplanted by an aspatial conceptualisation of the built form (Green, 2007). Polycentricity, argue Kloosterman and Musterd (2001), has become one of the defining characteristics of the urban form in advanced urban economies. Thus, the city-region, asserts Bontje and Kepsu (2013), is increasingly becoming the geographical unit of concern for urban planning with and between multiple urban centres, especially for those seeking to attract creative knowledge economies. Within polycentric city-regions, Musterd and van Zelm (2001) find that the core city becomes less important for residential households and the neighbourhood sub-centres gain traction in residential decision-making, especially among the affluent and mobile populations which are on the rise in these urban environments.

The Phoenix, Arizona city-region remains a quintessential polycentric metropolis, boasting 13 defined economic centres within the region (Leslie, 2010). Its exponential growth occurred in the post-Second World War automobile era, with the population more than doubling every 20 years between 1930 and 1990. The region had a 2010 population of 4.2 million, representing the addition of 2 million people since 1990. With few topographic barriers, Phoenix is defined by its suburban centres of low-density, single-family suburban housing and freeway interconnectivity (VanderMeer, 2011). While this form of development engendered affordable home ownership and business opportunities for decades, the costs are beginning to outweigh the benefits. With commute times between urban centres on the rise in polycentric cities (Alqhatani et al., 2014), and growing demand for dense, vibrant pedestrian oriented development (especially among Millennials), city-regions like Phoenix are looking to the past – or an idealized version of it – to rethink their twenty-first-century urban form.

Urban planners increasingly see transit-accessible nodes of high-density development as critical to reduce auto-congestion through increased transit ridership *and* to create vibrant, walkable communities. But with the momentum of decentralizing and homogenizing forces at work in auto-centric, polycentric city-regions like Phoenix, dense hubs of activity must be strategically planned and incentivized. Correlations between density and diversity in urban form, and social vibrancy and diversity, as explored by Talen (2006), present real opportunities for strategic planning. Zoning tools remain the primary tool for polycentric cities to facilitate the kind of urban diversity and vitality Jane Jacobs (1961) observed in Greenwich Village during the 1950s when short neighbourhood blocks housed diverse building types and ages with multiple uses.

The use of zoning to *facilitate* diversity and density in the social and built environment heralded by form based-codes, smart growth and sustainability codes today marks a notable effort to reverse the historical legacy of zoning intended to homogenize, segregate and disperse land uses in the US (Talen, 2008, 2012). In the first decade of the twentieth century, American cities began employing two different types of comprehensive land-use zoning: one type designed to prohibit undesirable physical attributes of the built environment, and the other to restrict people, largely based on race (Williams, 1956). Racial zoning ordinances were designed to spatially exclude racial minorities whereas land-use zoning was intended to exclude attributes of the built environment that negatively impacted health and aesthetics through restricting the density of development and separating residential and commercial land uses. The pursuit of entirely residential districts, especially those zoned for single-family homes, was seen as an effort to improve housing and social conditions for both low-income and wealthy communities. The intended separation effect of these exclusionary zoning efforts was in many instances achieved, and communities became more homogenized and less dense.

But as Talen (2012) attests, the nuanced and fine-grained detail of early land-use zoning actually included mixed-use commercial nodes and moderate density residential options in street-car suburbs. These instances of pre-Second World War zoning, provided access to the full suite of urban amenities such as transit, shopping, health services, education and recreation for virtually everyone in the community (while exposure to disamenities, such as heavy industry, were minimized). But the continued influence of modernist and auto-centric design further simplified and segregated land-use zoning into the kinds of developer-driven single-use zoning that creates the sprawling, low-density and unsustainable urban form we now see today. Additionally instances of exclusionary zoning intended to indirectly exclude certain types of people from a particular location persists (Bogart, 1993). Whether the land is developed or not, most cities are entirely zoned, and thus historical land-uses persist in the present. To alter this inherited built environment, municipal governments must creatively employ land-use zoning as both a reactive and proactive tool to engender new forms of urban development (Campbell et al., 2014). Land-use zoning can provide both incentives and constraints to development (Bates & Santerre, 1994; Cheshire & Sheppard, 1995; Grant, 2002). The overall effect of zoning on housing and land prices is varied due to conflicting costs and benefits (Netusil, 2005; Ihlanfeldt, 2007) which can both restrict options for property owners but simultaneously encourage the development of compatible land uses deemed attractive or desirable to the area.

Amenity driven development (ADD)

Two pervasive types of amenity-driven zoning have been at the fore of urban regeneration around the country and especially influential in Phoenix: historic district preservation (reactive zoning) and transit-oriented development (proactive zoning). In the sections that follow, we outline the lessons learned from each of these amenity-driven development strategies for sprawling, polycentric cities where high-density development is the exception, rather than the rule. We also highlight the limitations of these approaches in achieving *both* place-making and density-making, the ideal features of amenity-rich, walkable nodes that attract residents and tourists alike.

Historic district (HD) development: Phoenix case study

In Phoenix, like many Western cities without a history of historic preservation, transportation construction and development pressures inspired the use of historic districts (HD) as a reactive neighbourhood survival strategy (Johnson, 2007). The threat of disamenities, such as freeway proximity and the loss of residential streetscapes and character, was impetus for conceiving collections of old homes and their historic charm *as* potential cultural amenities. In 1974–1975 the construction of Interstate 10, through the heart of central Phoenix, resulted in the destruction of 600 older homes, and plans to build State Route 51 were underway. Contestation over the rapid urbanization of residential neighbourhoods resulted in the 1985 Phoenix Historic Preservation Ordinance, which established the Historic Preservation Commission and local preservation guidelines. In 1986, the first two residential historic districts were created in the Roosevelt and Coronado neighbourhoods. Ten years later, in 1996, Phoenix had designated 40 per cent of its eligible building stock as historic (structures at least 50 years old), the highest percentage of any large American city at the time (Kossan, 1998). Today, 35 residential historic districts cover much of central Phoenix in an incongruous patchwork, lending the quintessential 'ahistoric' metropolis a sense of cultural heritage.

While the use of historic zoning overlay to control the pace and character of urban landscape change burgeoned following the passage of the 1966 National Historic Preservation Act, the tool was first employed in South Carolina several decades prior. The Charleston preservation movement catalysed around the construction of a new-fangled Standard Oil service station, whose auto-centric land use and was perceived as an affront to the city's historic charm (Datel, 1990). The Old and Historic Charleston District (circa 1931), the nation's first historic district, was created using a zoning ordinance to establish the protection of the entire cultural landscape; all the visible features of the urban streetscape, rather than individual structures. While the historic preservation movement began as an effort to protect individual sites of national significance to an elite class of Americans, historic districts became a community development strategy to protect place-based amenities in ordinary neighbourhoods (Alanen & Melnick, 2000). While the practice of residential historic preservation is not without criticism, especially in regards to gentrifying and exclusionary outcomes (Duncan & Duncan, 2001, 2003), the nation's 8,500-plus residential historic districts attest to its widespread appeal (J. Byrne, email communication with the National Register of Historic Places, 1 April 2013).

Today, the popular appeal of historic districts is largely attributed to the suite of lagging amenities that revolve around the nostalgic ambiance of historic places (expressed as 'historic', 'green' and 'urban' living) more so than a concern for the leading amenity, historic preservation (DeLyser, 1999; Cameron & Gatewood, 2000; Levi, 2005; Kitson & McHugh, 2015). These findings speak to historic districts as an overwhelmingly successful place-making tool capable of attracting and retaining residents and a heritage tourism base (Stipe, 2003). In Phoenix, for example, the annual touring of ordinary historic homes has become a popular and generative tourist attraction and community-building event (Kitson, 2015). As an amenity driven development strategy, historic districts generate significant economic, environmental and social benefits. There is now widespread agreement on the long-term economic benefits of historic preservation both nationally and at the state and local levels, in terms of jobs, income, wealth, output and taxes (Listokin et al., 2010, 2011; Ijla et al., 2011). In the last decade, residential historic preservation has adopted environmental sustainability as a critical goal in preserving walkable places, rehabilitating built resources and ensuring energy efficiency (Young, 2012). Ultimately, historic preservation is one of the most successful and enduring practices in generating place-based identity (sense of place), cultural heritage and community building (Page & Mason, 2004).

As a twenty-first-century municipal development tool, however, historic districts have significant limitations. First, there is limited availability of historic structures, and in many cities they have already been preserved. The eligibility criteria require that structures be at least 50 years old (with time, more properties become eligible), the collection of structures must demonstrate historical significance (though places can be significant for their ordinariness, as is the case for most districts in Phoenix) and the majority of the structures must possess historic structural integrity (intact historic features, visible from the street). *In situ* historic residential resources can also pose challenges for transit accessibility given that the built environment around them has changed significantly. For example, in many cities, including Phoenix, what are now residential historic districts were formerly street-car suburbs. After the removal of the street-car trolleys that the neighbourhoods were built in tandem with, these communities were left only with limited bus access. Other historic districts were built as some of the first automobile suburbs, and despite a more dense or compact form (and a carport for one car) than the modern variety, these communities are preserved as such. Lastly, and most importantly, official historic district designation limits the height and intensity of new construction in accordance with the period of significance. So, while historic districts are lauded for their demonstrated place-making abilities, for incentivizing a bundle of strong lagging amenities, they do no result in increased density or intensity of development. Low density can then prevent such communities from becoming transit hubs.

Transit oriented development (TOD): Phoenix case study

TOD typically involves the encouragement of high-density development imme-diately surrounding the transit stop (Boarnet & Compin, 1999). This type of development harkens back to the notions of dense urban places by attempting to create a microcosm of New York- or Chicago-style development. The intro-duction of new amenities, such as light rail stations, will typically require the reactive zoning of the incentive type (Knight & Trygg, 1977), especially in auto-dependent city-regions like Phoenix. The current Phoenix light rail system opened in 2008, consisting of 28 stations along a 20-mile line, and cost $1.4 billion to build. In 2014, the line was extended approximately 3 miles, with 4 stations being added. Typically, land values surrounding a transit node will increase due to the transportation amenity; if the higher zoning were not allowed, the land would likely remain undeveloped or underdeveloped as high-intensity development would be needed to turn a profit on the higher valued parcels. Changing property value associated with TOD raises questions of transit-equity and ethnic residential segregation (Folch, 2012).

The premise of TOD is grounded on a Venn diagram of factors that do not necessarily have a large overlap. There are clearly residents interested in dense urban housing options *and* residents interested in efficient transit options, but what is less clear is if these are the same people. On the face of it, the success of TOD in a wide variety of cities would seem to confirm the assumption of a large overlap. So why would residents pay premium to live near transit, but not use it? The answer could be that they are not paying the premium for the transit but simply for the amenities high density brings. In the era before automobiles, high-density development was the only option, as most people moved around by foot. Ironically, TOD in the nineteenth and early twentieth centuries ushered in the era of lower density residential development by allowing people to 'rapidly' com-mute from streetcar suburbs into the central city. Like many cities in the United States, Phoenix had electric streetcar service that operated from the late nine-teenth century through the mid-twentieth century. For approximately 60 years, beginning in 1948, public transit was exclusively offered by buses. As average metro area densities have decreased over the decades, TOD in Phoenix and else-where is now a policy approach for increasing average densities. But is the draw of modern TOD, especially in polycentric sprawling city-regions like Phoenix, actually transit accessibility? Or is a nostalgic longing for 'lost' urbanity at work?

The challenge of disentangling leading and lagging amenities makes isolat-ing the success (or lack thereof) of TOD a difficult endeavour. New nodes of potential development are typically embedded within an already complex urban fabric. This is certainly the case of the Central Avenue corridor in Phoenix, a prominent thoroughfare that links the downtown, historic bungalow-filled neighbourhoods and ranch-style homes on curvilinear streets without sidewalks. Since the 2000 public vote that approved the funding to build the initial light rail system, including ten stations on Central Avenue, this corridor has seen considerable redevelopment. A particularly interesting intersection is at Central

Avenue and McDowell Road. This 5.46-acre lot on a prime corner across from the art museum, one block from the main public library, and across from a light rail station, has sat vacant for decades. After many attempts to build high-rise office or residential towers, in 2015, the construction of a four-storey apartment complex began on the site.

While there has been some success in generating increased housing intensity and density at TOD sites in Phoenix, there have also been many instances, such as the Central and McDowell intersection, which have not. Moreover, TOD has not generated a boom in transit ridership as the increase in overall ridership (bus and rail combined) is essentially on the same trajectory as it was before the introduction of rail. With empty mixed-use TOD storefronts and undeveloped parcels along the entire rail line, it is clear that transit proximity is not enough to attract and keep residents.

Canal oriented development (COD): Scottsdale case study

Along with rivers and harbours, canals have become important sites of waterfront development in cities. While harbour sites are situated in one large area, canal sites offer the advantage of multiple, potential sites of development of various scales and footprints, depending on the type of canal and community the canal is bisecting. These multiple site developments, termed COD, create hubs of activity that vary in size and function based on the community (residential, mixed-use, commercial), transportation network (transit stops, arterial roads, neighbourhood streets, bike paths) and type of canal (waterway or aqueduct). COD presents a malleable framework for the place-based and site-specific context. Key design elements, such as the linear connectivity of the canal, create a unifying mechanism to organize the urban form while also connecting public and private spaces. COD finds its inspiration in many of the design concepts of TOD, which includes 'moderate and high-density housing, along with complimentary public uses, jobs and services, concentrated in mixed-use developments along strategic points along the regional transit system' (Calthorpe, 1993, p. 41).

The evolution of the Scottsdale Waterfront in the city of Scottsdale (a key Phoenix-region economic centre) illustrates the canal infrastructure transformation in many cities with COD: from working agricultural or industrial waterway, to derelict disamenity and ultimately, to an economic, cultural and environmental amenity. For most of the twentieth century the 180-mile canal system in the Phoenix-Scottsdale region was viewed as a banal and uninspired landscape feature, much like a residential or commercial alleyway, best used for refuse. This view of the canal banks began to wane in the late 1990s and early 2000s as organizations and cities rediscovered the canal banks as both a source of recreation and economic development. During this time the Salt River Project (SRP), the region's key utility company and steward of the canal system, began to explore the recreation potential of the canal system and worked to improve over 50 miles of canal, including the portion which would later become known as the Scottsdale

Waterfront. In 1993 the derelict canal area, in the heart of an otherwise prosperous downtown Scottsdale, was declared a slum by the city. This paved the way for the canal waterfront redevelopment over the next decade (Bartman, 2010). The ambitious Scottsdale Waterfront COD project involved a long-term partnership of the City, the Salt River Project, business owners, public leadership, the community and developers (Buckman, 2014). The result has been a mixed-use, 1.1 million square foot development of upscale condos housed in two separate towers, as well as shops, restaurants and bars along the waterfront.

For non-harbour or non-riverfront communities like Scottsdale, COD represents an opportunity to construct water-driven, place-based development by creating dense, walkable districts for leisure and recreation, as well as economic growth and environmental stewardship. Importantly, COD success lies in its place-based emphasis, including the creation of vibrant public spaces (Buckman et al., 2013). Rather than being simply a node of transit or arterial roads, COD is built to reflect the values and heritage of the community, often around a particular theme (Carmona et al., 2010), in this case, water. Scottsdale's COD leverages the nostalgic role of water in the 'desert oasis', including the necessity of water for biological and cultural life to survive and thrive in desert environs. The idea of water has long impacted the human psyche, generating a natural pull as a source of biological, psychological, cultural and economic life (Kotval & Mullin, 2001; Millspaugh, 2001; Martin, 2003). In this way, COD draws on the heritage place-making legacy of historic preservation, but not the legal limitations and strict requirements of designation. The popular annual four-day Canal Convergence festival at the Scottsdale Waterfront celebrates the theme of water through illuminated artwork along with a marketplace and live performances.

Importantly, COD is waterfront place-making; it requires the canal to be a critical dimension in a larger holistic development initiative that takes into account access and linkages, comfort and image and social activities. A place that promotes both walkability and activity cultivates an engaging social environment with diverse uses and people-watching opportunities so that people come, stay and generate meaning (Gehl, 2010; Carmona et al., 2010). COD creates a public–private space for cultural and leisure activities that attracts residents and tourists, and keeps them there. The Scottsdale Waterfront has become one of the most important regional sites for civic, cultural and tourism activities. For example, the internationally known desert-based architect Paolo Soleri was commissioned to design an iconic pedestrian bridge and public plaza. During the 2008 Super Bowl, almost all of the main Super Bowl gala parties and the home base of the ESPN television sports channel were located at the Waterfront, some 30 miles away from University of Phoenix stadium in Glendale, Arizona (where the game was actually hosted). Above all else, CODs should encourage density, economic growth and place-making via strategic integration into the larger built and cultural environment. When carried out in this way, COD holds the potential to be a critical aspect of a city's future economic development strategy.

Beyond the rail station

Ross (2011) concludes that if a sustainability initiative or policy tool can work in Phoenix (the world's exemplar for low-density suburban sprawl), it will surely thrive elsewhere. Toward this point, our study of three improbable urban development strategies (HD, TOD, COD) in Phoenix reveals the strength of zoning as an urban planning tool and its continued evolution in polycentric Phoenix. *Historic* districts are particularly evocative in Phoenix, a city whose namesake speaks to perpetual newness and rebirth. In a city synonymous with sprawl, *transit* oriented development, seems downright oxymoronic. It is only fitting then, that *canal* oriented development would blossom in the nation's premier desert metropolis. Without these targeted urban planning interventions to make meaningful communities, perpetual waves of unregulated growth would have left the city void of character and cultural significance. While the benefits of HD and TOD are not without tremendous merit, these amenity development strategies face significant logistical and financial limitations for *future* use in polycentric Phoenix and neither approach successfully twins place-making and density-making. The future of COD, as an exemplar of amenity driven high-density development (ADHD) in the Phoenix metro region is promising because it leverages place-based heritage in the built environment (without the restrictions of HD) in tandem with higher density, mixed-use development (without the rail infrastructure costs). New COD efforts in Phoenix are currently underway to develop recreational amenities and employ canal oriented zoning tools at an important downtown section of the canal. But canals need not be the only focal point of ADHD.

ADHD is a framework for strategically incentivizing the development of dense, amenity rich places beyond the rail station. These are developments that attract residents, regional visitors and tourists alike, through leveraging their place-based assets and meanings in tandem with dense, walkable public–private spaces. Other forms of built infrastructure, such as defunct elevated rail systems, can become the meaningful catalyst for ADHD (e.g. High Line, New York City; Beltline, Chicago; Reading Viaduct, Philadelphia). Trivers (Chapter 2 in this volume) discusses the High Line in New York City, but his approach focuses on how the travelling urban imaginary creates an accretive narrative of the urban renewal experience through popular discourses. In this case of greater Phoenix, the ADHD framework outlined proposed here is intended to build upon the urban amenity concept as a strategy for directing compact urban form in polycentric cities beyond the rail station.

References

Agnew, J. A. (Ed.). (1997). *Political geography: A reader*. London: Arnold.

Alanen, A. R., & Melnick, R. Z. (Eds.). (2000). *Preserving cultural landscapes in America*. Baltimore, MD: Johns Hopkins University Press.

Alqhatani, M., Setunge, S., & Mirodpour, S. (2014). Can a polycentric structure affect travel behaviour? A comparison of Melbourne, Australia and Riyadh, Saudi Arabia. *Journal of Modern Transportation, 22*, 156–166.

Badoe, D. A., & Miller, E. J. (2000). Transportation–land-use interaction: Empirical findings in North America, and their implications for modeling. *Transportation Research Part D: Transport and Environment, 5*, 235–263.

Bates, L. J., & Santerre, R. E. (1994). The determinants of restrictive zoning: Some empirical findings. *Journal of Regional Science, 34*, 253–263.

Bartman, D. (2010). *Canal urbanism.* Master's thesis, Arizona State University, Tempe.

Boarnet, M. G., & Compin, N. S. (1999). Transit-oriented development in San Diego County: The incremental implementation of a planning idea. *Journal of the American Planning Association, 65*, 80–96.

Bogart, W. T. (1993). 'What big teeth you have!': Identifying the motivations for exclusionary zoning. *Urban Studies, 30*, 1669–1681.

Bontje, M., & Kepsu, K. (2013). Creative knowledge strategies for polycentric city-regions. In S. Musterd & Z. Kovács (Eds.), *Place-making and policies for competitive cities* (pp. 191–208). Somerset, NJ: John Wiley & Sons.

Buckman, S. (2014). The development feasibility of canal oriented development in the arid Southwest: Opinions of key stakeholders. *Land Use Policy, 39*, 342–349.

Buckman, S., Ellin, N., & Proffitt, D. (2013). Desert urbanism: Canalscape for Metropolitan Phoenix, Arizona. *Journal of Urban Regeneration & Renewal, 7*, 42–54.

Calthorpe, P. (1993). *The next American metropolis: Ecology, community, and the American dream.* New York: Princeton Architectural Press.

Cameron, C. M., & Gatewood, J. B. (2000). Excursions into the un-remembered past: What people want from visits to historical sites. *The Public Historian, 22*, 107–127.

Campbell, H. E., Kim, Y., & Eckerd, A. (2014). Local zoning and environmental justice: An agent-based model analysis. *Urban Affairs Review, 50*, 521–552.

Carmona, M., Tiesdell, S., Heath, T., & Oc, T. (2010). *Public places urban spaces: The dimensions of urban design.* Oxford: Architectural Press.

Cashman, R. (2006). Critical nostalgia and material culture in Northern Ireland. *Journal of American Folklore, 119*, 137–160.

Cervero, R., & Landis, J. (1997). Twenty years of the Bay Area Rapid Transit System: Land use and development impacts. *Transportation Research Part A: Policy and Practice, 31*, 309–333.

Champion, A. G. (2001). A changing demographic regime and evolving polycentric urban regions: Consequences for the size, composition and distribution of city populations. *Urban Studies, 38*, 657–677.

Chatman, D. G. (2013). Does TOD need the T? *Journal of the American Planning Association, 79*, 17–31.

Cheshire, P., & Sheppard, S. (1995). On the price of land and the value of amenities. *Economica, 62*, 247–267.

Cresswell, T. (2015). *Place: An introduction.* Malden, MA: Wiley-Blackwell.

Datel, R. E. (1990). Southern regionalism and historic preservation in Charleston, South Carolina, 1920–1940. *Journal of Historical Geography, 16*, 197–215.

DeLyser, D. (1999). Authenticity on the ground: Engaging the past in a California ghost town. *Annals of the Association of American Geographers, 89*, 602–632.

Diamond Jr, D. B., & Tolley, G. S. (1982). The economic roles of urban amenities. In D. B. Diamond Jr & G. S. Tolley (Eds.), *The economics of urban amenities* (pp. 3–54). Cambridge, MA: Academic Press.

Dostrovsky, N., & Harris, R. (2008). Style for the zeitgeist: The stealthy revival of historicist housing since the late 1960s. *The Professional Geographer, 60*, 314–332.

Duany, A., Plater-Zyberk, E., & Speck, J. (2000). *Suburban nation: The rise of sprawl and the decline of the American dream.* New York: North Point Press.

Duncan, J., & Duncan, N. (2001). The aestheticization of the politics of landscape preservation. *Annals of the Association of American Geographers, 91,* 387–409.

Duncan, J., & Duncan, N. (2003). *Landscapes of privilege: The politics of the aesthetic in an American suburb.* New York: Routledge.

Ewing, R., & Hamidi, S. (2015). Compactness versus sprawl: A review of recent evidence from the United States. *Journal of Planning Literature, 30,* 413–432.

Folch, D. C. (2012). *The centralization index as a measure of local spatial segregation.* Dissertation, Arizona State University, Tempe.

Florida, R. (2002). *The rise of the creative class: And how it's transforming work, leisure, community and everyday life.* Princeton, NJ: Basic Books.

Gehl, J. (2010). *Cities for people.* Washington, DC: Island Press.

Glaeser, E. L., Kolko, J., & Saiz, A. (2001). Consumer city. *Journal of Economic Geography, 1,* 27–50.

Grant, J. (2002). Mixed use in theory and practice: Canadian experience with implementing a planning principle. *Journal of the American Planning Association, 68,* 71–84.

Green, N. (2007). Functional polycentricity: A formal definition in terms of social network analysis. *Urban Studies, 44,* 2077–2103.

Hoyt, H. (1972). *The structure and growth of residential neighborhoods in American cities.* St Clair Shores, MI: Federal Housing Administration/Scholarly Press.

Ihlanfeldt, K. R. (2007). The effect of land use regulation on housing and land prices. *Journal of Urban Economics,* 61, 420–435.

Ijla, A., Ryberg, S., Rosentraub, M. S., & Bowen, W. (2011). Historic designation and the rebuilding of neighborhoods: New evidence of the value of an old policy tool. *Journal of Urbanism: International Research on Placemaking and Urban Sustainability, 4,* 263–284.

Jackson, J. B. (1994). *Sense of place, sense of time.* New Haven, CT: Yale University Press.

Jacobs, J. (1961). *The death and life of great American cities.* New York: Vintage Books.

Jivén, G., & Larkham, P. J. (2003). Sense of place, authenticity and character: A commentary. *Journal of Urban Design, 8,* 67–81.

Johnson, I. P. (2007). Historic preservation in the Phoenix Metro Area: History, current challenges, ongoing struggles. Master's thesis, Arizona State University, Tempe.

Kitson, J. (2015). Home touring as hospitable urbanism. *Journal of Urbanism,* doi: 10.1080/17549175.2015.1111924.

Kitson, J., & McHugh, K. (2015). Historic enchantments – Materializing nostalgia. *Cultural Geographies, 22,* 487–508.

Kloosterman, R. C., & Musterd, S. (2001). The polycentric urban region: Towards a research agenda. *Urban Studies, 38,* 623–633.

Knight, R. L., & Trygg, L. L. (1977). Evidence of land use impacts of rapid transit systems. *Transportation, 6,* 231–247.

Knox, P. L. (2005). Creating ordinary places: Slow cities in a fast world. *Journal of Urban Design, 10,* 1–11.

Kossan, P. (1998). Phoenix ranks highest in historic preservation. *The Arizona Republic,* 16 January.

Kotval, Z., & Mullin, J. (2001). Waterfront planning as a strategic incentive to downtown enhancement and livability. In M. Buraydi (Ed.), *Downtowns: Revitalizing the centers of small urban communities* (pp. 179–196). New York: Routledge.

Leslie, T. F. (2010). Identification and differentiation of urban centers in Phoenix through a multi-criteria kernel-density approach. *International Regional Science Review, 33,* 205–235.

Levi, D. J. (2005). Does history matter? Perceptions and attitudes toward fake historic architecture and historic preservation. *Journal of Architectural & Planning Research*, *22*, 148–159.

Light, A., Smith, J. M., & Roberts, D. (1998). Introduction. In A. Light & J. M. Smith (Eds.), *Philosophy and geography III: Philosophies of place* (pp. 1–20). Lanham, MD: Rowman & Littlefield.

Listokin, D., Lahr, M. L., Heydt, C., & Stanek, D. (2010). *First annual report on the economic impact of the Federal Historic Tax Credit*. New Brunswick, NJ: The State University of New Jersey.

Listokin, D., Lahr, M. L., Heydt, C., & Stanek, D. (2011). *Second annual report on the economic impact of the Federal Historic Tax Credit*. New Brunswick, NJ: The State University of New Jersey.

Lowenthal, D. (1998). *The heritage crusade and the spoils of history*. Cambridge: Cambridge University Press.

Lowenthal, D. (1999). *The past is a foreign country*. Cambridge: Cambridge University Press.

Lund, H. (2006). Reasons for living in a transit-oriented development, and associated transit use. *Journal of the American Planning Association*, *72*, 357–366.

Lynch, K. (1960). *The image of the city*. Cambridge, MA: MIT Press.

Lynch, K. (1995). *City sense and city design: Writings and projects of Kevin Lynch*. (edited by T. Banerjee & M. Southworth). Cambridge, MA: MIT Press.

Martin, D. (2003). Place-framing as place-making: Constituting a neighborhood for organizing and activism. *Annals of the Association of American Geographers*, *93*, 730–750.

Millspaugh, M. (2001). Waterfronts as catalysts for city renewal. In R. Marshall (Ed.), *Waterfronts in post-industrial cities* (pp. 74–85). London: Spon Press.

Musterd, S., & Murie, A. (Eds.). (2010). *Making competitive cities*. Somerset, NJ: John Wiley & Sons.

Musterd, S., & van Zelm, I. (2001). Polycentricity, households and the identity of places. *Urban Studies*, *38*, 679–696.

Netusil, N. R. (2005). The effect of environmental zoning and amenities on property values: Portland, Oregon. *Land Economics*, *81*, 227–246.

Page, M., & Mason, R. (Eds.). (2004). *Giving preservation a history: Histories of historic preservation in the United States*. New York: Routledge.

Relph, E. C. (1976). *Place and placelessness*. London: Pion.

Ross, A. (2011). *Bird on fire: Lessons from the world's least sustainable city*. Oxford: Oxford University Press.

Seto, K. C., Sánchez-Rodríguez, R., & Fragkias, M. (2010). The new geography of contemporary urbanization and the environment. *Annual Review of Environment and Resources*, *35*, 167–194.

Smith, D. L. (1974). *Amenity and urban planning*. London: Crosby Lockwood Staples.

Stipe, R. E. (2003). *Richer heritage: Historic preservation in the twenty-first century*. Chapel Hill: University of North Carolina Press.

Talen, E. (2006). Design that enables diversity: The complications of a planning ideal. *Journal of Planning Literature*, *20*, 233–249.

Talen, E. (2008). *Design for Diversity* (1st Ed.). Oxford: Routledge.

Talen, E. (2012). Zoning and diversity in historical perspective. *Journal of Planning History*, *11*(4), 330–347.

Tuan, Y-F. (1990). *Topophilia: A study of environmental perception, attitudes, and values.* New York: Columbia University Press.

Tuan, Y-F. (2001). *Space and place: The perspective of experience.* Minneapolis: University of Minnesota Press.

VanderMeer, P. (2011). *Desert visions and the making of Phoenix, 1860–2009.* Albuquerque: University of New Mexico Press.

Williams, N. (1956). The evolution of zoning. *The American Journal of Economics and Sociology, 15,* 253–264.

Young, R. A. (2012). *Metropolitan planning + design: Stewardship of the built environment: Sustainability, preservation, and reuse.* Washington, DC: Island Press.

6 Creating third places

Ethnic retailing and place-making in metropolitan Toronto

Zhixi Cecilia Zhuang

Introduction

Toronto is one of Canada's longest established gateway cities for immigration. According to 2011 figures, roughly 2,537,400 immigrants lived in Toronto's Census Metropolitan Area (CMA), accounting for 46.0 per cent of the total population and representing the largest immigrant population (37.4%) in Canada (Statistics Canada, 2013). A CMA is one or more adjacent municipalities with a central population core of at least 100,000 (with 50,000 or more residing in the core) (Statistics Canada, 2015a). The Toronto CMA comprises the City of Toronto and 23 surrounding suburban municipalities. Recent immigrants tend to bypass inner-city neighbourhoods and directly settle in suburban areas, or 'ethnoburbs'. 'Ethnoburbs' is a term that refers to suburban concentrations of immigrant groups (Li, 2009). This trend is apparent in Toronto where earlier waves of immigrants to Toronto created a significant presence in the inner city, but more recent immigrants have tended to settle in the inner and outer suburbs of the city (Qadeer et al., 2010; Wang & Zhong, 2013). The increasing suburban presence of various immigrants is visible in 'ethnic' retail clusters that are transforming suburban landscapes. Among various ethnic groups, Chinese and South Asian shopping clusters are by far the most prominent and rapidly increasing type of ethnic retailing in the Toronto area (Wang, 1999; Wang & Zhong, 2013; Zhuang et al., 2015; Zhuang, 2016; Zhuang & Chen, 2016).

Suburban Chinese and South Asian retail clusters not only serve as shopping destinations that offer diversity and choice in the general market, they can also play an important role in the social lives of immigrants and create 'third places' as informal public gathering places. 'Third place' is a concept popularized by Ray Oldenburg, mostly notably in his book *The great good place* (see Oldenburg, 1999). According to Oldenburg (1999), third places are social spaces that exist outside the 'first place' of home and the 'second place' of work. As sites for informal gatherings, third places are essential to a community's social vitality and public life. Because of their combination of retail, dining, entertainment, personal and business services and community functions, ethnic retail locations can serve as community places as well as contribute to the revitalization of existing suburban neighbourhoods.

In this chapter, I examine how suburban Chinese and South Asian retail clusters in Toronto have evolved over time and created a sense of place and community. Previous studies have typically focused on ethnic business enclaves located in Toronto's inner city, such as Chinatown, Little Italy, Little Portugal, India Bazaar and Greektown (Buzzelli, 2001; Hackworth & Rekers, 2005; Teixeira, 2006; Bauder & Suorineni, 2010; Zhuang, 2015, 2017). Insufficient attention has been paid to the city's emerging suburban ethnic retail developments (see the following exceptions: Wang, 1999; Preston & Lo, 2000; Linovski, 2012; Zhuang, 2016; Zhuang & Chen, 2016). Suburban ethnic retail sites are creating new meaning and identity in stereotypically homogeneous suburban landscapes. The rapid expansion of these sites requires more research and municipal attention because the development of these locations holds the potential for local municipalities to revitalize local economy, retrofit existing neighbourhoods and enhance community life. The study described in this chapter is one of the few that not only explored place-making with respect to ethno-cultural diversity (Hayden, 1995; Wood, 1997; Lin, 2011; Loukaitou-Sideris, 2002), but also examined the effects of new waves of immigration on suburban landscapes (Relph, 2014; Linovski, 2012; Zhuang, 2016; Zhuang & Chen, 2016).

Through extensive field research, I explored over 100 suburban Chinese and South Asian retail clusters with 3,800 businesses in five municipalities across

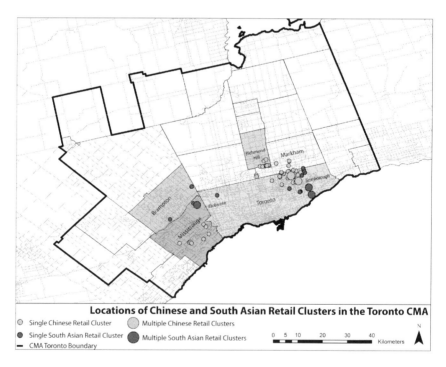

Locations of Chinese and South Asian Retail Clusters in the Toronto CMA

◯ Single Chinese Retail Cluster   ◯ Multiple Chinese Retail Clusters
● Single South Asian Retail Cluster   ● Multiple South Asian Retail Clusters
▬ CMA Toronto Boundary

0 5 10   20   30   40
                                  Kilometers

Figure 6.1 Locations of Chinese and South Asian retail clusters in the Toronto CMA (map produced by Fei Yeung Ivan Cheung).

the metropolitan Toronto area (Mississauga, Brampton, Richmond Hill, Markham and Toronto; Figure 6.1). This chapter is also the first to explore how third places are created within these sites and across two ethnic groups. As such it will serve as the basis for future research and theoretical work in the area.

Understanding third places and place-making

Place can be understood as 'both a physical/built environment at the neighbourhood scale and the subjective feelings its inhabitants harbour towards each other as an emplaced community' (Friedmann, 2010, p. 149). Using this conceptualization of place as an 'emplaced community', place-making can be described as 'the art of making places for people' (Sepe, 2013, p. 63). Visionary urbanists like Jacobs (1961) and Whyte (1980) advocated a people-oriented approach to create meaningful urban places (as opposed to 'spaces') that support diverse activities, promote human interactions and ultimately sustain lively and vibrant neighbourhoods. Their groundbreaking ideas and the people-oriented approach embedded in place-making process were echoed and enhanced by a variety of urban design and planning studies (see Lynch, 1960; Cullen, 1971; Alexander, 1977; Jacobs, 1985; Gehl, 2010). For example, from a physical design point of view, Lynch (1960, p. 119) argued that incorporating landmarks and symbols in place-making creates a place that can 'speak of the individuals and their complex society, of their aspirations and their historical tradition, of the natural setting, and of the complicated functions and movements of the city world'. The presence of physical landmarks in a space that reflect people's experiences of that space and of society helps create a sense of place there. When adopting a people-oriented approach in planning for multicultural communities, understanding people's diverse needs, values, cultural identities and social norms is critical in the making of meaningful places. In many cases, ethnic communities use cultural symbols, architectural or structural features, and ethnic events to (re)identify and (re)shape the space and create a sense of place and community (Olson & Kobayashi, 1993; Hayden, 1995; Wood, 1997; Loukaitou-Sideris, 2002; Rath, 2007; Lara, 2012; Dieterlen, 2014; Zhuang, 2015).

In addition to understanding a place from a user's point of view, creating community spaces is also considered vital to place-making practice. Cilliers et al. (2015, p. 351) defined place-making as 'the process by which people transform the locations they inhabit into the places where they live'. The authors referred to place-making as the creation of a strong sense of community by offering spaces to socialize and interact, provide security, create an inclusive public realm and establish destinations that attract users and invite them to return. In these ways, the goals of place-making parallel many of the characteristics of third places.

Third places are described as 'inclusively sociable, offering both the basis of community and the celebration of it' (Oldenburg, 1999, p. 14). It can be applied to many types of places, from private businesses, such as barbershops, cafes, restaurants, bars and shopping plazas, to public spaces, which may host 'regular, voluntary, informal, and happily anticipated gatherings' (Oldenburg, 1999, p. 16).

These sites are well-integrated into daily life, such that regulars feel a sense of ownership over the locale. Third places are not, however, necessarily notable or interesting to outsiders (Oldenburg & Brissett, 1982).

Although some scholarship about third places addresses ethno-cultural diversity, it is rarely the central focus despite the fact that the opportunity to interact with diverse people and opinions is part of the value of third places. According to Oldenburg (1999), culture matters when considering whether it is possible to create a third place in a community, what form a third place could take, and what function it needs to serve. Any exploration of third places created for and/or used by particular ethno-cultural communities should be rooted in the culture, politics and history of that group. Furthermore, Oldenburg and Brisset's (1982) assertion that third places are inclusive and offer a remedy to the malaise of everyday life suggests that these sites could be of particular importance to communities that are racialized or otherwise marginalized in spaces primarily occupied by the dominant culture. The place-making practices of immigrant communities have been recognized as means to manage alienation and isolation, while establishing a place of belonging in a new environment (Phillips & Robinson, 2015). This chapter's exploration of how ethno-cultural diversity impacts the use, value and operation of third places will contribute to the literature on diversity-oriented place-making practices.

Place-making in ethnic suburbs

Suburban landscapes are commonly characterized as areas of segregated land use with characterless streets lined with cookie-cutter homes, big box stores and seas of parking lots (Duany, 2010). Suburban sprawl has created a reliance on cars to the detriment of walkable neighbourhoods and pedestrian accessible amenities and places for people to meet. The suburbs are often thought of as 'placeless' unsustainable developments with underperforming spaces, dead malls and degenerating strips (Relph, 1976; Duany, 2010; Dunham-Jones & Williamson, 2011). I suggest, however, that underused suburban spaces hold untapped place-making possibilities and the potential to retrofit existing neighbourhoods.

Over the past decade, planners have started to retrofit suburbia across North America through the reinhabitation, redevelopment and regreening of abandoned or underused spaces such as strip malls, business parks, parking lots and disconnected residential subdivisions (Talen, 2010; Dunham-Jones & Williamson, 2011). The goals of suburban retrofitting are similar to those of place-making, in that they both seek to improve places for human activity and interaction. However, the effects of increasing suburban immigrant settlement on the social and economic fabric of existing suburban communities has been overlooked in current retrofitting practices (Zhuang, 2016; Zhuang & Chen, 2016).

Ethnoburbs are emerging across North America, where stereotypically homogeneous suburban landscapes have been transformed with unique forms of ethnic retailing and places of worship (Li, 2009; Wang & Zhong, 2013). Various ethnic groups have readapted former facilities or (re)developed existing areas to create vital community spaces that embody the social, cultural and political meanings of the respective community (Wood, 1997; Li, 2005; Zhou, 2013; Lung-Aman, 2015). Accordingly, these suburban ethnic places are helping to forge a sense of community and create new third places for social life and community functions. These community-building processes present a novel approach to place-making within a suburban context and deserve further empirical study.

Setting the context

The research I present here was based on a case study approach, through which I examined the dynamics of place-making practices in ethnic retail neighbourhoods. The Toronto area is an ideal site to study suburban ethnic retailing because of its numerous ethnoburbs; their high concentration of immigrant populations and ethnic-oriented institutions are significantly changing conventional suburban landscapes 'not only in the social and cultural domains, but also in the economic and political realms' (Wang & Zhong, 2013, see abstract). I focused on Chinese and South Asian business communities because these two immigrant groups have established the most visible and sizeable ethnic retail facilities across the Toronto region and represent one well-established immigrant group in Canada (Canada's second largest visible minority group is Chinese) and one relatively new but rapidly growing group (South Asians are Canada's largest visible minority group) (Statistics Canada, 2013). As defined by the Employment Equity Act, visible minorities are 'persons, other than Aboriginal peoples, who are non-Caucasian in race or non-white in colour' (Government of Canada, 2015, p. 2). Statistics Canada adopts this definition and the Canadian Census currently includes the following visible minority groups: Chinese, South Asian, Black, Arab, West Asian, Filipino, Southeast Asian, Latin American, Japanese and Korean (Statistics Canada, 2015b). As the two largest visible minority groups in the Toronto CMA, Chinese and South Asians represent 9.6 per cent and 15.1 per cent of the total population, respectively (Statistics Canada, 2015c). I developed an inventory of Chinese and South Asian business clusters in the suburban regions of Toronto, including Markham, Richmond Hill, Brampton, Mississauga and inner suburbs of Toronto (Etobicoke and Scarborough). Both immigrant groups have established a similar suburban settlement presence with their respective retail clusters being located in close proximity to where these communities reside (Figures 6.2 and 6.3). The Chinese communities and retail clusters are concentrated in north Scarborough, Markham, Mississauga and Richmond Hill, and South Asian clusters are primarily in east Scarborough, north Etobicoke, Mississauga and Brampton.

Through extensive field surveys, 112 Chinese and South Asian clusters in these suburban areas were identified (Table 6.1). The ethnic retail clusters were carefully selected based on the following criteria: 1) each cluster had at least 10 individual businesses sharing the same property; and 2) each cluster featured a strong presence of ethnic-oriented (i.e. Chinese and South Asian) signage, products and services. Retail clusters were grouped into three categories (strip mall, plaza and indoor mall), based on the type of retail building (Linovski, 2012). Strip

LEGEND
☐ 0 - 355
▨ 356-995
▨ 996-2005
▨ 2006-3695
■ 3696 - 6480
○ Single Retail Cluster
◎ Multiple Retail Clusters

N
0 10 20 30 40 KM
Source: Statistics Canada, 2006

Figure 6.2 Chinese population by ethnic origin and retail clusters in the Toronto CMA (map produced by Fei Yeung Ivan Cheung).

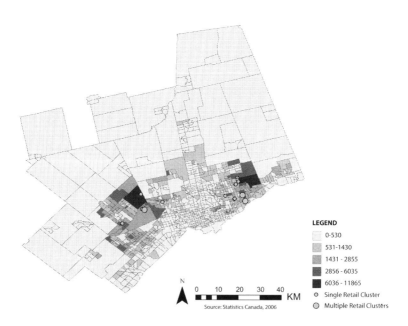

LEGEND
☐ 0-530
▨ 531-1430
▨ 1431 - 2855
▨ 2856 - 6035
■ 6036 - 11865
○ Single Retail Cluster
◎ Multiple Retail Clusters

N
0 10 20 30 40 KM
Source: Statistics Canada, 2006

Figure 6.3 South Asian population by ethnic origin and retail clusters in the Toronto CMA (map produced by Fei Yeung Ivan Cheung).

malls are 'multiple, conjoined rental units arranged parallel to the street' with parking abutting the right-of-way (Linovski, 2012, p. 84). Plazas are set farther back from the street, with a large parking lot in the middle and individual businesses opening inward towards the parking lot instead of the street. Indoor malls have become a popular form of ethnic retailing, especially for Chinese communities. These are a relatively innovative retail form compared with mainstream retail structures because they tend to be part of a condominium development, with many constructed since the 1980s. This condominium format means developers can create smaller units within the malls, which business owners can purchase an individual unit directly instead of leasing. A Chinese condominium mall typically has the following features that distinguish it from a mainstream shopping centre: a concentration of Asian/Chinese-oriented and operated businesses; condominium ownership (versus leasehold); an absence of conventional anchors (e.g. the Bay, Sears) with restaurants or grocery stores acting as anchors; variable store hours (versus traditional norms and practices); no control of tenant mix; and smaller store size (Qadeer, 1998; Wang, 1999; Preston & Lo, 2000). Though a more recent phenomenon, South Asian shopping malls and plazas with similar features to their Asian/Chinese predecessors are also rapidly increasing, as observed during my field surveys.

Field surveys were conducted in order to observe the following: site visitors and social interactions, business activities, retail building form, site accessibility, public/private space allocation, architectural features and ethnic expressions (signage, decoration, window displays, etc.). Site visits allowed for the assessment of variances/diversities between locations as well as the development of an understanding of these spaces. At least one Chinese and one South Asian case study from each retail form category (i.e. strip, plaza, indoor mall) were selected for in-depth research, with at least one from each of the municipalities listed above. The following eight case studies were selected based on the observed variety and intensity of social and economic activities as well as physical characteristics: Jaipur Gore Plaza in Brampton, Great Punjab Business

Table 6.1 Retail forms and profiles (SA = South Asian; CHN = Chinese)

Retail forms		Strip	Plaza	Indoor mall	Total
# of clusters		41	48	23	112
	SA	38	7	1	46
	CHN	3	41	22	66
# of businesses		468	1,411	1,930	3,809
SA clusters	SA	207	267	55	529
	non-SA	194	101	0	295
CHN clusters	CHN	48	826	1,790	2,664
	non-CHN	19	217	85	321

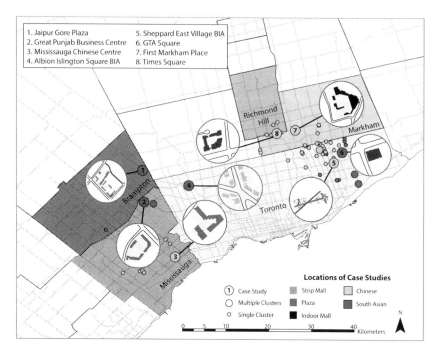

1. Jaipur Gore Plaza
2. Great Punjab Business Centre
3. Mississauga Chinese Centre
4. Albion Islington Square BIA
5. Sheppard East Village BIA
6. GTA Square
7. First Markham Place
8. Times Square

Locations of Case Studies

① Case Study   ▨ Strip Mall   ▨ Chinese
○ Multiple Clusters   ■ Plaza   ▨ South Asian
○ Single Cluster   ■ Indoor Mall

0   5   10   20   30   40 Kilometers

N

Figure 6.4 Locations of case studies (map produced by Fei Yeung Ivan Cheung).

Centre and Mississauga Chinese Centre in Mississauga, Albion Islington Square in Etobicoke, Sheppard East Village and GTA Square in Scarborough, First Markham Place in Markham, and Times Square in Richmond Hill (Figure 6.4). The most prominent place-making features observed in these case studies will be discussed in the following sections. Overall, the presence of Chinese and South Asian retail clusters provides several implications for suburban ethnic place-making practices.

Ethnic place-making practices and strategies

The following sections describe how ethnic businesses operate in a concentrated format, and how the study sites are featured with strong ethnic identity and used as community space. The analysis reveals effective ethnic place-making strategies including spatial concentrations as place markers, ethnic expressions to inscribe a place with meaning, and the creations of suburban ethnic retail sites as third places.

Concentrated ethnic businesses as place markers

The spatial concentration of ethnic businesses operates not only as a resource, or a form of 'spatial capital', but also 'make(s) and mark(s) ethnic places' (Kaplan & Li, 2006, p. 7). The Chinese and South Asian retail clusters in this study reflect these spatial concentration effects by readapting, modifying and transforming the existing suburban landscapes. As shown in Table 6.1, the Chinese enterprises feature 66 clusters with nearly 3,000 businesses, while their South Asian counterparts were concentrated in 46 clusters with over 800 businesses; 38 out of 46 (82.6%) observed South Asian retail clusters are shopping strips, while Chinese businesses are found in 41 (62.1%) shopping plazas and 22 (33.3%) indoor malls. Most of the strip malls observed were located along major suburban arterial roads and were often older post-Second World War buildings. Although the buildings appeared to be in disrepair, the strong presence of Chinese and South Asian signage and merchandise display (e.g. jewellery, textiles, clothing, kitchenware, groceries, music records, videos) made the storefronts stand out visually from the surrounding built environment. In the cases of Albion Islington Square and Sheppard East Village, South Asian and Chinese businesses have replaced the mainstream businesses that once occupied the strips, and created economic opportunities to revitalize local economy. Both areas have grown to 200 and 500 businesses, respectively. Compared with strip malls, many shopping plazas and indoor malls were developed after the 1980s and tend to have larger business capacity. With stronger concentration effects, some of the ethnic plazas and indoor malls (e.g. Jaipur Gore Plaza, Great Punjab Business Centre, Times Square, First Markham Place) have become the catalyst for residential developments adjacent to the retail sites.

The concentration of Chinese and South Asian businesses in the studied clusters also reveals how these retail places can serve as intercultural social and commercial spaces for different ethnic groups, although this was slightly less so for the Chinese clusters, in which 89.2 per cent of the total businesses were considered co-ethnic (i.e. Chinese signage, products and services) compared with 64.2 per cent for the South Asian clusters. Although the majority of South Asian businesses tended to mix with non-South Asian businesses, the GTA Square indoor mall, in which 100 per cent of the businesses were South Asian-oriented, was an exception. For example, in Albion Islington Square and Jaipur Gore Plaza, African, Caribbean, Latino and mainstream businesses co-existed with the most prominent South Asian businesses. Signage advertising various shops including Las Palmas Latin Restaurant, African and West Indian Market, Caribbean Oriental Speciality Food, Basmaties Caribbean Grocer and African Super Market were just a few markers of the multi-ethnic business environment. Chinese businesses tended to mix with other Asian-oriented businesses (e.g. Vietnamese, Korea, Japanese, Filipino) in the studied clusters, but the food courts and restaurants in the Chinese indoor shopping malls (e.g. First Markham Place, Times Square) tend to be frequented by nearby office workers regardless of their cultural backgrounds who often socialize with their co-workers during lunch time.

The spatial concentration of ethnic businesses plays an important role in attracting diverse customers and retailers and making the retail places more recognizable than the rest of the built environment. The Chinese and South Asian clusters demonstrate how concentrated ethnic businesses as place markers have maximized this spatial resource, transformed the suburban spaces, and continue to shape the retail places.

Ethnic expressions to reinforce 'a sense of place'

In addition to using signage and merchandise displays that are ethnically unique, other place-making strategies such as distinct and symbolic architectural features, public art, streetscape improvements and cultural festivals were adopted by businesses in the case studies. In many cases these strategies were facilitated by the Business Improvement Area (BIA) programme, which also governed what strategies could or could not be undertaken. For example, although the built form (e.g. older, rundown building stock with limited on-site parking) of both the Albion Islington Square (Figure 6.5) and Sheppard East Village strip malls impedes physical makeover and public gathering opportunities, the local BIAs greatly facilitated the place-making process. A BIA is generally in the form of main streets where local business people and property owners voluntarily work together in partnership with the municipality to improve and promote their business area. The city collects a special tax levy and the funds are returned to the BIA to manage, for instance, streetscape improvement, event planning, marketing and promotional campaigns. With the involvement of the BIAs, local businesses can access 50/50 matching funds from the City of Toronto for street beautification, festivals, and marketing and promotion (e.g. street festivals up to $50,000 (all monetary figures in this chapter are in Canadian dollars), murals and signage up to $4,000 each, and commercial facade improvement up to $10,000 (see Toronto Association of Business Improvement Areas, 2016). The Albion Islington Square BIA has paid homage to the area's historic name, Thistletown, by putting up thistle lights on lampposts and a 'Thistletown Village' sign to define the district. Similarly, the Sheppard East Village BIA installed banners on lampposts to promote the area and had a mural painted to 'reflect some of the area's heritage, as well as depict people from around the world, who now live and work here' (Sheppard East Village BIA, 2016a). Both BIAs have been attempting to attract geographically dispersed and ethnically diverse customers and visitors by promoting the areas as multicultural communities that offer a global flavour of unique products and services. The Sheppard East Village BIA website invites visitors to drop by the area and 'discover the world at your doorstep', while the Albion Islington Square BIA hosts the annual street festival, Fusion of Taste, to celebrate the diversity of the community (Albion Islington Square BIA, 2016; Sheppard East Village BIA, 2016b).

Elaborate architectural features and distinct public artwork that convey ethno-cultural meanings were observed in two shopping plaza case studies: the Mississauga Chinese Centre and the Great Punjab Business Centre (whose names also explicitly assert their respective ethnic identities). The Mississauga Chinese Centre has remarkable architectural features that reflect Chinese history and architectural and cultural traditions. Among notable features are the following: a 43-feet tall entrance gateway (Paifang in Mandarin); Chinese garden features such as a pavilion and stone sculptures located in the centre of the courtyard, and covered walkways connecting businesses surrounding the courtyard; and replicas of a pair of steles, corner towers, a fortress at the Great Wall of China, and the famous nine dragon wall (Lo, 2006; Mississauga Chinese Centre, 2016;

Figure 6.5 Strip storefronts in Albion Islington Square BIA (photo by author).

Figure 6.6). Although these features mix-and-match elements of Chinese art and architecture 'typically found in imperial Chinese palaces, together with Southern China vernacular gardening elements' and are not uncommon in other Chinese retail developments (Zhuang, 2015, p. 689), such ethnic expressions create a strong sense of place within the plaza's boundary.

Similarly, the Great Punjab Business Centre uses public art and architectural motifs to commemorate Punjabi Sikh history and heritage, while providing the place a unique identity (Figure 6.7). For example, a statue of Maharaja Ranjit Singh, the founder of the Sikh Empire, riding on a warrior horse stands at the entrance of the plaza. Engravings from Singh's throne can be found on the upper walls of the two-storey buildings to signify the legacy of the emperor. Another important piece of public art is the Komagata Maru monument that depicts the 1914 incident when a boat carrying over 350 Punjabi migrants from India (the majority were Sikh) was not allowed to port at Vancouver due to Canada's discriminatory immigration policies and was forced to return to India. The monument not only invites visitors to congregate in the space, but creates a historical attachment to the place by reminding people of how the Punjabi Sikh community claimed their space and rights in Canada. The buildings of the plaza also use continuous arches with lotus flower motifs, a significant cultural symbol of Sikhism. Combined, these architectural and public art features convey both explicit and subtle meanings of the Sikh

Figure 6.6 Ethnic expressions through elaborate architectural features in Mississauga Chinese Centre, pavilion (left) and nine dragon wall (right) (photos by author).

culture and history, leaving powerful marks on the retail landscape and making the business centre identifiable and distinct.

By contrast, the three indoor shopping malls, Times Square, First Markham Place and GTA Square, reflect only generic suburban architecture with no ethnic expressions except for store signage and ethnic merchandise. Their exteriors look no different than any other shopping mall; yet, inside their culturally unique merchandise attracts customers who have social, cultural or economic attachments to the place. For example, GTA Square mainly caters to the Tamil community who reside in the adjacent area of Scarborough, while Times Square and First Markham Place are the Chinese commercial landmarks in Richmond Hill and Markham, respectively.

Suburban ethnic retail sites as third places

Another major finding of my research was that the Chinese and South Asian retail clusters can serve as third places because they are conducive to social interactions among regulars. Some of the retail places in my sample were actively facilitating and promoting community functions beyond retailing.

Despite differences in business size, retail form and the mix of ethnicities (Table 6.1), both Chinese and South Asian retail clusters share similarities with respect to business composition. Approximately half of the Chinese (47.0%) and South Asian (52.8%) businesses are service-oriented, which include personal and professional services, such as health clinics, hair and beauty salons, and offices for law, immigration, accounting, educational training, real estate and travel (Figure 6.8). These businesses cater specifically to the diverse cultural needs of the ethnic communities. I observed that the majority of the clientele in the studied sites were from the co-ethnic community who were seeking services without linguistic or cultural barriers. Some of these businesses, such as beauty salons and educational institutions (e.g. cultural centres, senior clubs, extra-curricular learning centres for school-age children) have become local destinations inviting social

Figure 6.7 Ethnic expressions through public art and architectural motifs in the Great Punjab Business Centre, continuous arches (top left); Singh's throne engraved on the walls (bottom left); the Komagata Maru Monument (top right); statue of Maharaja Ranjit Singh (bottom right) (photos by author).

interactions among the regulars. At the time, the retail sector accounted for nearly one-third of the businesses for both Chinese (29.8%) and South Asian (28.0%) groups, and food-related businesses had a slightly smaller market share of 23.2 per cent and 19.2 per cent, respectively (Figure 6.8). Businesses in these two sectors also provided space (e.g. storefront, food court) for social interactions among business operators, regulars, and strangers during their shopping and dining experiences. It is interesting to note that many seniors used the interior spaces of the Chinese shopping malls (e.g. food court, hallway, and lobby) for social activities and group exercises (e.g. chatting, walking, chess, fan dance, Tai chi) rather than primarily for commercial activities. Because of the important role these retail places play in the everyday lives of the ethnic groups, they not only serve as retail destinations, but also integrate other community functions (e.g. community and religious services, schools, housing).

Figure 6.8 Business compositions (produced by Fei Yeung Ivan Cheung).

The two most established community places in my sample were the South Asian shopping plazas, Great Punjab Business Centre and Jaipur Gore Plaza. The Great Punjab Business Centre in Mississauga was developed right next to Sri Guru Singh Sabha, a long-established Sikh gurdwara and the Khalsa School, a private religious school from Junior Kindergarten to Grade 10 mainly serving the Sikh community. A Sikh Heritage Museum of Canada is also a prominent feature of the mall. The museum is a public exhibition and educational facility that aims to 'celebrate the Canadian Sikh experience and its vibrant history, explore the richness and complexities of Sikh spirituality and identity, and commemorate and honour Sikh history' (Sikh Heritage Museum of Canada, 2016). The museum has two rooms showcasing a collection of photographs, war artefacts, model soldiers, paintings and other items that commemorate the Sikh history and culture, as well as contemporary Sikh experiences in Canada. At public events and exhibitions, the museum uses the foyer of the plaza to engage visitors. During my observations, I noted that people from various cultural backgrounds and geographical limits freely exchanged their viewpoints, with museum staff actively facilitating the interactions. These interactions turned the museum space into a public forum allowing for the intercultural exchange of ideas and community engagement opportunities.

The Jaipur Gore Plaza in Brampton was developed in 2005. Its location was strategically chosen for its close proximity to the Hindu Sabha Temple – a long-established religious institute located in an industrial zone. The Jaipur Gore Plaza provides an onsite place of worship, the Bharat Mata Mandir, alongside retail stores. Recent developments to the retail site include a newly built banquet hall facility and an ornate Sikh temple, the Gurdwara Dasmesh Darbar. The Brampton Seniors and Youth Recreation Centre (BSYRC) was under construction at the time of my research. The BSYRC is intended to 'support an intergenerational mix of South Asian and Indo Caribbean cultural and multicultural recreational activities further contributing to the diversity of our communities' (Brampton Seniors & Youth Recreation and Cultural Centre, 2016). Another religious service organization, the Brampton and Regional Islamic Centre (BARIC), also occupies a storefront in the plaza complex. According to the BARIC's website in 2016, the organization has plans to build a mosque 1 kilometre away from the retail site (Brampton and Regional Islamic Centre, 2016). During my site visit, I observed that a planning public notice had been posted showing a zoning amendment proposal to permit the development of a new subdivision with 73 townhouse units, 17 live-work townhouse units, and a 0.23-hectare park. These development trends suggest that a complete community is being planned with retailing, places of worship, community services, housing and park space. The retail plaza has been the catalyst for the series of later developments and has become the centre of the community space that will bring together people of different cultural and religious backgrounds, but especially those of South Asian descent.

Conclusions

The increasing suburban immigrant settlements in the Toronto region have created retail development opportunities reflective of the changing demographics, as well as place-making opportunities for suburban municipalities. My analysis revealed how suburban ethnic retail space evolves and is shaped, how cultural identity is expressed through ethnic retail activities and inscribes a place with meaning, and how ethnic retail places contribute to community-building via the creation of third places. Municipalities need to understand the dynamics and concentration effects of suburban ethnic retailing and how they can create a sense of place and community. This will help municipalities integrate ethnic retailing into suburban retrofitting schemes and maximize their social and economic contributions to community-building.

This research provides municipalities with empirical data about existing ethnic retail places and effective place-making strategies. Additional research is needed to clarify ways to nurture and sustain emerging ethnic markets and make them more inclusive, which could be a lucrative tool for the broader economy and could contribute to place-making and community-building. Clarifying these aspects of the ethnic retail phenomenon will better accommodate the growing immigrant population, facilitate their retail activities, and importantly, improve the community as a whole.

References

Albion Islington Square BIA. (2016). Fusion of taste. Retrieved from www.fusionoftaste. com/index.html.

Alexander, C. (1977). *A pattern language: Towns, buildings, construction*. New York: Oxford University Press.

Bauder, H., & Suorineni, A. (2010). *Toronto's Little India: A brief neighbourhood history*. RULA Digital Repository. Retrieved from http://digitalcommons.ryerson.ca/ immigration/3.

Brampton and Regional Islamic Centre. (2016). Funding request. Retrieved from http://baric.ca/fundrequest.html.

Brampton Seniors & Youth Recreation and Cultural Centre. (2016). Our project. Retrieved from http://bsyrc.com.

Buzzelli, M. (2001). From Little Britain to Little Italy: An urban ethnic landscape study in Toronto. *Journal of Historical Geography, 27*, 573–587.

Cilliers, E. J., Timmermans, W., Van Den Goorbergh, F., & Slijkhuis, J. (2015). Green place-making in practice: From temporary spaces to permanent places. *Journal of Urban Design, 20*, 349–366.

Cullen, G. (1971). *The concise townscape*. London: Architectural Press.

Dieterlen, S. (2014). Hidden in plain sight: Design approaches to Midwestern Mexican-American landscapes. *Journal of Urbanism: International Research on Placemaking and Urban Sustainability, 7*(2), 109–129.

Duany, A. (2010). *Suburban nation: The rise of sprawl and the decline of the American dream*. New York: North Point Press.

Dunham-Jones, E., & Williamson, J. (2011). *Retrofitting suburbia: Urban design solutions for redesigning suburbs* (updated edition). New York: Wiley.

Friedmann, J. (2010). Place and place-making in cities: A global perspective. *Planning Theory and Practice, 11*, 149–165.

Gehl, J. (2010). *Cities for people*. Washington, DC: Island Press.

Government of Canada. (2015). Employment Equity Act. Government of Canada. Retrieved from http://laws-lois.justice.gc.ca/PDF/E-5.401.pdf.

Hackworth, J., & Rekers, J. (2005). Ethnic packaging and gentrification: The case of four neighborhoods in Toronto. *Urban Affairs Review, 41*, 211–236.

Hayden, D. (1995). *The power of place: Urban landscapes as public history*. Cambridge, MA: MIT Press.

Jacobs, A. (1985). *Looking at cities*. Cambridge, MA: Harvard University Press.

Jacobs, J. (1961). *The death and life of great American cities*. New York: Vintage.

Kaplan, D., & Li, W. (2006). Introduction: The places of ethnic economies. In D. Kaplan & W. Li (Eds.), *Landscapes of the ethnic economy* (pp. 1–14). Lanham, MD: Rowman and Littlefield.

Lara, J. J. (2012). Patterns and forms of Latino cultural landscapes: Southwest Detroit, a case of incremental re-adaptive use. *Journal of Urbanism: International Research on Placemaking and Urban Sustainability, 5*, 139–156.

Li, W. (2005). Beyond Chinatown, beyond enclave: Reconceptualizing contemporary Chinese settlement in the United States. *GeoJournal, 64*, 31–40.

Li, W. (2009). *Ethnoburb: The new ethnic community in Urban America*. Honolulu: University of Hawaii Press.

Lin, J. (2011). *The power of urban ethnic places: Cultural heritage and community life*. New York: Routledge.

Linovski, O. (2012). Beyond aesthetics: Assessing the value of strip mall retail in Toronto. *Journal of Urban Design, 17*, 81–99.

Lo, L. (2006). Suburban housing and indoor shopping: The production of the contemporary Chinese landscape in Toronto. In W. Li (Ed.), *From urban enclave to ethnic suburb: New Asian communities in Pacific Rim countries* (pp. 134–154). Honolulu: University of Hawaii Press.

Loukaitou-Sideris, A. (2002). Regeneration of urban commercial strips: Ethnicity and space in three Los Angeles neighborhoods. *Journal of Architectural and Planning Research, 19*, 334–350.

Lung-Amam, W. (2015). The vibrant life of Asian malls in Silicon Valley. In J. Archer, P. J. P. Sandul, & K. Solomonson (Eds.), *Making suburbia: New histories of everyday America* (pp. 208–226). Minneapolis: University of Minnesota Press.

Lynch, K. (1960). *The image of the city*. Cambridge, MA: MIT Press.

Mississauga Chinese Centre. (2016). Architectural features. Retrieved from http://miss issaugachinesecentre.com/architect.html.

Oldenburg, R. (1999). *The great good place: Cafes, coffee shops, bookstores, bars, hair salons and other hangouts at the heart of a community*. Cambridge, MA: Da Capo Press.

Oldenburg, R., & Brissett, D. (1982). The third place. *Qualitative Sociology*, 5, 265–284.

Olson, S. H., & Kobayashi, A. (1993). The emerging ethnocultural mosaic. In L. Bourne & D. Ley (Eds.), *The changing social geography of Canadian cities*. Montreal: McGill-Queen's University Press.

Phillips, D., & Robinson, D. (2015). Reflections on migration, community, and place. *Population, Space and Place*, *21*, 409–420.

Preston, V., & Lo, L. (2000). Asian theme malls in suburban Toronto: Land use conflict in Richmond Hill. *Canadian Geographer*, *44*, 182–190.

Qadeer, M. (1998). Ethnic malls and plazas: Chinese commercial developments in Scarborough, Ontario. Working paper, Joint Center of Excellence for Research on Immigration and Settlement (CERIS), Toronto.

Qadeer, M. A., Agrawal, S. K., & Lovell, A. (2010). Evolution of ethnic enclaves in the Toronto Metropolitan Area, 2001–2006. *International Migration and Integration*, *11*, 315–339.

Rath, J. (2007). *The transformation of ethnic neighbourhoods into places of leisure and consumption*. San Diego: Centre for Comparative Immigration Studies, University of California.

Relph, E. (1976). *Place and placelessness*. London: Pion.

Relph, E. (2014). *Toronto: Transformations in a city and its region*. Philadelphia: University of Pennsylvania Press.

Sepe, M. (2013). *Planning and place in the city: Mapping place identity*. New York: Routledge.

Sheppard East Village BIA. (2016a). Mural unveiled at CP overpass. Retrieved from www. sharesheppard.ca/node/424.

Sheppard East Village BIA. (2016b). You're always welcome in Sheppard East Village. Retrieved from www.sharesheppard.ca.

Sikh Heritage Museum of Canada. (2016). Our mission. Retrieved from http://shmc.ca/about/.

Statistics Canada. (2013). Immigration and ethnocultural diversity in Canada. Retrieved from www12.statcan.gc.ca/nhs-enm/2011/as-sa/99-010-x/99-010-x2011001-eng.cfm#a2.

Statistics Canada. (2015a). Census metropolitan area (CMA) and census agglomeration (CA). Retrieved from www12.statcan.gc.ca/census-recensement/2011/ref/dict/geo009-eng.cfm.

Statistics Canada. (2015b). Visible minority of person. Retrieved from http://www.statcan. gc.ca/concepts/definitions/minority-minorite1-eng.htm.

Statistics Canada. (2015c). NHS focus on geography series. Retrieved from www12.statcan. gc.ca/nhs-enm/2011/as-sa/fogs-spg/Pages/FOG.cfm?lang=E&level=3&GeoCode=535.

Talen, E. (2010). Fixing the mess we made. *Planning*, *76*, 32–36.

Teixeira, C. (2006). Residential segregation and ethnic economies in a multicultural city: The Little Portugal of Toronto. In D. Kaplan & W. Li (Eds.), *Landscapes of the ethnic economy* (pp. 49–66). Lanham, MD: Rowman and Littlefield.

Toronto Association of Business Improvement Areas. (2016). Financial incentives for BIAs. Retrieved from www1.toronto.ca/wps/portal/contentonly?vgnextoid=59473725 2e3bc410VgnVCM10000071d60f89RCRD.

Wang, S. (1999). Chinese commercial activity in the Toronto CMA: New development patterns and impacts. *Canadian Geographer, 43*, 19–35.

Wang, S., & Zhong, J. (2013). *Delineating ethnoburbs in Metropolitan Toronto*. Toronto: Joint Centre of Excellence for Research on Immigration and Settlement (CERIS).

Whyte, W. H. (1980). *The social life of small urban spaces*. Washington, DC: Conservation Foundation.

Wood, J. (1997). Vietnamese American place making in northern Virginia. *Geographical Review, 87*, 58–72.

Zhou, M. (2013). The transformation of Chinese American communities: New York vs. Los Angeles. In D. Halle & A. Beveridge (Eds.), *New York and Los Angeles: The uncertain future* (pp. 358–382). New York: Oxford University Press.

Zhuang, Z. C. (2015). Construction and reconstruction of ethnicity in retail landscapes: Case studies in the Toronto Area. *Journal of Urban Design, 20*, 677–697.

Zhuang, Z. C. (2016). Planning for diversity in a suburban retrofit context: The case of ethnic shopping malls in the Toronto Area. In R. Thomas (Ed.), *Planning Canada: A case study approach*. Toronto: Oxford University Press, Canada.

Zhuang, Z. C. (2017). The intersection of place and ethnic entrepreneurship: The role of ethnic entrepreneurs in the making of three Toronto neighbourhoods. *Journal of Architectural and Planning Research* (accepted).

Zhuang, Z. C., & Chen, A. X. (2016). The role of ethnic retailing in retrofitting suburbia: Case studies from Toronto, Canada. *Journal of Urbanism: International Research on Placemaking and Urban Sustainability* (DOI: 10.1080/17549175.2016.1254671).

Zhuang, Z. C., Hernandez, T., & Wang, S. (2015). Ethnic retailing. In H. Bauder & J. Shields (Eds.), *Immigrant experiences in North America* (pp. 223–247). Toronto: Canadian Scholars' Press.

7 Place-making and place-breaking on the banks of the Clyde

Georgiana Varna

Introduction

Place matters and today, more than ever, there is a global recognition that our urban quality of life is highly dependent on the quality of place. In October 2016, the United Nations met in Quito to launch a New Urban Agenda, while the European Union is close to finalizing its own urban strategy. In the UK, a strong city devolution movement has seen new funding arrangements put in place, such as the City Deals, agreements between the government and several cities in the United Kingdom giving them increased control over public finances and their economic growth.

These past decades have seen positive increases in both research and practice aimed at creating more livable, friendly and vibrant urban places. Foundation work from the late 1950s and early 1960s pioneered the field of contemporary urban design research (e.g. Whyte, 1959/2000; Lynch, 1960; Jacobs, 1961). Although there are voices questioning the validity of urban design as a 'real science' (Marshall, 2012), there are many examples indicating that this new way of looking at cities, as people-friendly environments and as networks of lively, high-quality public spaces, has had a significant positive impact on the physical environment. Writing at the turn of the century, European urbanists Gehl and Gemzøe (2000, p. 20), instrumental in Copenhagen's regeneration, concluded that:

> Public life has blossomed on the streets and squares of the city in a way not seen 20 or 30 years ago, certainly not in the form it has today which is not even a new version of an older tradition, but a truly new phenomenon. The overwhelming interest in and backing for the new public life in public spaces is certainly thought provoking.

However, it can be argued that accelerating urban competition has had considerable negative effects on 'non-important' or 'Second Tier' cities (ESPON & EIUA, 2012), as the focus of policy, at both national and supranational levels, has mainly concentrated on strengthening capitals and major urban areas. New evidence suggests that foreshadowing a few, key locations, causes the other cities to fall behind, primarily in terms of economic growth; there is overall weaker territorial cohesion, and large cities suffer from sky-rocketing real-estate prices, congestion, environmental pressure, skill shortages and wage inflation (see ESPON & EIUA, 2012). In the United Kingdom, a strong city devolution movement has seen new funding arrangements put in place, such as the City Deals. These are agreements between the government and several cities giving them increased control over public finances and their economic growth. In parallel to the creation of new, more livable and vibrant urban spaces in some cities, there is also a commodification and virtualization of urban public space, which leaves many city centres depleted and desolate. Looking beyond the winners in the urban competition, it is evident that there are also numerous cities struggling to create a people-friendly environment, and provide a high quality of life.

Regeneration has been especially difficult in the last few years, as the severe economic crisis has put high pressure on public budgets, with many local authorities struggling to deliver not only the pre-crisis agendas of urban growth, but even basic public services. This shortage of public funds is paralleled by a diminished influx of private money, due to the collapse of the building and financial sectors, the main engines of the urban development process. As a result, a key reason for many cities seeking to improve their urban environment and their image, is to prevent the loss of inhabitants and businesses (moving to the big centres), and hopefully to attract flows of capital, tourists and new residents. The reality for many Second Tier cities is an acute loss of population, weakening their taxation base and therefore putting increased pressure on revenues, already tightened after budget cuts. Consequently, local city governments are forced to make difficult choices and prioritize other key areas of intervention such as housing, health and education. This is resulting in urban public spaces, the gravitational nodes of the urban fabric and the stage where the communal life of the city unfolds, dying out in many cities worldwide. They are either poorly managed by the public authorities or they have been taken over by private actors, leading to semi-private urban spaces, 'inversions of public life that kill genuine urban experience' (Dovey, 1999; Stevens, 2006). In addition, the increase in cross-border migration has brought together more visibly than ever, different groups with different religions and ways of life, among which frictions are increasing, showing at once the fragility of public space, but also its crucial importance in facilitating social cohesion.

Glasgow is an example of a Second Tier city that had struggled for many decades to revert the trends of population and income loss, high levels of unemployment and high inequality. This chapter concentrates on Glasgow's experience of 'place-making' and 'place-breaking' as the local administration has striven for the past three decades to create new public spaces and change the city's identity from a declining industrial centre to a more vibrant urban environment. Moreover, it focuses on the banks of the River Clyde, and aims to uncover to what extent Glasgow's transformation into a post-industrial city has been centred on place and people. Based on document analysis and 15 semi-structured interviews with key actors from the public and private sectors involved in the development of the city, this study addresses how the transformation was imagined and delivered, in addition to noting the main compromises affecting the overall outcome. This chapter also aims to explain why, despite a concentrated effort of the public authority to revitalize the river, there is still no continuous public walkway today on the banks of the River Clyde, which is generally devoid of life. It briefly presents three regenerated areas and shows why these failed to match the initial plans and visions. The chapter ends by reflecting on the key lessons of the past decades in relation to current initiatives, particularly the recent City Deal and assesses if indeed a meaningful regeneration took place on Glasgow's waterfront. It also offers some practical thoughts on which areas need to be prioritized in terms of public realm and urban design in the next years to ensure Glasgow truly becomes a liveable, inclusive and vibrant city.

Waterfront regeneration and Glasgow's experience

One key focus in urban regeneration strategies has been the creation of new indoor and outdoor public spaces – especially on the site of former industrial waterfronts, which are often characterized by large, centrally located tracks of land, disconnected physically and psychologically from the main urban thoroughfares. Concerning the regeneration of Melbourne's waterfront, Dovey (2005, p. 10) states that waterfronts represent 'a new urban frontier with opportunities for significant aesthetic, economic, social and environmental benefits' but they are also the new battleground between public and private interests. The spark that ignited the global process of waterfront regeneration was Baltimore Harbor in the 1960s. A key reason for its success was a good working relationship between public and private actors, cemented by the creation of public–private partnerships (PPPs) to manage the regeneration process in a democratic but also market-efficient manner; these brought a strong sense of leadership, a consistent vision and continuity in the development process (de Jong, 1991). Being large-scale and complex undertakings, waterfront regeneration projects are difficult for one single actor to manage successfully and, as such, PPPs became popular in many projects (for instance, London Docklands Development Corporation in England, Cardiff Bay Development Corporation in Wales, Darling Harbour Authority in Sydney and Ria 2000 in Bilbao). These can be described as examples of new forms of urban governance, having emerged as a response to new forms of development, on a background of globalization and urban competition (Desfor & Jørgensen, 2004).

Researchers from around the world have discussed urban waterfront regeneration (see, for example, Kilian & Dodson, 1996; Gomez, 1998; Gehl & Gemzøe, 2000; Hoyle, 2001; Marshall, 2001; Rodriguez et al., 2001; Wu, 2004; Doucet, 2010). In the United Kingdom specifically, the controversial market-led development of the London Docklands in the 1980s was followed by projects all over the country (Wood & Handley, 1999; Miles, 2005; Punter, 2007). The existing literature demonstrates that waterfront regeneration differs from a typical mixed-use development in three key ways, being more time-consuming, costly and risky (Millspaugh, 2001). Post-industrial waterfronts often occupy large tracts of land, in various degrees of contamination and both land assembly and cleaning measures are lengthy and costly processes that can span decades (Marshall, 2001). In addition, their success is dependent on the involvement of the wider urban community (Cook et al., 2001) along with the implementation of a strong vision involving all key stakeholders. The Waterfront Communities Project Toolkit (2007) report concluded that 'big regeneration projects, like waterfronts, are a key opportunity to foster sustainable economic and social development and should not be lost to short-term thinking or solely commercial interests'.

Even taking into consideration the numerous issues that influence the success of waterfront regeneration schemes, the context of each location leads to different outcomes. Sometimes they are dependent on local factors such as the Olympic Games in 1992 in Barcelona or the Loma Pietha Earthquake in 1989 in San Francisco. In Glasgow, post-Second World War development was dominated by slum clearance and the rebuilding of the housing stock, in a city marked extensively by overcrowding and poor quality living conditions.

A fundamental change happened in the 1980s, with three key factors laying the foundation for the city's waterfront transformation in the following decades. First, in 1983, the 'Glasgow's Miles Better' campaign was launched, aimed at changing negative perceptions of the city. This was followed by 'Glasgow Scotland with Style' (in 2004) and 'People Make Glasgow' (in 2013) to promote and brand the city. Paddison (1993, p. 346) described the 'Glasgow's Miles Better' campaign as 'premised on a well-established technique of indirect promotion used in advertising, of altering the image of a product in order (hopefully) to alter the pattern of its consumption'. He points out though that unlike products, cities are not new and a new post-industrial image for Glasgow needed to reconcile with its industrial legacy.

Second, the publication of the McKinsey and Co. Report in 1985, commissioned by SDA, became the red line that defined the city's transformation during the 1990s and 2000s (Tiesdell, 2010). As a local politician describes:

> Away back in the 1980s Glasgow's leadership had McKinsey Consultants look at the city and they recommended that we develop retail, that we develop tourism, that we diversify into service industries, etc. and despite all the changes of leadership since then, we've stuck with essentially the same strategy.

The report suggested that the city should focus on improving its image of crime, poverty and dilapidation through place-marketing campaigns and the creation of a coherent vision for its post-industrial development. In the early stages of regeneration in Glasgow there was a strong hesitancy to focus on the river, which was the location of the shipbuilding yards and docks that fuelled the city's economy for decades. Based on the McKinsey recommendations, Glasgow City Council (GCC) concentrated its efforts on creating an attractive environment for businesses and tourists alike, promoting the city's image in a series of festivals, cultural and sport events (Booth & Boyle, 1993; Tucker, 2008; Tiesdell, 2010). As a result, the 1988 Garden Festival took place by the waterfront, at Plantation

Quay in Govan and on the site of the partially infilled former Prince's Dock. This was the third element that crucially influenced the regeneration of the waterfront as it brought people to the derelict banks of the Clyde for the first time in decades. It was followed by many other events such as the European City of Culture in 1990, City of Architecture and Design in 1999, European Capital of Sport in 2003 and the Commonwealth Games in 2014. The building of new large venues on the riverside has supported this strategy. For example, the Scottish Exhibition and Convention Centre in 1985, the extension the Clyde Auditorium in 1997, the Glasgow Science Centre in 2007 and the SSE Hydro in 2013. The latest addition is the Riverside Museum, hosting the relocated Museum of Transport into a new, 'iconic' building by the River Clyde, designed by the famous architect Zaha Hadid and opened in 2011.

The research undertaken here shows that the defining element for the current physical configuration of the Clyde waterfront is Glasgow's pursuit of business-led regeneration. The local authority's approach to urban development has often been 'Glasgow is open for business', as a local GCC councillor describes:

> I have been to a public event where the leader of the city council was speaking to the commercial sector and he was saying: 'If you come to me with a planning application and tell me when you need the planning approval for I can guarantee to have it for you for that date.' I'm sure from some directions it seems to work very nicely but I don't think we ask for half enough.

This is similar to what Tiesdell (2010, p. 278) found to be the norm for the public sector in Glasgow, they describe 'a scattergun approach to maximize annual receipts' rather than prioritizing certain areas and directing the market towards certain anchoring projects for holistic place-making. In his opinion, second-order urban design, which refers to shaping the decision environments of development actors (George, 1997; Adams & Tiesdell, 2013), has been weak in Glasgow, as the city channelled its efforts into becoming primarily a commercial and business centre (Tiesdell, 2010). As Mooney (2004, p. 337) writes:

> The type of strategy adopted in Glasgow – 'the Glasgow model' – has contributed to the worsening levels of poverty and deprivation and to the deepening inequalities that characterise the City today. It has done this primarily by constructing Glasgow's future – and the future for tens of thousands of Glaswegians – as a low paid, workforce grateful from the breadcrumbs from the tables of the entrepreneurs and investors upon which so much effort is spent in attracting and cosseting – and by marginalising and ruling out any alternative strategy based upon large-scale public sector investment in sustainable and socially necessary facilities and services.

Indeed, today although Glasgow has reversed its trend of population decline, and is the home of approximately 600,000 people, it still has the poorest health profile of any city in the United Kingdom, with a mortality rate 15 per cent higher than the average among cities in the United Kingdom and almost half of its residents living in the 20 per cent most deprived areas in Scotland. As Kerevan writes in the *Sunday Herald* at the turn of the century:

> Glasgow is a victim of its own propaganda. It believed it was a world-class city with a world-class economy. But in over a quarter of a century and after perhaps three billion pounds of public subsidy, not one world-beating company has emerged from the second city [. . .] The culprits in Glasgow's long decline are threefold. The dispirited middle classes who fled the city. The Pol Pot planners whose social engineering halved the city's population. And one-party city government – introverted, sectional, arrogant, parochial and incapable of appealing outside its own narrow constituency.
>
> (Kerevan, 2000, cited in Garcia, 2005, p. 856)

In a nutshell, the evidence reviewed here shows that fundamentally the regeneration of Glasgow's waterfront has been part of a larger strategy focused on promotion campaigns, attraction of festivals, supported by the building of large indoor cultural venues and securing business at all costs; it has not been about 'people' and about creating a vibrant, friendly and sustainable urban environment. Nordic cities such as Copenhagen, Helsinki or Stockholm, for instance, are widely recognized as being livable people-friendly places, having focused on developing waterfronts with well-connected vibrant public spaces where anyone can join in the life of the city. The Clyde riverside, which could become one of the main thoroughfares of Glasgow and its central public space, is still highly disconnected from the central area, although only a five-minute walk from the main business and commercial districts of the city. A walk along the banks of the Clyde today shows a fragmented landscape, with large structures and car parks. The area lacks basic amenities such as benches and public toilets. The remaining part of this chapter will take a more in-depth look at the reasons behind this and zoom in on three case study areas: Glasgow Harbour, Pacific Quay and Broomielaw.

Urban design, place-making and new public spaces on the Clyde

Glasgow is today a city of red and honey-coloured sandstone, with a tight rectangular grid overlaid on a medieval core and with large tracts of derelict land scarring the overall city landscape. Despite the transformation of Glasgow into a dynamic retail, office, cultural and tourism centre, almost 7 per cent of the city still lies vacant or derelict. This wasted land resource amounts to a total of 1,171 hectares distributed on 837 separate sites. Much of the city's physical transformation has been founded on the above-mentioned 1985 McKinsey Report, which contained a comprehensive spatial regenerative framework proposed by the urbanist Gordon Cullen (Tiesdell, 2010). His ideas were promoted and developed by the consultant firm Gillespies in the report titled 'Glasgow & The Clyde, Continuing the Renaissance' in 1990 (see Gillespies, 1990). Although the report was not followed precisely, it represented the blueprint for much of the city's urban design projects in the past decades. The city centre's transformation was envisioned as anchored by a stronger Buchanan Street, seen as a development axis, flanked by the Merchant City to the east and Blythswood New Town to the west while the river was to be punctuated by a 'string of pearls', or outdoor rooms, each with a different spatial identity (Gillespies, 1990). Several of the interviewees mentioned this metaphor, showing that the narrative proposed in the 1980s has had a great impact on the local authority's thinking about the river's transformation. However, it was over a decade later that significant change started to happen on the waterfront, when Glasgow elected a new city leader. This former leader notes:

> When I became leader in the summer of 1999, the council had only recently secured the future of the city centre as our main retail and cultural destination with the advent of Buchanan Galleries in spite of out-of-town shopping centres such as Braehead. So we could see that we had secured the future of the city centre, so we began to look elsewhere for the next big project. And I decided as leader that I wanted a big project of my own that I would be taking the lead on. The logical one was the river because the river is in the city centre, is part of the city centre, and links parts of the city and the level of activity on the river and beside the river had reached an absolute rock-bottom.

Under this leadership, the Council started to invest in infrastructure works, by repairing the quay walls and providing pontoons and decontaminating land, but even according to a local planner 'this has come incrementally and kind of piecemeal in certain sections' (GCC planner). Another GCC planner explained this as follows:

> We have a working river which is very long with lots of decay, quay walls. Some of the sections on the north side aren't open just because it's so dangerous that there is a big public liability if you open those sections. We have to find the money to do these sections up before people can go there and restore quay walls, put all the infrastructure that sometime nobody will see, you know just building the quay walls again, which is an infrastructure project it's not an environmental enhancement project. Then you've got to find the money for resurfacing it and the public realm and creating the green space.

In 2003 a *River design framework* was published by GCC, almost a decade later than the public realm strategy for the city centre by Gillespies (1995). This put forward a series of proposals to create a better designed, more inviting and more lively waterfront, focusing on issues such as the type of materials, the quality of pavements and lighting, comfortable street furniture and well-kept green space, and the importance of connectivity and visibility. The framework has never been put in place (GCC planner) however, a number of new developments appeared on the river. Many of them were piloted and undertaken by the Clyde Waterfront Strategic Partnership, created in 2002, an alliance between: GCC, Renfrewshire Council and West Dunbartonshire Council, Scottish Enterprise (including Dunbartonshire,

Renfrewshire and Glasgow) and the Scottish Government. Its aim was to take the lead in co-ordinating the main public bodies involved in the regeneration of the Clyde, from Glasgow City Centre to Dumbarton and provide a much-needed overarching body to control and promote development. The partnership has been instrumental in delivering several key infrastructure projects such as three new bridges, The Millennium Bridge in 2002, The Clyde Arc (referred to as The Squinty Bridge) in 2006 and The Broomielaw–Tradeston Bridge (referred to as The Squiggly Bridge) in 2009. However, several interviewees argued that although it was a strong body in its beginning years, in time, the partnership did not provide the needed leadership and its position has diluted to a more promotional role (former city design advisor). The need for a strong body to lead and support the river's development is still a crucial issue:

> What ought to be the delivery vehicle? If you have an up to date robust planning framework then how do you deliver that? You're going to deliver that, yes, in partnership with the private sector, deliver it on the basis of partnership working, but you're then into the politics of the city. I think what the city has been reluctant to embrace, if I'm being honest, is some idea of a multi-purpose vehicle, sort of autonomous. In other words, an urban development cooperation, which is the model that most British cities adopted. Particularly with regard to the regeneration of dock areas – we didn't have the political appetite for that.
>
> (GCC planner)

Pacific Quay, Glasgow Harbour and Broomielaw can be seen as representative for Glasgow's re-invention as a post-industrial city (see images in Figure 7.1). Tables 7.1, 7.2 and 7.3 give an overview of the regeneration of the three cases: Pacific Quay shows the focus of the city towards enhancing its media services, Glasgow Harbour is illustrative for the new trend of creating upmarket, luxury housing developments, while Broomielaw's new public realm is illustrative of Glasgow's ambitions to establish itself as an international financial and business centre.

Table 7.1 Regeneration timeline of Pacific Quay

1970s	Prince's Dock is closed and infilled
1988	Glasgow Garden Festival takes place; Bell's Bridge is built
1995	Pacific Quay Developments is formed and becomes the main private landowner on site
2001	The Science Centre is built; Millennium Bridge is built
2006	The Clyde Arc Bridge is built at the north-eastern part of the site
2007	BBC Scotland headquarters open
2008	The start of the 'Digital Media Quarter' project
2009	Science Centre and Scottish Enterprise Glasgow bring improvements to the public space
2010	The 'floating village' application for the Canting Basin is submitted; Scottish Enterprise Glasgow regains the ownership of the central part of the site

Table 7.2 Regeneration timeline of Glasgow Harbour

1988	Meadowside Granaries cease operation
1999	Glasgow Harbour Ltd is formed
2000	Kohn Pederson Fox is appointed to design the masterplan
2001	Outline planning consent granted for masterplan; demolition of the granaries begins
2003	Residential Phase 1 construction begins; Clydeport becomes part of Peel Holdings
2004	Riverside walkway and park opened to the public
2005	Residential Phase 2 construction begins; Meadow Road underpass improved; major road work begins
2007	The new Riverside Museum construction begins; Residential Phase 1 is completed
2009	Stages 1 and 2 of Residential Phase 2 are completed

Table 7.3 Regeneration timeline of Broomielaw

1812	Henry Bell's launch of *The Comet* paddle steamer; Broomielaw becomes the main departure point for passenger steamboats
1976	Broomielaw Quay Gardens is created
2001	The International Financial Service District is launched
2003	A design competition is held and won by Richard Rogers Partners and Atkins – the plans include an improved public space, a series of pavilions and a new bridge
2005	Construction of the project starts
2006	The project is stopped due to rising costs and a new competition is organized won by Nuttal and Halcrow in partnership with Dissing and Weitling
2007	Construction is restarted without the pavilions; Wilson Boden (later Capella) appointed to build the pavilions
2009	The new public space and the bridge are opened to the public

Pacific Quay

Pacific Quay is located on the south bank of the River Clyde, approximately one mile southwest from Glasgow's centre. This is where the Garden Festival was held in 1988. The area stretches over 25 hectares on the former site of Prince's Dock, closed down and partly infilled in the 1970s; it includes the Canting Basin, a five-hectare water surface, and the last remaining large pocket of water on the Clyde.

The redevelopment of this site spanned several decades, starting in the 1970s when Prince's Dock was closed and infilled. The main landowners involved were the City Council and Scottish Enterprise, representing the public sector, and a series of private actors. The vision was the creation of a media quarter, and a vibrant cultural area with the BBC Scotland and the Science Centre anchoring the public spaces in between. However, the river walkway is highly disconnected from Festival Park, which remained onsite from the Garden Festival, and is still owned by GCC. This fragmented ownership, combined with the private sector's reluctance to develop their sites without a significant return on their investment, are key reasons for its current disjointed development; there is very little

Figure 7.1 The Clyde waterfront at Broomielaw and Glasgow's financial district
            (top left); along the Clyde waterfront: view of Pacific Quay and Scottish
            Exhibition and Conference Centre (top right); iconic regeneration on the
            Clyde, the view south from Glasgow Harbour with the new Transport
            Museum (bottom) (photos by author).

vibrancy here and connectivity has been only ensured with the north bank through
Millennium Bridge and Bell's Bridge. In addition, the two main public bodies
did not collaborate harmoniously; as one Building Design Partnership architect
interviewed described:

> If you could start again, with someone in real control but also have the money
> to put in the proper infrastructure, you'd have to do that. Scottish Enterprise
> weren't up for that, they couldn't get the City Council to agree with them, so
> if the two biggest contributors, two big players have funding to say: 'Yeah,
> we're really going to do this well,' set it up and then allow the developers to
> move in and at the back of that you create this fantastic place.

The two views below support this:

> Pacific Quay was in a way the first regeneration project because it was the Garden
> Festival in 1988, but now it has become the last and I'm still not clear what the
> master plan is for Pacific Quay. What you have to understand about Pacific
> Quay is that the lead developer there has always been Scottish Enterprise. And
> I think that they have chopped and changed their plans so often. I know the area
> well. When you are at Pacific Quay, you feel far from the city, you feel isolated.
> Don't get me wrong, I believe that Pacific Quay could be a great location, it's
> just that I think that Scottish Enterprise's leadership has been poor.
>
> (Former GCC leader)

I think as a whole, once ownership has become fragmented, the people, the owners tend to go off and do their own thing and we've made various attempts over the years to try to bring a bit of cohesion to the stakeholder group and we had proposals for a common infrastructure approach which we'd look at the central boulevard, look at upgrading the park, we'd also be looking at upgrading the public utilities servicing in the area so that when we are ready to start delivering the scale of development that is proposed, there are no restraints in that sense, and that's an area that hasn't worked quite as well as we would have liked but it tends to be driven by the economic cycle as well.

(Scottish Enterprise representative)

There are several planned schemes to create a stronger sense of place at Pacific Quay, including a large boulevard connecting the river with Festival Park, housing units that would bring permanent residents to the area, and a possible marina on the canting basin, but so far nothing has been started.

Glasgow Harbour

This project is a 52-hectare development, twice the size of Pacific Quay, totalling over £1 billion public and private investment to date, and stretching on the north bank of the river, between the Clyde Tunnel and the Scottish Exhibition and Convention Centre. It lies in the West End of Glasgow, the wealthiest area of the city, in between two historically working-class neighbourhoods: Partick to the north, and across the river to the south, Govan, home of one of the last remaining shipyards on the Clyde, Fairfields. During Glasgow's industrial heyday, this was the heart of the city's harbour activities, particularly regarding the import of maize and wheat from North America for the local mills and distilleries, which were stored in four large brick granaries.

The site is entirely owned by Clydeport, the former Harbour Authority, now a private company, a subsidiary of Peel Holdings; in 1999 they decided to redevelop the area and created Glasgow Harbour Ltd. The granaries were demolished overnight, much to the dissatisfaction of locals, for whom they represented a landmark and a symbol of the past glory of industrial Glasgow. A phased development was undertaken, framed by a masterplan created by the international company Kohn Pederson Fox. This proposed a fragmented and permeable development along the river, so that the mass of buildings would not become a new barrier along the waterfront. However, this was never respected, and the subsequent upscale, expensive flats were built higher and denser, with a basic public space, represented by an improved walkway along the river, and a park at the back of the development, meant as a buffer towards the busy expressway that runs along the site. No shops, no ground uses, nothing to attract people to the former industrial area were built.

To this day, only Phase 1 and Phase 2 have been delivered, the site being surrounded by a sea of derelict land, where the New Riverside museum was sited in 2011. The economic crash stopped the development midway and it remains to be seen how this area of the city will evolve in coming years and if a vibrant community will develop here. This will rely fundamentally on bringing active, ground-floor uses to the housing units, which was a point of contention between the private owner, Clydeport, and the Council:

> I deliberately didn't put them in the first phase. I think if you do that at the early stages, you're dooming those businesses and units to failure. Homes for the Future, you know the ground floor use units, commercial units – not a success. Quite deliberately the first phase, which is the pink bits here, it's something like 650 houses, I fought quite hard with Ethel May etc., not to have any shop units or commercial units in here, and I would do that time and time again. You need a mass of people to support this.
>
> (Managing Director of Glasgow Harbour Ltd)

> In the original masterplan, we talked about these squares, you know the three squares coming down from the West End, and when they hit the river, they were meant to be active uses, but it's very difficult to try, and you see a lot of developments that are being built and the ground floor units are all boarded up with you know 'Lease.' It takes ages for these areas to become established before they become attractive to the market, that they actually want to open a coffee shop. But ultimately, yeah, that's exactly what it needs.
>
> (GCC planner)

Broomielaw

Broomielaw is a narrow strip of land, stretching along the Clyde in the city centre, the waterfront of the International Financial Services District (IFSD), launched in 2001, to boost Glasgow's financial services. Historically it became a major harbour in the eighteenth century, when the canalization of the river allowed deep-sea transatlantic vessels of 200 to 300 tons to sail upstream (Pacione, 1985). After the famous launch of Henry Bell's paddle-steamer *The Comet* in 1812, Broomielaw became the point of departure for passenger steamboats taking Glaswegians to coastal resorts such as Largs, Rothesay or Ayr (Riddell, 2000). During the first half of the twentieth century, with the background of the general deindustrialization of the Clyde, the area slowly fell into disrepair and dereliction. The first major improvement took place in 1976, when the council created Broomielaw Quay Gardens which, although an award-winning scheme at the time, fell into disrepair through the 1980s and 1990s. In 1996 the Riverboat Casino was brought here and a series of office developments started to be built, creating a critical urban mass in this area of the city.

After the launch of the IFSD, a series of public space works were delivered for the entire area of Broomielaw, comprising two phases. Phase 1 was concerned with upgrading the street environment, and creating small 'pocket' public places. This was the largest streetscape project awarded by GCC with a value of £6 million, undertaken between 2004 and 2006 by Land Engineering, a Scottish firm specializing in public realm works. Phase 2 of the Broomielaw public realm improvements was a much larger project and it concerned the redevelopment of the public place along the water's edge. The vision was to create a high-quality public place, a 'postcard view' for Glasgow and the IFSD that would further help in marketing the district for business. As the developer hired to deliver it put it:

> I want lots of banners which again we're not very good at doing in this country. You'd have to go to Disneyland and I'm kind of seeing this as a little bit of Disneyland. I don't mean Disneyland, but it's got to feel like that, it's festive. You go to places like Baltimore or like Boston, they're brilliant at doing this. I want kites, I want balloons, I want activity. I want to see something is happening down here. We've got all these break-out bits in between, one bit which is enclosed, two bits that aren't. I could see, during the summer a little jazz band playing there or pipe shows I want to see activity, and we can license that out you know, there's all sorts of things you can do.

In term of users, apart from giving the workers in the IFSD a place to enjoy having lunch or spending leisure time after work hours, 'a kind of lung for the people working in the IFSD' (GCC development officer), the central idea was to create a *destination* for tourists and Glaswegians alike that was missing on the Clyde waterfront:

> I think it is more than the people from the IFSD, I mean the IFSD is a major part of the city centre economic activity and we see it as one of the thoroughbreds for the city's economy but it's more than that. Obviously this is the frontage to the river but it is supposed to serve not just the people living and working there but also tourists coming to Glasgow, people coming in visiting, they might come for business or they might just come and stay in the IFSD. It is to be a part of the city's experience.
>
> (GCC planner)

Apart from an improved public space along the river, the development involved also a series of pavilions, upgrading the quay walls, placing a pontoon on the river to attract boat traffic, a new bridge linking the place with the south bank area of Tradeston. In addition to a contribution from Scottish Enterprise, the council succeeded in securing £4.7 million from the European Regional Development Fund (ERDF). The time-dependent nature of this grant was crucial in the delivery of the project, and when the developer did not provide the pavilions in time, the council went ahead as it needed to finalize the development on time. The winning design bridge by Lord Rogers and partners was abandoned for a cheaper option which became the new Tradeston 'Squiggly' Bridge. As the economic recession hit, the pavilions were never built, and the Tradeston area across the river never benefitted from improvements. Out of the three areas analysed, this was the most successful in terms of place-making. This stretch of waterfront is fairly vibrant, and many people use the new pedestrian and cycle bridge.

The future of Glasgow's waterfront

As Keating (1988) noted, Glasgow is 'a city that refused to die' and overcame its post-industrial decay. However, it should be asked at what cost this change has happened? From what has been presented in this chapter it appears that place-making has not been a priority for the local authority in its efforts to regenerate the waterfront and the city's environment. In order to achieve a good balance between conservation and new uses and structures, between private and public interests, between preserving identity and place re-branding, those who are in charge of the regeneration of waterfronts (and generally large urban development projects) need a strong vision, political leadership to support this and good working relations among key actors. To sum up, these were all problematic in Glasgow, for three main reasons.

First, the local authority's public purse seems to be permanently empty, especially in recent years of austerity and severe cuts in public funding. This is similar to the trend existent in many Second Tier cities, as presented at the beginning of the chapter. With little funds, the GCC approach has been pump-priming development, as the former city leader states:

> I thought that the City Council should 'prime-the-pump' as I call it of ten percent of the development costs. But most of it should come from private investment. The City Council is not in the business of building apartments. Or the City Council certainly isn't in the business of running restaurants or running water buses. So we've got to create the conditions where people see the opportunity and they invest.

This meant that the few resources were part spent in delivering infrastructure works and in the heavy advertising and promoting of city areas, making them attractive for the private sector. Glasgow's waterfront regeneration, heavily dependent on private funds, has been particularly susceptible to market fluctuations. This is a key characteristic of waterfront projects in general, as discussed in the first part of this chapter, and as previous experience shows, for these fluctuations to be successfully bypassed, the local authority needs to show a strong vision and the commitment to carry it through different market cycles.

Second, although the vision was present in Glasgow and supported in different stages, there has been a lack of strong will on the part of GCC to enforce 'good development' and to apply this in a meaningful and strategic way on the ground. As a GCC planner describes:

> We don't even have a strategy for the spaces. We're just saying we want to leave this space for the private developer, we don't even have in our head: 'Why are we leaving that space? Do we want to have soft amenity, do we want to have amenity or do we want it big enough to hold a concert out there?' Nobody is actually thinking 'Well maybe now and then we need a node that will do this or a space that will do that.' Nobody is thinking at all.
>
> (GCC planner responsible for the river)

This is one of the key reasons why there is no continuous walkway and cycle route along the Clyde although this is safeguarded in the City Plan. The GCC planner responsible for the river commented that often developers who do not want to follow the design principles set in this document will apply for planning permission only for an area excluding the river walkway. She is of the opinion that two main elements frustrate the river's development and the public space creation on its banks: lack of funding and weak political leadership.

> There's lots of reasons but I would say the main reason this doesn't work, 'cause if you go to any city, people are not looking for something that is pristine all the time, they just wasn't to know it's there and that is walkable and I think we're a long way off of making it comfortable because we don't manage it at all as a single unit. [. . .] There's nobody, one single person and one single budget. I am the only one single person contact but I have no control over everybody at all; there is nobody leading on a strategic level.
>
> (GCC planner)

Third, divided ownership and power struggles, especially between the public and the private sectors, have led to more place-breaking rather than place-making on Glasgow's waterfront. This is also one of the key reasons for the lack of activity on the river. Most waterfront development projects show revitalized rivers filled with boats, yachts, water taxis and other water activities. The Clyde is devoid of activity for most part of a year, except for when events such as the River Festival take place. The GCC holds the view that Clydeport does not promote activity on the river and has stopped dredging upstream, in the city centre area. Clydeport's property director blames the Council and declared that:

> I wrote to the Council on this, four years ago, saying you know 'We all want more leisure and activity in most of the river, how do we do this? We need to properly resource it.' So what happens now is Ethel tends to meet a lot of madcap people with daft schemes and that what happens and none of them work. And a lot of time gets taken up and eventually the Harbour Master, and this has happened recently, gets fed up and says 'You know, I've got a job to do.'

More activity on the water would lead to a more animated public space on the waterfront; this seems to be lacking mainly from a combination of factors, fundamental among which is the distrust between the public and private sectors (former city planner, now private sector consultant). There seems to be an overwhelming view that the tough decisions and meaningful regeneration, focusing on place-making, will happen sometime in the future, but nobody seems to take a clear and determined stand today, as a GCC planner notes: 'Sometime in the future we will have to make very difficult decisions. I think there will come a point and we'll have to just grab the bull by the horns.' A key point that has not been touched so far is that successful city re-branding, fundamentally changing a city's identity in a meaningful and sustainable way, can only succeed when all the various publics that live and make up the city are involved in the process of transformation. This has happened very little in Glasgow, and the most quoted example of successful place-making in the city is the housing area of the Gorbals (Tiesdell, 2010). Developing upscale, expensive flats and 'iconic buildings' such as the New Transport museum, does not mean place-making.

Several policy initiatives have emerged recently on a Scottish national level that will hopefully help the success of the Clyde's waterfront regeneration. The recently published Community Empower Bill and the ongoing Land Reform can help, if well implemented, both with the issues of divided ownership on the banks of the Clyde and the lack of empowerment of communities (however we may choose to define these). Moreover, as part of a wide city empowerment movement taking place in the UK, Glasgow secured a City Deal for the Clyde Valley in 2014, a partnership between GCC and the other seven councils that share the banks of the Clyde. Among goals such as creating jobs and alleviating unemployment, the deal promises to secure £1 billion of Scottish Government and United Kingdom Government capital funding for infrastructure projects and spread the benefits of growth, tackling particularly deprived areas (Scottish Government, 2014). It remains to see how this will be delivered in terms of urban design and the creation of vibrant and inclusive places and how much it will help with the delivery of more place-making and less place-breaking along the banks of the Clyde.

References

Adams, D., & Tiesdell, S. (2013). *Shaping places: Urban planning, design and development.* New York: Routledge.
Booth, P., & Boyle, R. (1993). See Glasgow, see culture. In F. Bianchini & M. Parkinson (Eds.), *Cultural policy and urban regeneration* (pp. 21–47). Manchester: Manchester University Press.
Cook, A., Marshall, R., & Raine, A. (2001). Port and city relations: San Francisco and Boston. In R. Marshall (Ed.), *Waterfronts in post-industrial cities* (pp. 117–133). London: Spoon Press.
de Jong, M. W. (1991). Revitalizing the urban core: Waterfront development in Baltimore, Maryland. In J. Fox-Prezerworski, J. Goddard, & M. de Jong (Eds.), *Urban regeneration in a changing economy* (pp. 185–198). Oxford: Clarendon Press.
Desfor, G., & Jørgensen, J. (2004). Flexible urban governance. The case of Copenhagen's recent waterfront development. *European Planning Studies, 12*, 479–496.
Dovey, K. (1999). *Framing places: Mediating power in built form.* London: Routledge.
Dovey, K. (2005). *Fluid city: Transforming Melbourne's urban waterfront.* London: Routledge.
Doucet, B. (2010). *Rich cities with poor people. Waterfront regeneration in the Netherlands and Scotland.* PhD thesis, Utrecht University.
ESPON & EIUA. (2012). *Second Tier cities in Europe: In an age of austerity why invest beyond the capitals?* Retrieved from http://www.ljmu.ac.uk/EIUA/EIUA_Docs/Second_Tier_Cities.pdf.

Garcia, B. (2005). Deconstructing the city of culture: The long-term cultural legacies of Glasgow 1990. *Urban Studies*, *42*, 841–868.

Gehl, J., & Gemzøe, L. (2000). *New city spaces*. Copenhagen: The Danish Architectural Press.

George, R. V. (1997). A procedural explanation for contemporary urban design. *Journal of Urban Design*, *2*, 143–161.

Gillespies, in association with Price & Cullen; P A Cambridge Economic Consultants; Douglas Baillie Associates & Drivers Jonas. (1990). *Glasgow City Centre and The Clyde: Continuing the Renaissance*. Report for Scottish Development Agency and Glasgow District Council, Glasgow.

Gillespies. (1995). *Glasgow public realm, strategy and guidelines*. Prepared for Strathclyde Regional Council, Glasgow City Council and Glasgow Development Agency, Glasgow.

Gomez, M. V. (1998). Reflective images: The case of urban regeneration in Glasgow and Bilbao. *International Journal of Urban and Regional Research*, *22*, 106–121.

Hoyle, B. (2001). Lamu: Waterfront revitalization in an east African port-city. *Cities*, *18*, 297–313.

Jacobs, J. (1961). *The death and life of great American cities*. New York: Random House.

Keating, M. (1988). *The city that refused to die – Glasgow: The politics of urban regeneration*. Aberdeen: Aberdeen University Press.

Kerevan, G. (2000). The sick city. *Sunday Herald*, 12 March.

Kilian, D., & Dodson, B. J. (1996). Forging a postmodern waterfront: Urban form and spectacle at the Victoria and Alfred Docklands. *South African Geographical Journal*, *71*, 29–40.

Lynch, K. (1960). *The image of the city*. Cambridge, MA: MIT Press.

Marshall, R. (Ed.). (2001). *Waterfronts in post-industrial cities*. London: Spon Press.

Marshall, S. (2012). Science, pseudo-science and urban design. *Urban Design International*, *17*, 257–271.

Miles, S. (2005). 'Our Tyne': Iconic regeneration and the revitalisation of identity in Newcastle Gateshead. *Urban Studies*, *42*, 913–926.

Millspaugh, M. L. (2001). Waterfronts as catalysts for city renewal. In R. Marshall (Ed.), *Waterfronts in post-industrial cities* (pp. 74–85). London: Spon Press.

Mooney, G. (2004). Cultural policy as urban transformation? Critical reflections on Glasgow, European city of culture 1990. *Local Economy*, *19*, 327–340.

Pacione, M. (1985). Renewal, redevelopment and rehabilitation in Scottish cities, 1945–1981. In G. Gordon (Ed.), *Perspectives of the Scottish city* (pp. 280–305). Aberdeen: Aberdeen University Press.

Paddison, R. (1993). City marketing, image reconstruction and urban regeneration. *Urban Studies*, *30*, 339–349.

Punter, J. (2007). Design-led regeneration? Evaluating the design outcomes of Cardiff Bay and their implications for future regeneration and design. *Journal of Urban Design*, *12*, 375–405.

Riddell, J. F. (2000). *The Clyde: The making of a river*. Edinburgh: Birlinn.

Rodriguez, A., Martinez, E., & Guenaga, G. (2001). Uneven redevelopment: New urban policies and socio-spatial fragmentation in metropolitan Bilbao. *European Urban and Regional Studies*, *8*, 161–178.

Scottish Government. (2014). *Scottish planning policy*. Edinburgh: St Andrew's House.

Stevens, Q. (2006). The design of urban waterfronts: A critique of two Australian 'Southbanks'. *Town Planning Review*, *77*, 173–203.

Tiesdell, S. (2010). Glasgow: Renaissance on the Clyde? In J. Punter (Ed.), *Urban design and the British renaissance*. London: Routledge.

Tucker, M. (2008). The cultural production of cities: Rhetoric or reality? Lessons from Glasgow. *Journal of Retail and Leisure Property, 7*, 21–33.

Waterfront Communities Project Toolkit. (2007). *The cool sea.* Edinburgh: WCP.

Whyte, W. H. (1959/2000). Securing open space for urban America: Conservation easements. In A. LaFarge (Ed.), *The essential William H. Whyte* (pp. 141–158). New York: Fordham University Press.

Wood, R., & Handley, J. (1999). Urban waterfront regeneration in the Mersey Basin, North West England. *Journal of Environmental Planning and Management, 42*, 565–580.

Wu, W. (2004). Cultural strategies in Shanghai: Regenerating cosmopolitanism in an era of globalization. *Progress in Planning, 61*, 159–180.

8 Urban renewal in Tehran's neighbourhoods

Displacement or potential for identity-building and place-making?

Azadeh Hadizadeh Esfahani

Introduction

Tehran has grown exponentially in terms of area and population in the past three decades. It is currently considered a megacity in the Global South, not in the same tier as Delhi, Sao Paulo or Mexico City, but certainly comparable to Rio de Janeiro, Istanbul and Shanghai. Tehran's population has doubled in the past two decades (reaching almost 11 million) as a result of high birth rates, but more specifically, migration from other urban and rural areas of Iran. This increase in population has been accompanied by the physical expansion of the city (reaching around 700 square kilometres). Tehran, as many other Southern cities, evolved gradually from the pattern of clustered residential settlements of people who had ethnic or religious commonalities or possessed similar economic status in neighbourhoods (Mousavi, 2008). However, rapid growth of urbanization and emergence of modern forms of city management subdued these informal social areas into formal administrative or planning units in order to make them manageable (Fanni & Saremi, 2008; Abdollahi et al., 2010). It is naïve to think of a smooth transition from an old to a modern city. Today, Tehran is a mishmash of narrow alleyways and massive highways, deteriorated neighbourhoods and wealthy gated communities, informal shacks and enormous skyscrapers. Despite substantial formal city administration and planning, Tehran's unplanned (Roy, 2005) and emergent urban dynamics in addition to its rapid growth and its vulnerability to highly predicted earthquakes, demand urgent renewal for the sake of sustainability, liveability and enhanced livelihoods. Moreover, Tehran's old urban texture is experiencing immense relative devaluation that has exposed its inner-city neighbourhoods to increased poverty, crime and degradation.

In recent decades, urban renewal projects, both in the developed and emerging countries, have been criticized for intensifying the commodification of urban properties, nourishing urban growth coalitions and subsequently escalating processes of accumulation by dispossession. In addition, urban renewal projects have resulted in the gentrification of neighbourhoods and displacement of disadvantaged residents (Smith, 1996; Fraser, 2004; Lees et al., 2008; Munzner & Shaw, 2015). Urban planners have endeavoured to reduce this latter undesired outcome by adding a democratic and participatory dimension to renewal processes.

Their success in doing so is controversial among planners, geographers and other assessors of urban renewal projects. The controversy hinges upon the different ways that displacement is understood, conceptualized and measured. While some critiques emphasize preventing any material change and dislocation of residents, others highlight the complex process of renewal, which can include transformation of identities and meanings that are tied into place.

In this chapter I will develop a conceptual framework for understanding displacement by utilizing ongoing debates about space, place and place-making. I will employ this framework to look into the renewal practices in Tehran and, in particular, two renewal experiences in the city to illustrate how urban renewal can be associated with processes of identity-building and place-making. Following a discussion of urban renewal and forced displacement in the next section, I will distinguish two conceptions of displacement, based on loss of space and loss of place. In the third section, I will explore two experiences of urban renewal in Tehran and discuss them in terms of displacement typology. Finally, in the last section, I will discuss venues for identity-building and place-making in urban renewal processes.

Urban renewal and displacement: From North to South

Urban renewal can be described, in general terms, as an interventionist activity to transform an urban area through improving its built environment and infrastructure, and consequently, increasing the quality of life and provision of social services, enhancing economic conditions, improving social and cultural characteristics, and advancing environmental and ecological conditions. The focus of urban renewal initiatives on each of these dimensions varies between different projects, as well as across time and space. Urban renewal processes can be distinguished according to the focus and drivers of renewal (people and social goals or property and economic goals), geographical location and scale (inner cities versus outer cities, and small-scale versus large-scale renewals), and governance system (varies among public, public–private partnership and private) (Hadizadeh Esfahani, forthcoming).

Europe and North America have long histories of urban renewal. But since the 1980s, with the decline of the welfare state and expansion of neoliberalism, a significant shift was observed in the urban renewal practices, especially in terms of the drivers of the renewal and its governance system. This rise of market-oriented renewal, especially in less wealthy neighbourhoods, has led to gentrification. Upgrading low-income neighbourhoods, in the name of urban renewal, results in the influx of middle- and upper-class households. The presence of a new population, in addition to an increase in property values and rents, brings a shift in the culture of the neighbourhood and the life-styles of inhabitants. As a result, the prior poor and often marginal residents of the neighbourhood can be left socially alienated and economically impoverished, and even be dispossessed of their homes. This displacement phenomenon is one of the most criticized outcomes of urban renewal projects.

Under the neoliberal rubric, the role of the state as the key driver and actor in the renewal process declined and was replaced by the private sector. Prominence of neoliberal ideas, in tandem with globalization, amplified the 'growth' discourse within urban policy and practice. As a result, strengthening the competitiveness of cities in order to attract global investment became the main agenda in North America and Europe, and then disseminated to cities all around the world. For these entrepreneurial approaches, urban renewal is linked to opportunity, and city governments and planners seek to elevate their place within globalized urban hierarchies. They are also appealing instruments for bringing together the local growth coalitions that propel urban growth machines. This has led to the emergence of public–private partnerships and market-led (in contrast to previous state-led) renewal projects. Examples of pro-growth and competitiveness-oriented renewal can be found in numerous event-based and culture-led strategies, centred on place-marketing and place-branding agendas (Ho, 2006; Friedmann, 2010). In this new order, the role of the state switched from planning, formulating, financing and leading the renewal process to facilitating and promoting renewal by creating attractive environments, encouraging subsequent investment and development. In this new cooperative model, local politicians, developers, urban entrepreneurs and many other stakeholders often favour private interests over public interests. The intensified role of developers and private sector investors in the renewal processes also has socio-political influences. By focusing on private interests, most entrepreneurial and private renewal creates private spaces and thus instils a specific form of civility and citizenship. The extension to include the marginal and excluded groups in these private and gated spaces is under question. So, while developers and entrepreneurs become more and more 'flexible citizens' (Lepofsky & Fraser, 2003, p. 133) who shape the renewal process in different places, the original residents, especially more marginal groups, are increasingly excluded and disenfranchised from both process and influencing.

In the Global South, urban renewal has even more complex dynamics. Northern urban models such as growth machines (Logan & Molotch, 1987) and urban regimes (Stone, 1989) have been less useful in explaining the underlying mechanisms that drive urban renewals in Southern cities. Desire for development, modernization and improving the ranking of the city among the world cities hierarchy is a driver of much urban renewal in the Global South. Besides this, the reality of insufficient or weak provisions of basic services and infrastructure, such as clean water, sewage systems, electricity and roads, makes renewal desirable for many disadvantaged groups. The need for urban renewal is further amplified by the rapid growth of many of these cities, along with an increasing need for housing, more efficient transportation modes and routes, and a vulnerability to disasters like earthquakes and floods. Additionally, renewal projects targeting provision of infrastructure and basic services provide a ground for building relationships with city and state officials for claiming other social and political rights. What is really important in these renewal practices is considering the local context and environment of each city, without taking for granted assumptions coming from the Global North neighbourhood. As similarly noted by Thurber (Chapter 11 in this volume), in the absence of state welfare policies, informal networks and relationships can be the main asset of the residents of the poor and disadvantaged neighbourhoods where urban renewal takes place. Intervening in these neighbourhoods without considering the effects of renewal on these networks and relations can lead to more marginalization of already disadvantaged people. Furthermore, the citizen–state relationship is also different in many of these cities. The absence of strong civil society, lack of transparency and accountability from state or city officials' corruption creates a very different dynamic, which needs particular attention. Cultural differences that imply different urban forms and processes also need to be considered. All these require attending to the local context that underlines the necessity of bottom-up participatory approaches in urban renewal. However, elaborating the distinct dynamics of urban renewal in the Global South compared to the Global North does not mean there is no similarity among urban renewal experiences in these two contexts. In fact, one common point of renewal practice in both contexts is the upsurge of private market-oriented renewals.

Displacement, space and place

Displacement is described as the physical relocation of previous residents of a neighbourhood (Hall, 2016). Thus, if there is no physical repositioning for the residents of the neighbourhood, it is not considered as displacement. Davidson (2009), criticizing this view, advocates adding a social dimension to displacement. He argues that displacement should be defined as the spatial *and social* displacement of previous residents of an urban area. This means the residents of a neighbourhood may not be physically relocated, but they may still be socially isolated and economically disadvantaged. In fact, due to the presence of a new population and formation of new social relations and interactions, the lived experience of previous residents may change and thus they may feel dispossessed from their homes and therefore claim displacement. What Davidson (2009) is emphasizing is attending to the lived experience based on Lefebvre's (1991) notion of lived space in approaching displacement. Davidson (2009, p. 222) argues that 'through a particular (spatial) understanding of displacement, the loss of place [or lived space] has been mistakenly equated to a loss of (abstract) space'.

At the core of this argument is conceptualizing displacement based on the concept of 'place' rather than that of 'space'. Space and place are key terms in geography (Agnew, 1987; Massey, 1994; Cresswell, 2004). Both concepts point to the geographical dimension of the world and are used to signify the geographical extent of processes, practices and events. Reviewing geographical scholarly works reveals that space and place are sometimes used interchangeably, while often are employed pointing out two distinct dimensions of the material world. The following sub-section briefly reviews conceptualizations of space and place in geographical theory to critique the duality of space, place and place-based displacement. My argument is to move beyond these static views on displacement and to recruit a relational and emergentist approach to the reproduction and transformation of space and place for an enhanced critical assessment of the effects of renewal processes on displacement.

Space and place in geography

Different conceptualizations of space and place attribute different elements of subjectivity, objectivity, agency and structure to each concept. In one approach, space is often used to describe the general and the objective of the phenomena under study, while notion of place often refers to the particularity of the spatial dimension attached to the particular subjectivity. For example, 'spatial science' uses the term 'space' as a container, within which, events and phenomena occurred to represent the geographical dimension of a process or practice. These spatial studies, criticizing the idiographic approaches and their descriptive nature, offers an objective understanding of the spatial dimension of processes, relations and events, based on a Cartesian view of the world (Cresswell, 2004). On the other hand, humanist geographers (e.g. Tuan, 1996; Buttimer, 1976; Relph, 1976) have been influenced by the works of philosophers like Martin Heidegger, who argued that place is part of human experience. To humanists, place is a constitutive element of human existence and becoming. Thus, place is an essential characteristic of humanity, and therefore, understanding 'place' requires attending to and realizing human experience.

Radical human geographers use space and place interchangeably by attending to the macro-structures that influence spatial dimensions – and argue that place is socially constructed. As a seminal scholar employing this approach, Lefebvre (1991) emphasizes the structural forces constituting space, distinguishing abstract space from social space. He defines three dimensions of social space: conceived space which is the realm of conceptualization; perceived space, which can be recognized through our senses; and lived space, which is the space we live in and experience. Harvey (1996) highlights the social construction of place, and puts emphasis on the association of this construction with politics. Therefore, what is important is how place is produced and who gets included and excluded in this process. Again, for Harvey (1996) place does not have any authenticity or generality; rather, it is produced and reproduced by structural forces in a political process.

While these constructivist approaches mostly attend to structural forces produce space and place, structurationist scholars ask for considering both structure and agency in this production process. According to these scholars, place is neither a frozen scene, produced by structures for action, nor is it an essential dimension of humanity in association with particular human experience. It is always in the process of becoming, influenced by both structural forces and agents' actions (Pred, 1984).

More recent conceptualizations of place argue for a relational understanding of space and place. Massey (1994), as a pioneer in this approach, argues that we can recognize a place through relations and the connections that produce place. Thus, for her, place is a bundle of time-space trajectories coming together in a conjuncture of event and practices. In other words, place is constituted by a temporary constellation of relations, which are continuously changing. As a consequence of this view, place is neither static nor fixed; rather, it is dynamic and continuously changing, with multiple identities. This does not mean that place is not particular, but its specificity comes from the particular bundle of relations that produce it not from any essence or rootedness. The next section further defines displacement by either space (the spatial science perspective or the Lefebvrian perspective) or place (the phenomenological and humanistic geography approach) and addresses the complexity of reproduction or transformation of place-making processes.

Displacement beyond 'loss of place' or 'loss of space'

As stated earlier, the dominant understanding of displacement is physical reloca-tion of an area's previous residents. In this regard, the house, neighbourhood or census tract are considered as containers in which people live; they are understood as three-dimensional locations in which social relations and interactions happen. Therefore, if as a result of urban renewal, transformation or other drivers, people change the house, neighbourhood or census tract in which they live, it can be argued that, since they are changing their geographical location, they are dis-placed. However, this objective view of the geography where people live, does not take into account the lived experience of people in their homes, neighbourhoods or census tracts. If we instead attend to the lived experiences of people (the rela-tionships they develop in their homes and neighbourhoods, their interaction with their neighbours and other residents, their attachment to buildings and the built environment they live in) then a new understanding of displacement is developed. In this view, displacement is not limited to 'loss of space', but is seen in a broader sense as 'loss of place'. In this regard, 'space' is somewhere there, a location in the Cartesian environment that is connected to the physical world while 'place' is produced through relations and interactions and is connected to the lived world. As a result, displacement is not only a change in the geographical location of the physical world or space; rather, can be understood as a change in the socio-spatial constellation of the lived world or place. Beyond this phenomenological view, if we define a place as the bundle of materiality, relations and emotions which includes physical, natural, mental and social realms, then any imposed change in this constellation can be considered displacement. Thus, the influx of new peo-ple into an area which changes the social environment of the neighbourhood, the increase in property values and rents which shifts the everyday life experience of residents, and transformations in the built environment that destroys the memories and sentiments of residents, all can induce a sense of displacement even when residents are not being physically relocated. In this view, displacement is not only 'loss of space', but also 'loss of place'.

If we employ the conceptualization of displacement based on the notion of relational place, then the question that comes to mind is what are the implications of this new conceptualization? First, this chapter would argue that people, their lived experiences and their sense of place need to be prioritized in urban planning and decision-making practices relating to renewal and area transformation. This implies the necessity of the involvement of people who inhabit or experience a neighbourhood in any decision that aims to produce place. The direct control and participation of inhabitants in the production process of place can be considered an actualization of Lefebvre's 'right to the city' (Mitchell, 2003; Purcell, 2002).

Second, if we consider place as a bundle of materiality, social relations emotions and memories, then displacement will be an inevitable outcome of any change in an area. Thus, in cases where urban renewal of neighbourhood seems necessary and publicly accepted, neighbourhood displacement is unavoidable. To take an extreme case: what of neighbourhoods with old and degraded infrastructure, where the lives of the residents are in danger? The question raised here is whether we should accept the resultant displacement and loss of place or dismiss the whole renewal process, potentially at the risk of residents' lives? Changes are inescapable and the desire to improve people's quality of life always exists. Hence, instead of ignoring the renewal process, it should be accompanied by a place-making process in order to prevent loss of place. This, reemphasizing the importance of involvement of inhabitants in the renewal process, implies attending to meaning-making and identity-building process of place-making.

Displacement and place-making

In the previous section, the relational approach to place (and place-making) was briefly discussed. Grounded on this framework, Pierce et al. (2011) introduce a relational place-making process which highlights three points: 1) both structural forces and agency are involved in the bundling process of place-making; 2) the bundling process and thus place-making is not only individual, but also involves collective processes; and 3) politics are involved in the place-making process through negotiations and conflicts about different bundles. This means that individual bundles of time-space trajectories come to the contestation with each other. The politicized negotiation of different bundles to reach a common place frame signifies the relational place-making process.

Although this framework argues to consider both structural forces and agentic actions, in its operationalization – by focusing on how individuals do bundling and the politics involved in it – puts the focus on agency. In order to overcome this imbalance, I argue for an emergentist relational place-making process. By adding the emergentist element, I emphasize the need to consider both structural and agentic forces, but as they cannot both be realized in one moment, changes over time need to be taken into account. As we need two moments to consider both agency and structure, two geographical contexts also need to be represented. Thus, space represents the geographical reach of structural forces, while place represent the geographical reach of the agents' agency. This means space and place are not two separate things, nor they are a unitary; they represent the geographical reach of two different moments. When we focus on structural forces and their realization in space, we consider how they reproduce or transform place. On the other hand, when we emphasize agents and their action at place, we realize how space is reproduced or transformed. This reproduction or transformation of space/place through reproduction or transformation of structural and agentic forces may lead to emergent characteristics such as new identities and meanings.

As discussed above, changes in any of material, emotional and social realms of our lived geography is inevitable. This means we cannot prevent changes of space nor of place. What needs to be attended is the continuous process of place-making which can build new identities and bring new meanings for those living in the area under change. Hence, in addition to prevention of loss of space (physical relocation) and loss of place (changes in emotional and social realms with(out) material change), place-making can be targeted. In this collective process, through negotiation and contestation by attending to both structures and agency and their subjective and objective dimensions of the geographical reach, identities can be built and meanings may be made.

Urban renewal in Tehran

Tehran, the capital of Iran and Tehran Province, is the largest city of Iran. Tehran's population, experiencing continuous growth in the past decades, is almost 11 million, while its area is around 700 square kilometres. Tehran holds about 15 per cent of Iran's population, while more than 40 per cent of the nation's economic activities take place in Tehran. Tehran's modern development started in the 1920s and continued to the 1960s. Public infrastructures including water pipes, electricity, pavements and widening of streets was the main focus of development. Moving on, from 1960 to 1979, development was linked to industrialization, which was disproportionally concentrated on big cities like Tehran. Because of Tehran's role as a political, economic and cultural centre, what resulted was inward immigration from smaller cities and rural areas. This influx of population was not accompanied by the provision of sufficient services, which resulted in an increase of informal settlements around Tehran, especially in the city's south. The revolution in 1979 and the Iran–Iraq war till 1988 temporarily removed development from the agenda, as the redevelopment of war-degraded areas became the main focus of urban planning in Tehran after war until 1995. In 1995 Tehran Renovation Organization (TRO) was founded by Tehran Municipality in order to supervise the city's renovation. The performance and approach of TRO can be divided in two phases, one from 1995 to 2006 and the other since 2006.

Urban renewal in Tehran: phase I, 1995–2006

The main urban renewal project implemented by TRO during this phase was renewal of the Navvab Highway. Navvab was one of the key north–south streets of Tehran which played an important role in Tehran's traffic. Due to the heavy load of vehicles using this street, there was a plan to broaden it and turn it to a highway to facilitate high traffic volumes. This meant the surrounding neighbourhoods, which were mostly lower- and medium-income residential areas, had to be demolished to provide space for the transversal street expansion. In order to operationalize this project, TRO identified an area large enough for necessary expansion, informing the area's residents about this project, and then approached building by building for the possession of buildings. Thus TRO representatives or developers, signed contracts with TRO, contacted owners of each building in order to offer them a price for buying their building. The owner would receive cash money in the exchange of the building and moved to another neighbourhood.

As the result of the renewal project some of the neighbourhoods were demolished completely since there was a need for more space in order to widen Navvab Street to Navvab Highway. The buildings right next to the highway were changed from residential to commercial. Neighbourhoods that remained also underwent a significant revitalization in which most of the one- or two-floor buildings were changed to four- and five-floor buildings. In addition, most of the previous residents that had lived there for more than 15 years, on average, did not come back to the renewed neighbourhoods primarily because they could not afford it. Based on the distinction discussed above, these residents have become (physically) displaced. The new residents who moved into the renovated neighbourhoods considered them temporal and transitionary settlements, living there for an average of five years.

As mentioned above, the old buildings in the neighbourhoods were bought by developers in cash. The increase in fluidity of money because of cash transfers led to growth of inflation in the housing market which made not only the Navvab area but also other adjacent areas unaffordable for the previous residents of Navvab. Thus, many of the previous residents ended up in lower-income neighbourhoods or informal settlements. Furthermore, not all of the residents used the cash money they received for buying a new home and some of them spent it on other short-term consumption. After a decade they faced the situation that they had lost the main capital of their life, their home, and they were not successful in replacing it. Finally, the social fabric of the neighbourhoods changed significantly. Previously, the residents of these neighbourhoods were families who had been living there for a long time and most of them knew each other and had, at least, greeting relations with each other. These relations made them perceive their neighbourhood as a safe place. After renewal, especially since the demolition and rebuilding of buildings in one neighbourhood occurred at different times, new people moved to the neighbourhood. Because many were thinking about short-term residency in the neighbourhood, they did not develop the kind of relations that existed previously. This unfamiliarity among residents in the neighbourhood led to perceptions of an unsafe neighbourhood.

Urban renewal in Navvab Highway project

The renewal process in the Navvab Highway project can be analysed based on three dimensions. The first refers to the level of renewal process (macro and micro). On one hand, in renewal planning, the whole area including Navvab Street and all adjacent neighbourhoods, were considered for renewal. This area covered neighbourhoods from different municipal districts. Thus, TRO employed a macro-level urban renewal process. On the other hand, in operationalizing the renewal, they targeted each building and entered a negotiation process with individual owner of each building. Hence, their view was focused on the micro-scale of buildings. The second dimension is the renewal approach (referring to possession). The approach of TRO in Navvab renewal project was possession. This means the TRO's or developers' representatives contacted homeowners in order to purchase their buildings. The only option offered to the homeowners was selling their homes and they could only, at the best case, negotiate on the price. The third dimension here is the actors (the TRO and the developers). As a result of level of renewal and also the approach employed by TRO, the only actors involved in the renewal process were TRO and developers. Residents were not involved in any of the planning, decision-making and implementation phases. They were informed about the renewal project when the project began and their only involvement in the project was through the buildings that they either owned or resided in – not themselves and their social relations.

Urban renewal in Tehran: phase II, 2006–onward

Although the Navvab Highway renewal played a significant role in facilitating traffic in Tehran, at least for north–south trips in the west of Tehran, this project received severe criticism due to its social and economic outcomes. The displacement (physically) of large amount of residents, rise of property values and rents, increase in informal settlements, and growth in crime rate and unsafety are among the main points of critique. In the rise of these critiques, a terrible earthquake happened in Bam, Kerman, south-centre of Iran, in which more than 25,000 died. One of the main factors reported for the large death toll was vulnerability of buildings and their lack of strength against natural disasters (such as earthquakes). This terrible event brought up the issue of safety, accessibility and strength of buildings to the centre of attention in the whole country, including the municipality of Tehran.

Much of the critique linked to the Navvab renewal redevelopment referred to raising the issue of safety. With the change of mayor in Tehran in 2006, a new approach to urban renewal began. The new approach, referred to as the 'Renovation of Deteriorated Neighbourhoods', put emphasis on revitalization of neighbourhoods. The identification of deteriorated neighbourhoods was based on the strength of buildings, accessibility and size of buildings. According to these criteria, three types of deteriorated neighbourhoods were recognized: 1) those neighbourhoods with historical sites; 2) those neighbourhoods without historical sites; and 3) informal and marginal settlements. The focus here would be on the second type: urban deteriorated neighbourhoods without historical sites.

Foremost, TRO identified deteriorated neighbourhoods and established a Neighbourhood Renovation Office (NRO) in each neighbourhood. Representatives from the private sector or NGOs who signed a contract with TRO constitute these NROs. The first task of these NROs is to identify the buildings and document different degrees of intervention needed. Documenting and recording was a technical process where buildings are examined based on specific criteria, for instance, accessibility, age of buildings, their strength against earthquakes, accessibility and the number of dead-end alleys. NROs then used this opportunity to make initial contacts with neighbourhood residents to brief and sensitize them about the problem of the existing old buildings and the necessity to take appropriate action. Based on the evaluation of the buildings, three types of intervention were recognized: 1) *behsazi*, 2) *nosazi* and 3) *bazsazi*. *Behsazi* (improving) means the least amount of intervention needed; there is a tendency to keep the building as much as possible by repairing and strengthening the parts that are weak. *Nosazi* (renewing) refers to no tendency to keep the building – if there are parts that need to be renovated, they will be rebuilt. Finally, *bazsazi* (rebuilding) suggests there is no need for keeping and maintaining any part, the whole building will be demolished and rebuilt from the beginning. Preparing technical reports were part of a bigger process of neighbourhood identification. Thus, at the surface level, technical information is collected by experts, but at the deeper level, NRO staff are attempting to become familiar with the neighbourhood and its residents by making connections with them and trying to understand their concerns to become familiar with the neighbourhood.

In the next step, which is in many cases implemented in parallel to the identification step, NROs hold introductory sessions and meetings in the neighbourhoods to explain their mission and goals to residents – an attempt to strengthen their relations with residents. As they progress they present the results of their technical investigation to residents and the recommended renewals. They also explain the whole renewal process, the financial mechanism developed particularly for assisting renewal of deteriorated neighbourhoods, the facilities they can use, and, in short, they describe the whole renewal process from the first to last step. There is a main difference between the NRO's approach and the approach employed in the Navvab project. In the new approach, residents will move to a temporary location during the renewal process, and after renewal is done, they will come back to a renewed home in the neighbourhood.

In the deteriorated neighbourhoods the size of (many) houses were too small, or many of the alleys were narrow. Some buildings could not be renovated individually, so collaborations between a few landlords was necessary. Thus, NRO's staff, instead of having one-to-one meetings with landlords, would have group meetings with a number of landlords and residents together. This does not mean that there were no one-to-one meetings between NRO staff and residents. When issues regarding financial mechanisms and finding the temporary location for the renewal period were discussed, there were individual meetings between NRO staff and residents. The point made here puts emphasis on the general approach of renewal, particularly in comparison to the Navvab project, which is collective interaction and relation. Of course, moving from individual level to a group level adds complications when reaching agreements and collective action are aimed at, since all residents need to come to agreement about the starting time, the duration of project and the assignment of renewed units. There are also positive points in moving to the collective level that can facilitate collaborative action and contribute to building new collective identities or constructing new collective meaning for the neighbourhood. There are cases in which one or two landlords disagreed with the renewal process, however through collective discussions and justifications of their adjacent neighbours not NRO staff, they consented to the renewal process. There are also instances in which the successful experience of one project spread through word of mouth in the neighbourhood and made other residents interested in the renewal process.

This renewal process in not without challenges. Two big groups that contend renewal are older people and renters. The old people usually are against the renewal process since they do not want to move twice in a short period in this stage of their life. Another issue that makes renewal a less attractive option for older people is the legal problem of inheritance if they were to pass away during the renewal process. In addition, the general trend of being more risk averse in the later stages of life is true for the old residents of these neighbourhoods. Another notable big group of opponents to renewal process are renters. Due to lack of an organized recording system that provides the information of the landlords, tenants are the main route to reach landlords and contact for the renewal process. Thus, their lack of collaboration in sharing their landlord's information and informing them about the renewal process (in various stages) can pose a significant barrier to the renewal process.

Urban renewal by NROs

Three dimensions are considered to describe the NRO's approach (level of renewal process, renewal approach and actors), which were also employed to analyse the renewal process of the Navvab Highway. The first is the level of renewal process (meso). Unlike the Navvab Highway project that targeted renewal of a large area and then approached each building individually, the NRO focuses on neighbourhoods and approaches the whole neighbourhood. Although renewal of the whole neighbourhood was not possible (nor desired), NRO's approach is through collective meetings, public hearings and collaborative projects. Thus, the level of renewal process is neither the macro-level of districts or combination of neighbourhoods nor individual buildings. The next renewal approach is in contrast to the Navvab Highway project, where NROs prevent possession of buildings. Learning from the Navvab Highway project and its undesired outcomes (e.g. inflation in housing market, enforced dislocation of residents, destruction of social relations and networks), they attempted to keep residents of the neighbourhoods. Thus, residents of the area under renewal process were temporarily to live in another place till their renewed unit is ready. The meso-level approach of NROs which requires a collective approach and its approach to bringing residents back to the neighbourhood made involvement of residents a necessary part of renewal process. Third, there are three actors (TRO, the developers and the residents). As a result of level of renewal and also the approach employed by TRO, in addition to TRO and developers, residents were engaged in the renewal process. In practice, the rate of participation of residents varies in different projects but in general, the nature of NRO's approach was a participatory approach which had the potential for involvement of residents in different stages of planning, decision-making and implementation.

A summary: displacement in Tehran's renewal processes

This chapter introduces a typology of displacement that occurs in urban renewal processes. The most obvious and often discussed displacement is spatial and physical relocation of residents. This type of displacement, discussed as space-based displacement in this chapter, has happened in the Navvab Highway project. In this project, buildings were taken possession of by the agents of the renewal process and residents were free to decide wherever they wanted to move. There was no plan to bring the previous residents back to the neighbourhood, and after renewal it was open to the market for whoever could afford to live in the neighbourhood. The residents of the neighbourhood were only involved in the pre-renewal phase (purchasing the buildings). They had no interaction and no relation existed after acquisition of the buildings by the renewal agency.

The second type of displacement, discussed in the critique of space-based displacement, is place-based displacement. This view argues for attention to the lived experience of people and the whole combination of materials, emotions and social relations tied to a place. From this view, displacement has both physical and social dimensions and any changes in either dimension cause displacement. The NRO's approach attempted to prevent the space-based displacement by designing the renewal process in a way that brought the residents back to the neighbourhood. But still, changes were made in both the physical and social realms. Not only the materiality of the neighbourhood is changed in the renewal process (with new buildings, new alleys and new infrastructures) but by changing a one-floor building to a four-floor building, new households come to the neighbourhood changing its social dynamics. Due to the influx of new residents, new relations and interactions will influence the place. Therefore, NRO's approach, while successful in preventing space-based displacement, was unsuccessful in preventing place-based displacement.

The third viewpoint considered displacement via place-making, realizing that changes in physical and social realms are inevitable. Here, the emphasis is put on the collective and participatory process of place-making. The emergentist relational place-making approach, introduced in this chapter, accepts the continuous change occurring in our geography prompted either by structural forces or agentic actions; and argues that the focus should be on making place collectively which can bring about new meaning and identity. In this view, both objective and subjective dimensions of our geography are taken into account and changes in them may occur through reflection on either structural forces or agentic actions. According to this view, any renewal process should be intertwined with place-making attempts. Although the basis of NRO's approach and its attempt in returning residents to the neighbourhood were mainly towards preventing space-based displacement, in some neighbourhoods place-making attempts could be recognized. Holding public meetings where residents could discuss their concerns, their memories of the neighbourhood, the importance of some buildings, the services or infrastructures they need in their neighbourhood, plays an important role in this regard. In some NROs, the staff organized the first few meetings but then facilitated more and more meetings initiated by the residents to discuss different issues such as lack of green space in the neighbourhood, improvement in school services or collective cleaning of the neighbourhood. Many of these meetings were held in residents' houses not in local NRO offices. All these collective discussions and actions provide space for negotiating different place frames and making a collective place frame. As they represent, place-making is a collective process requiring time and energy and it should be the priority of NRO's staff in order for this to occur. It involves interaction between, and collective reflection on, structural and agentic forces in the renewal process that may lead to new meaning and identity.

References

Abdollahi, M., Sarafi, M., & Tavakolinia, J. (2010). Barresi nazari mafhoom mahaleh va baztarif an ba takid bar sharayet mahalehaye Iran [Theoretical interrogation of neighbourhood concept and its redefinition based on Iran urban neighbourhoods' conditions]. *Human Geography Research, 72*, 83–102.

Agnew, J. (1987). *Place and politics*. Winchester, MA: Allen and Unwin.

Buttimer, A. (1976). Grasping the dynamism of lifeworld. *Annals of the Association of American Geographers, 66*, 277–292.

Cresswell, T. (2004). *Place: A short introduction*. Malden, MA: Blackwell.

Davidson, M. (2009). Displacement, space and dwelling: Placing gentrification debate. *Ethics, Place & Environment, 12*, 219–234.

Fanni, Z., & Saremi, F. (2008). Chaleshhaye nezam modiriyati mahaleh-mehvar dar toseye paydar kalanshahr Tehran [Challenges of neighbourhood-based management system in sustainable development of Tehran]. *Soffeh, 17*, 91–108.

Fraser, J. (2004). Beyond gentrification: Mobilizing communities and claiming space. *Urban Geography, 25*(5), 437–457.

Friedmann, J. (2010). Place and place-making in cities: A global perspective. *Planning Theory & Practice, 11*, 149–165.

Hadizadeh Esfahani, A. (forthcoming). Urban renewal. In B. S. Turner (Ed.), *The encyclopedia of social theory*. Oxford: Wiley-Blackwell.

Hall, D. (2016). Place and displacement: Introduction. *Urban Geography, 37*, 1–3.

Harvey, D. (1996). *Justice, nature, and the geography of difference*. Cambridge, MA: Blackwell.

Ho, K. C. (2006). Where do community iconic structures fit in a globalizing city? *City, 10*, 91–100.

Lees, L., Slater, T., & Wyly, E. (2008). *Gentrification*. London: Routledge.

Lefebvre, H. (1991). *The production of space*. Oxford: Blackwell.

Lepofsky, J., & Fraser, J.C. (2003). Building community citizens: Claiming the right to place-making in the city. *Urban Studies, 40*, 127–142.

Logan, J. R., & Molotch, H. L. (2007). *Urban fortunes: The political economy of place*. Berkeley: University of California Press.

Massey, D. (1994). A global sense of place. In D. B. Massey, *Space, place, and gender* (pp. 146–156). Minneapolis: University of Minnesota Press.

Mitchell, D. (2003). *The right to the city: Social justice and the fight for public space*. New York: The Guilford Press.

Munzner, K., & Shaw, K. (2015). Renew who? Benefits and beneficiaries of Renew Newcastle. *Urban Policy and Research, 33*, 17–36.

Mousavi, Y. (2008). Bazsazi mahalehaye shahri dar charchub barnamerizi toseye ejtemae mahaleyi [Renovation of urban neighbourhoods based on neighbourhood social development planning]. *Iran Social Studies, 2*, 99–123.

Pierce, J., Martin, D. G., & Murphy, J. T. (2011). Relational place-making: The networked politics of place. *Transactions of the Institute of British Geographers, 36*, 54–70.

Pred, A. (1984). Place as historically contingent process: Structuration and the time-geography of becoming places. *Annals of the Association of American Geographers, 74*, 279–297.

Purcell, M. (2002). Excavating Lefebvre: The right to the city and its urban politics of the inhabitant. *GeoJournal, 58,* 99–108.

Relph, E. (1976). *Place and placelessness.* London: Pion.

Roy, A. (2005). Urban informality: Toward an epistemology of planning. *Journal of the American Planning Association, 71*(2), 147–158.

Smith, N. (1996). *The new urban frontier: Gentrification and the revanchist city.* London: Routledge.

Stone, C. N. (1989). *Regime politics: Governing Atlanta, 1946–1988.* Lawrence: University Press of Kansas.

Tuan, Y-F. (1996). Space and place: Humanistic perspective. In J. Agnew, D. N. Livingstone, & A. Rogers (Eds.), *Human geography* (pp. 444–457). Oxford: Wiley-Blackwell.

9 When community and condos collide

The uneven geographies of housing wealth in mixed-income neighbourhood transformation

Charles Barlow

Introduction

Castells (1996, pp. 415–416) mentions: 'Elites are cosmopolitan, people are local. The space of power and wealth is projected throughout the world, while people's life and experiences is rooted in places, in their culture, in their history.' Mixed-income neighbourhoods, by definition, are populated with residents marked with differential experiences. These experiences – shaped by divergent sets of cultural, social and economic capital – present very real power differentials between tenure groups. Different groups include public housing residents, renters, and homeowners in mixed-income neighbourhoods. The influence of higher-income residents over elite actors (including policymakers, politicians and other stakeholders) to impose a particular neighbourhood aesthetic reinforces specific conceptualizations of rights and obligations and cements the difference inscribed in urban space by promoting a dialectic between the powerful and the powerless. This chapter seeks to investigate the specific practices through which public space is produced in mixed-income neighbourhoods and how the power to determine its use is arrayed.

Elwood et al. (2014, p. 126) assert that:

> place-making occurs in everyday acts through which individuals and social groups demand or seek the kind of residential neighbourhoods they desire, whether in terms of neighbours, sense of community, retail and recreation opportunities, housing options, and so on.

However, amidst the constructed socioeconomic difference inscribed in mixed-income neighbourhoods, place-making has come to represent a spatial and discursive practice through which higher-income residents impose their class identities upon their lower-income neighbours. The power of property and capital privileges these residents to influence elite actors and to assert their own aesthetic ideologies about how neighbourhood spaces ought to be. In turn, this privilege prevents lower-income residents from exercising their entitlements of citizenship – their right 'to urban life, to renewed centrality, to places of encounter and exchange, to life rhythms and time uses, enabling the full and complete *usage* of [. . .] moments and places' (Lefebvre, 1996, p. 179).

Mixed-income neighbourhood transformation in the United States

In the twenty-first century, a consensus has emerged in the housing policy arena that mixed-income neighbourhoods are desirable. Among the most committed to the adoption of mixed-income policies in the United States, the Chicago Housing Authority (CHA) has demolished more than 50 traditional high-rise structures since 2000 to make way for mixed-income housing developments in gentrifying areas of the city. Joseph et al. (2007) identify four theoretical propositions promoted by policymakers and public housing agencies to support mixed-income housing as a mechanism to counter the hyper-concentration of poverty in failed traditional public housing developments across the United States: 1) the expansion of *social networks* of low-income residents; 2) the increased *social control* and social organization afforded to low-income residents; 3) the presence of higher-income residents as *role models* transforming the behaviours and culture of low-income residents; and 4) the enhanced provision of public goods and services to low-income residents (*'political economy of place'*). The first of these takes its roots in Putnam's understanding of social capital. Putnam (2000) asserts that low-income residents lack social capital and that placing them in proximity with higher-income residents would increase both the quantity and quality of their social networks that allow them to lead fuller lives. The second and third propositions are grounded in Wilson's (1987) conceptualization of the 'underclass' and Lewis's (1975) 'culture of poverty' respectively. Here, it is argued that the creation of mixed-income neighbourhoods will reduce the social pathology associated with the 'physical concentration of poor households in multifamily projects' that is thought to cause 'severe problems for the residents, including joblessness, drug abuse, and welfare dependency' (Brophy & Smith, 1997, p. 6). Fourth, proponents of the political economy of place narrative maintain that the provision of public goods and services improves as neighbourhood residents become wealthier and assume that lower-income residents will benefit from the enhanced provision of amenities.

Since the United States Department of Housing and Urban Development (HUD) launched the HOPE VI programme promoting mixed-income housing as a revitalization strategy in 1992, there has been essentially no empirical work that supports the first three propositions and only limited evidence to support the fourth. These policies are often justified by painting low-income residents as a problem that calls for 'a benevolent gentry [. . .] to colonise their home space in order to create the conditions necessary to help the poor "bootstrap" themselves into a better socioeconomic position' (DeFilippis & Fraser, 2010, p. 136). But despite their popularity in policymaking spheres, a growing body of empirical research suggests that these transformation efforts fail to achieve the benefits proposed by their integrationist agendas (e.g. August, 2008; Hunt, 2009; Vale & Graves, 2010; Chaskin & Joseph, 2015). Indeed, much of the support for mixed-income policies comes not from evidence articulating the benefits of socioeconomic mix but from 'dissatisfaction with the previous thrust of low-income housing policy' (Schwartz & Tajbakhsh, 1997, p. 91).

While there is an established literature around place-making and the use of public space in urban settings, little attention is given to the struggles that emerge in the public spaces of mixed-income neighbourhoods. Empirical studies point to divergent cultural norms and social stigma as drivers of spatial conflicts in these neighbourhoods (Duke, 2009; Chaskin & Joseph, 2013). However, no study has investigated the reasons why particular ideological visions of urban space are able to prevail over others in the geographical contestations that play out in mixed-income neighbourhoods. Employing a mixed-methods approach drawing upon ethnographic observations over 12 months while residing in two mixed-income housing developments in Chicago's Oakland neighbourhood, supplemented by interviews with elite actors and residents as well as a systematic review of policy and design documents, this chapter contributes to our understanding of geographical contestations that exist between tenure groups by examining how property and capital mediate the power relations that shape the character and use of public space in mixed-income neighbourhoods.

Transforming a Chicago neighbourhood

Oakland is one of 77 community areas in Chicago, and is located four miles from downtown on the city's Mid-Southside (Figure 9.1). In the early 1950s, Olander Homes, a 15-storey federal aid housing project was constructed on a parcel of slum land. Five more high-rises were constructed in the decade that followed to complete the Lakefront Properties, home to more than 907 public

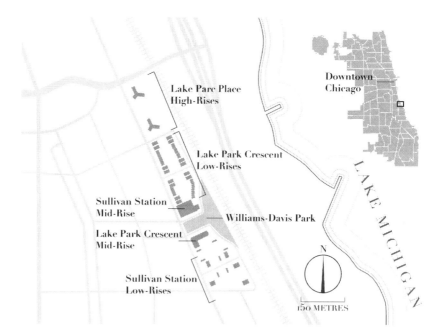

Figure 9.1 Map of Lakefront Properties redevelopment site in Oakland, Chicago.

housing families. Only two of these buildings still stand. Renovated in the early 1990s, Lake Parc Place is the earliest example of mixed-income housing in the United States with half of its 289 units reserved for public housing residents earning between 50 and 80 per cent of the area median income. The remaining four high-rises were imploded in 1998.

Where these public housing high-rise developments devastated by the deleterious consequences of urban poverty once stood, a vibrant mixed-income neighbourhood now commands the attention of affluent homeowners who are attracted to state-of-the-art recreational facilities. New million-dollar townhomes and private commercial development made possible by the unprecedented disposition of public lands once reserved for low-income residential development exist. As of early 2017, more than 300 replacement public housing units have been constructed in the surrounding area, mostly in new mixed-income residential developments at the site of the demolished buildings. The first on-site phase, Lake Park Crescent, began accepting residents in 2005. The latest development phase, Sullivan Station, opened in November 2013 and includes a mix of public housing (47 units), market-rate rental (34 units) and Low Income Housing Tax Credit (LIHTC) affordable rental units (51 units). Subsequent development phases are planned to deliver more than 140 market-rate and homeownership units at the site from late 2017 onwards.

Oakland has emerged from this transformation less as a site of participation and instead as one of expropriation by affluent, propertied citizens and allied distance elites that appear disinterested in making the neighbourhood a site for the cohabitation of socioeconomic difference. The significance of property and capital has imposed a geography of exclusion that leaves low-income renters and public housing residents to struggle over the shape of the neighbourhood, the terms of access to and use of its public spaces, and even their entitlements of citizenship.

Public space in mixed-income neighbourhoods

Open space first entered the redevelopment discourse at the Lakefront Properties in a 1999 Request for Proposals for mixed-income redevelopment issued by the CHA (Draper & Kramer & The Community Builders, 1999). The agency's inaugural Annual Report for its Plan for Transformation made a single mention of public space – presenting 'green space' as just one of a multitude of metrics upon which proposals would be evaluated. Proposals submitted to the agency were considered, among other criteria, upon 'the extent of non-housing benefits to residents such as funding for or provision of social services, business and employment opportunities, community facilities and *green spaces*' (Chicago Housing Authority, 2000). The agency presented no further guidelines or direction as to how these spaces might look. Even now, guidance from the agency remains sparse and gives no indication of how these open spaces are to be experienced by local residents. Its latest strategic initiative calls for developers to 'invest in spaces and partner with organizations that support educational,

Figure 9.2 Williams-Davis Park (photo by Maya Dukmasova).

community, recreational, and commercial purposes, including increasing public space' (Chicago Housing Authority, 2013, p. 16).

As noted, this chapter offers an ethnographic inroad into one of the newly constructed public spaces and the surrounding streetscape in Chicago's Oakland neighbourhood. Described by the Chicago Park District as 'a vibrant new park' (Chicago Park District, 2015), Williams-Davis Park was envisioned to provide a recreational space at the heart of the mixed-income redevelopment (Figure 9.2). According to the master planner, the 2.8-acre park was constructed at a cost of $2 million and includes several elements of creative change 'to account for the neighbourhood's rich ethnic heritage, and established an identity as a place to celebrate art', including a play area, educational butterfly garden, and native plants and bioswales (BauerLatoza Studio, 2015).

Originally named Park No. 532, several hundred residents petitioned the Chicago Park District to rename the park in 2012 to honour two local women, Dr Hattie B. Kay Williams and Ms Izora Davis, who were devoted to improving the lives of underprivileged citizens (Clarke, 2013). Dr Williams (1922–1990) was a community activist who played an important role in desegregating public schools. Her campaigning led to the resignation of the Superintendent of the Chicago Public Schools system, who had refused to integrate schools and installed substandard wagons to educate black schoolchildren separately from white children. Ms Davis (1952–2006) moved into the CHA's Lake Michigan Homes in 1983. Her activism with the Lakefront Community Organization was instrumental in securing a Memorandum of Accord that afforded public housing residents the right to return to the revitalized mixed-income housing. Williams-Davis Park is one of only 44 parks in Chicago named to honour black citizens, and is the only park named after two black women.

Geographies of exclusion: order and control

Imposing limits and control over spatial interaction and unconventional behaviours has long been the goal of urban planners (Harvey, 1989; Davis, 1990; Lefebvre, 1991). Public spaces in desirable neighbourhoods become places where 'a pacified public basks in the grandeur of a carefully orchestrated corporate spectacle' (Crilley, 1993, p. 147). In mixed-income neighbourhoods, planning practices sort and divide social groups according to the dictates of comfort and order. These planning strategies 'distribute the various social strata and classes (other than the one that exercises hegemony) across the available territory, keeping them separate and prohibiting all contacts – these being replaced by *signs* (or images) of contact' (Lefebvre, 1991, p. 375). Higher-income households increasingly accept signs and images of contact as more natural and desirable than contact itself in an effort to assert their desired aesthetic of place. These spaces of controlled spectacle narrow the list of people eligible to form 'the public' to exclude lower socioeconomic classes as undesirable and their behaviours as unconventional (see also Varna, Chapter 7 in this volume). Once excluded from these spaces, the legitimacy of lower-income residents as members of the public is called into question. Now *unrepresented* in the image of 'the public', these residents are prevented from fully asserting their right to use and shape urban public spaces.

In concert with distance elites, higher-income households are able to manipulate exclusion and entitlement to create an image of the city that 'reflects decisions about what – and who – should be visible and what should not' (Zukin, 1995, p.7). As these spaces undergo pseudo-privatization, these wealthy residents can 'move without obstruction, effort, or engagement' (Sennett, 1994, p. 18) with the social difference actually inscribed in mixed-income neighbourhoods. Empowered to foster the 'illusion of a homogenized public' by filtering out 'the social heterogeneity of the crowd, [and] substituting in its place a flawless fabric of white middle class work, play, and consumption' (Crilley, 1993, p. 154), elite actors are empowered to minimize higher-income residents' exposure to poverty and associated unconventional, undesirable behaviours that would otherwise bleed into the streetscape.

The public spaces in mixed-income neighbourhoods are constructed upon a premise grounded in a perceived need for social order, surveillance and control over the behaviour of their users. Elite actors, most visibly contemporary urban planners and policy practitioners, have forged environments founded upon a desire for control over interaction, for strictly organized recreational opportunities (Garreau, 1991; Sorkin, 1992; Crilley, 1993; Goss, 1993). But in these public spaces, the real danger comes not from children playing unsupervised, nor is it from the disorderly behaviour once darkness falls – as higher-income residents and elite actors have reasoned. Instead, the greatest threat comes from the erosion of the very ideal of the public and the steadfast promotion of private control of public spaces as the mechanism to make the neighbourhood a desirable place to live. Indeed, Vidler (2002) argues that urban life worth living consists of the very notion of publicness itself, but a fear of disorder and unconventional behaviour threatens the publicness of public spaces like Williams-Davis Park in mixed-income neighbourhoods. When anybody (of any class, race or income) is afforded freedom to use neighbourhood space, these higher-income residents perceive a threat to their privacy and property values. In concert with distance elites, tight controls that uphold their sense of ownership and control over urban space have become commonplace.

Unconventional behaviour

In cities around the world, people use public spaces to relax, to protest, to buy and sell, to experiment and to celebrate. The United States Supreme Court bases its public forum doctrine on the notion that since 'time immemorial' people have used the public spaces of the city – the streets, parks and squares – as gathering places for 'communicating between citizens' and 'discussing public questions' (Supreme Court of the United States, 1939, Hague v. Committee for Industrial Organization. *307 US 496*). Nevertheless, public space occupies an important but heavily contested ideological position in democratic societies.

Supporters of tight controls governing public spaces argue that 'disorder' is the primary threat facing urban neighbourhoods. Kelling and Coles (1996, pp. 14–15) define disorder as 'incivility, boorish and threatening behaviour' including the 'obstruction of streets and public spaces' and other offences generally prohibited by law that disrupt urban life. Wilson (1996, quoted in Wortley & Mazerolle, 2013, pp. 258–259) asserts that 'as the number of unconventional individuals increases arithmetically, the number of worrisome behaviours increases geometrically', suggesting that the threat is not so much 'disorder' but merely 'unconventionality'. 'Harm' in this case becomes nothing more than the presence of fear. This logic is evident in mixed-income neighbourhoods where higher-income residents reason that rules prohibiting unconventional behaviour are required if their desired aesthetic of place is to be preserved. This rationale comes from a fear that the actual use of space would otherwise deviate from their ideologies about what conventionality of use ought to be. Untended *disorderly behaviour*, according to Kelling (1987), communicates that nobody cares and thus may lead to increasingly aggressive *criminal behaviours*. Accordingly, merely the potential for citizens to be disorderly is sufficient grounds for enforcing rules that control the use of space. Ultimately, for higher-income residents and their allied elite actors, aesthetics of place take precedence over marginalized individuals' right to exercise their entitlements of citizenship if to do so would negatively impact upon their idealized quality of neighbourhood life.

For these wealthy residents, unconventional uses of public space have a 'devastating effect on a city's image' (Paisner, 1994, p. 1272) since this image impacts 'the quality of urban life, the general feeling of comfort, aesthetics, security, and freedom people should have in their urban public spaces' (Tier, 1998, p. 258). Indeed, many affluent newcomers attracted to mixed-income neighbourhoods would simply prefer that the neighbourhood be reserved for their exclusive use and seek to impose controls that curb undesirable behaviour that does not conform to their desired neighbourhood aesthetic.

The allied elites complicit to the de facto privatization and control of public spaces in mixed-income neighbourhoods ignore that some level of disorder and unpredictability might be necessary for a space to function democratically. Young (1990, p. 119) suggests, 'one should expect to encounter and hear from those who are different, whose social perspectives, experience and affiliations are different' in open and accessible public spaces. However, the functioning of urban public space in mixed-income neighbourhoods rarely aligns with this normative ideal. Instead, these spaces are always and everywhere places of exclusion (Fraser, 1990; Hartley, 1992) and in mixed-income neighbourhoods this exclusion has carefully constructed a homogenous, exclusive public comprising only those whose housing wealth affords them the attention of distance elites.

In contemporary democratic societies everywhere, these notions of the 'public' and the nature of public democracy have developed dialectically with the ideologies of private property rights and the private sphere, and the ability for some citizens to move between private property and public space has shaped the nature of interactions in public (Habermas, 1989; Fraser, 1990; Marston, 1990). In the United States, citizenship was initially claimed through a process where 'owners of private property freely join together to create a public' (Marston, 1990, p. 445). This process was possible because the private sphere represented a place from which white propertied men could venture out into the democratic arena of public space. Publicness was itself exclusionary since it required possession of the right to access private space. Consequently, the public sphere in the United States was a 'profoundly problematic construction' (Marston, 1990, p. 457) comprising a voluntary, exclusive community of private citizens that denied lower socioeconomic classes the right to even access public spaces in everyday life.

The divide between publicity and privacy was a fiction in which citizens 'willingly suspended disbelief' (Morgan, 1988, p. 15) as to the improbability of participation of all in the public sphere. While the normative idea of the Habermasian public sphere holds out hope that a *representative* public can meet (Hartley, 1992), the reality of the public sphere is little more than an 'ideological construction with respect to who belongs to the national community and the relationship of "the people" to formal government' (Marston, 1990, p. 450). Indeed, any re-examination of the normative ideals that frame the nature of public spaces makes plain that those who seek to control public spaces do so in contradiction to the very principles that define democracy itself.

Housing wealth and property rights

Contemporary urban planning principles inscribe difference in the socioeconomic ordering of tenure groups within mixed-income neighbourhoods. This constructed difference sparks a class conflict that triggers demands for control over space and the exploration of alternative ways of experiencing public space (Dennis, 2008, p. 144). This conflict is manifest in two opposing, and perhaps irreconcilable, ideological visions of the nature and purpose of public space made clear by the words of low-income residents and higher-income residents and their allied elites as they seek to explain the struggles that play out in public space. Low-income residents promote a vision of public space characterized by free and unmediated social interactions and the absence of coercion by the institutional influence of elite actors. Meanwhile, the vision of higher-income residents and allied elite actors is fundamentally different. For this latter group, public spaces are controlled – open for recreation by a public of their own choosing and only then to engage in a narrowly prescribed set of behaviours and activities considered 'conventional'. Indeed, while lower-income residents are willing to risk social disorder, the vision for the propertied and affluent is one of control that guarantees order and foregoes freedom of use. Under the vision of low-income residents, public space is also a representation of the *good* that comes from *public* control and ownership, as contested and problematic as these may be. Controlled public spaces, low-income residents argue, lack energy and dynamism – they feel too monitored to allow activity to simply unfold and *be*. This is a corollary of the vision of public space as a place of relatively unmediated interaction: it is a vision of public space that understands that the very publicness of space is a good in and of itself that understands the *collective* right to the city ought to be secured for all citizens.

Although there are exceptions in desirable, dense urban neighbourhoods where space is at a premium, household size, both in numbers and square footage, is predominantly a function of household income and wealth. Private space can be more generously arrayed between members of affluent households who can afford larger housing units. Lower-income households tend to be larger – their individual members have a smaller share of private space and are more dependent upon the opportunities that public space can offer. For public housing residents with limited private space, public space oftentimes becomes more valuable because it extends the lived experience of each resident. Wealthy residents with ample private space can afford for the function of public space to be purely aesthetic: neighbourhood parks should be orderly, quiet and enjoyed from a distance. Lower-income households, by contrast, need functional public spaces: parks should be lived-in, experienced and dynamic because their private space is more constrained.

Property rights are exclusive, which results in property owners choosing to exclude unwanted people from accessing their spaces (Blomley, 2007; Ostrom & Hess, 2008; Blomley & Sturgeon, 2009). But these exclusionary traits extend beyond exclusion of use to include exclusion from participation in the discourse that shapes space in mixed-income neighbourhoods. With the support of elite actors, propertied citizens are equipped to impose a particular geography of privilege governing the use of urban public space. For these privileged citizens, their lived experiences in the private sphere bleeds into their desired aesthetic of public space. In this way, their entitlement to control their experience of private space bleeds outward, expressing as exercise of privilege to control public spaces as well. By possessing property rights that control the use of their private spaces, these citizens are positioned to claim as an entitlement to control public spaces. Accordingly, the possession of private property rights positions higher-income residents to claim de facto property rights over public space, and distance elites are complicit to this claim. The sense of ownership afforded to propertied citizens enables them to control and exclude particular classes of people from these spaces.

When community and condos collide

The right of, or the ability for, representation for low-income residents is continuously challenged and struggled over in mixed-income neighbourhoods. Williams-Davis Park is a space where the entitlements of citizenship, including the rights to use and shape urban space, could be expanded to low-income households. But instead, in the name of comfort, safety and profit, Williams-Davis Park represents a highly commoditized spectacle, promoting the particular idealized vision of urban life desired by those privileged with housing wealth (Garreau, 1991; Boyer, 1992; Crawford, 1992; Mitchell, 1995, 2003; Mitchell & Van Deusan, 2002). The Williams-Davis Park Advisory Council (WDPAC), an elected body of local residents recognized by the Chicago Park District, offers a platform upon which this group's cry and demand can be heard and provides a space for representing their legitimacy within the broader public. According to its by-laws, the purpose of the WDPAC is to promote ways for the community to better utilize the Chicago Park District's programmes and facilities; to provide communication to the District on matters relating to the Williams-Davis Park community and all park patrons; and to increase community awareness by involving all segments of the community and all park patrons in the planning and implementation of WDPAC and Chicago Park District projects (Williams-Davis Park Advisory Council, 2014). Attendance records reveal that the majority of regular attendees are public housing residents, and only one homeowner attends on a semi-regular basis. These residents are joined by representatives from property management from the mixed-income sites, the Chicago Park District, the CHA and the local Alderman's office. I was elected President of the WDPAC at its September 2014 meeting. Three public housing residents filled the remaining board seats.

The battle of the barbecues

Early in the redevelopment process, local residents were invited to attend a series of community meetings. The first meeting was held on 8 September 2004 to present an overview of the park project to local residents, elite actors and other stakeholders interested in transforming the Oakland neighbourhood (BauerLatoza Studio, 2004a). Attendees expressed a desire to 'celebrate local heritage through educational/informational features [and] create a park that will be a regional draw' (BauerLatoza Studio, 2004b). At the second meeting held on 29 September 2004, attendees expressed that game tables would be a desirable feature in the new park. These discussions prompted a final meeting on 3 November 2004 to discuss incorporating a chess area for senior citizens and enlarging the entry area to the park which is now home to a public art installation designed by a local resident (BauerLatoza Studio, 2004c).

The final design of the park included two games tables located in a small paved section of the park immediately to the north of the playground (see Figure 9.3). While local residents expressed an awareness of the chess boards affixed to the table tops, over 80 per cent of those interviewed identified the tables as 'picnic tables' given their frequent appropriation as an eating place for groups barbecuing in the open area to the north of the playground. Unhappy that this behaviour did not adhere to their desired aesthetic of public space, several homeowners complained to allied elites and the Chicago Park District posted signage that stated that barbecuing was not permitted:

> It's unsightly for *them* to be out in the park barbecuing. The park was not designed for that, they should go elsewhere. If I see people barbecue, I'll go and tell them 'hey no, you can't barbecue here! This is a park for *our community*, and it's *not for you*'
>
> (Homeowner, emphasis in interview)

Low-income residents generally adopt more inclusive definitions of 'community' susceptible to the risk of disorder that certain behaviours might bring because they did not view behaviours such as barbecuing as problematic in and of themselves. These residents also tended to be more sympathetic to the reality that those barbecuing in the park had few other alternatives: they did not have private spaces of their own, and public spaces where barbecuing was permitted were several blocks away and, in the case of the nearby beach, charged users to use the car park:

> Williams-Davis Park is *a community park*, and it's *for everyone* to use. As long as people are behaving and cleaning up, what's the problem?
>
> (Public housing resident, emphasis in interview)

These divergent interpretations about the permitted uses of public space and who was afforded membership within the local community amplify the socio-economic difference inscribed in mixed-income neighbourhoods and deepens the geography of exclusion of low-income residents. Those without their own private property expressed resentment towards their propertied neighbours who garnered the support of distance elites to impose a controlled aesthetic over public spaces. One elected representative for local public housing residents blames these distance elites for contributing to the destruction of a sense of community in the new mixed-income neighbourhood:

Property management and the rules divide the community. The community is divided because of property managers and the CHA. It's one place, one voice, if your unit burns up, so does mine. You get a fire, you get a flood, those sprinklers go off, so do mine. If my pipes are backing up, that means yours are too because we're back-to-back. *So how can we be different?* We're breathing the same air – it's the management and the CHA that creates this difference, this divide.

(Public housing resident, emphasis in interview)

Several elite actors acknowledge the destructive potential of socioeconomic difference in mixed-income neighbourhoods and are sympathetic to the challenges that class conflicts can present:

A lot of the homeowners ask why [the public housing residents] can't just barbeque in their house or on their patio? They don't have that, that's the thing – the reality is not everyone has private outdoor space or open space. When people get frustrated, they have to consider that not everybody has access to that. People's concepts of home are different.

(Affordable housing legal professional)

But others dismiss any suggestion that they favour higher-income residents by promoting the controlled aesthetic vision of space held by higher-income residents and instead maintain that social control is universally desired: 'I don't think there's too much that's dissimilar about the people that live here because they're living here for a reason' (Property development professional). The ability to have one's needs and desires represented through a politics of representation in mixed-income neighbourhoods hinges upon who possesses the right to use, occupy and shape neighbourhood space. But when these place-making practices are not open to all residents, possessing cultural, social and economic capital becomes critical since it is those residents with the most who are positioned to influence elite actors' actions. The networks of affiliation associated with high cultural capital (Bourdieu, 1986), for instance, position higher-income residents to act more effectively in influencing elite actors than lower-income residents without these alliances to those with the power to effect neighbourhood change (DeKeseredy et al., 2003).

Common space without common ground

Contestations over competing visions of space exist not only in the public spaces between mixed-income housing developments but inside them as well. Property management impose strict controls over the use of the community room, the outdoor patio, the lobby, the hallways and other common areas. Residents are required to sign agreements holding them accountable to a list of 'house rules': no loitering, no barbecuing, no alcohol, no use of the kitchen adjoining the

Figure 9.3 Game tables in Williams-Davis Park (photo by author).

community room, and so on. These rules create tensions between residents of different tenure groups about what should constitute appropriate use of these shared spaces. Elite actors maintain that the strict regulations are needed to maintain functionality of space:

> It's easier to say that there's a rule for everyone, or just rules in general, and we have to abide by them.
>
> (Property management professional)

> I do believe there is a common core of shared expectations for behaviour that people should have that makes living in a place like this easier and more enjoyable.
>
> (Property development professional)

A blame culture emerges from these spatial contestations and amplifies the difference inscribed in mixed-income developments as residents and elite actors wrestle with competing visions of use. For most market-rate residents, these spaces are viewed as an extension to their private property and are therefore subject to their control. Many lower-income residents, by contrast, tended to desire more freedom to use and occupy these spaces in alignment with their vision for public space.

Some residents even call into question the very existence of these spaces if their use is so tightly controlled and mediated:

> Downstairs in the lobby area – residents should be able to sit. You got a lobby, you got a social room – why would you build a lobby with chairs where you can't sit and chat and build a social room that people can't use?
>
> (Public housing resident)

Market-rate residents generally expressed satisfaction with the house rules and the control that they afforded. These residents had limited interest in using the communal spaces, and preferred to participate in recreational activities in the confines of their own homes or outside of the immediate neighbourhood. Other market-rate residents were unsatisfied by the amenities available in the building, expressing dissatisfaction about the absence of fitness rooms and other amenities usually associated with new market-rate rental buildings elsewhere in the city.

Elite actors suggest that the divide is grounded in divergent perceptions of housing and home, and that socioeconomic mix will not ameliorate the way in which space is conceived:

> No matter how many regulatory agreements we draft, it's never going to get to the core of how people see home. For a lot of people, the lobby is part of their house, and for others, it's a thoroughfare to get to their mailbox and to their unit. Neither is right or wrong, they're just different. Mixed-income communities do not and cannot address that difference.
>
> (Affordable housing legal professional)

Elite actors and privileged residents have little desire to share their neighbourhoods with unconventional people in general, but even more unsightly to the privileged is the congregation of many unconventional people in the spaces they seek to control. The next development phase at Sullivan Station includes the construction of a number of owner-occupied townhouses. At mixed-income developments elsewhere, the presence of homeowners intensifies the socioeconomic divisions inscribed in space. Homeowners in these mixed-income developments justify their right to restrict and control the uses of these communal spaces upon their financial investment in the neighbourhood. By maintaining that these spaces ought to function as an extension of their private property, public housing residents face still greater barriers that prevent their freedom to use the spaces they consider 'public':

> You have some homeowners who think, just think 'I own this.' They think because they own that they have the right. But they only own the little section they pay for. They *don't* own the hallways, they *don't* own the parks, and they *don't* own the libraries – but they dictate to others anyway.
>
> (Elected representative for public housing residents,
> emphasis in interview)

More than half of the market-rate renters interviewed at Sullivan Station believe that the use of communal spaces ought to be restricted to behaviours that aligned with their 'conventional' social norms. It was not uncommon for these residents to justify their entitlement to control these spaces upon the fact they paid more in rent than subsidized residents for the same facilities. At the same time, a number of low-income residents were reluctant to raise complaints about the rules to elite actors fearing the loss of their housing subsidy. Unlike many of these low-income residents who may jeopardize their subsidy if they wanted to relocate, these market-rate residents could relocate without facing repercussions and could use their higher rent as currency in negotiations to claim control over the use of communal space. Elite actors acknowledge that rent can be used as currency in the 'social contract' inherent with occupying a rented housing unit:

> Honestly, my whole thing is, we got a lease – it's a contract. We have a building that is now your home – and my assumption is that you want to enjoy it, and have it be a nice place, and have people come here and think it's a great place [. . .] because part of what you're doing, in paying rent, is for a certain amount of uniformity in terms of behaviour, and like-minded people.
>
> (Property development professional)

> I think in the instances that we do have issues, we try to engage people in a constructive and rational dialogue about that kind of stuff, and see where we end up because it will cost us more money if it's a conflict . . . It's more to our benefit that we have retention than turnover because turnover costs money. So, our preference is to make this place the best place that it can be, so people stay, and we had them for more than one year, because, ultimately, the cost of turning over one unit ends up affecting the bottom line.
>
> (Property development professional)

Higher-income residents are undoubtedly better positioned to capture the interest and support of elite actors than low-income residents in mixed-income neighbourhoods. While they deny doing so, it does appear that elite actors align their efforts in support of the constructed idealized urban life sought by higher-income residents in mixed-income neighbourhoods because the loss of these residents adversely impacts their profits.

Geographies of privilege: influence and distance elites

Oakland residents come together across tenure lines to identify three 'hot spots' where individuals appropriate neighbourhood space for illicit purposes such as public drinking, drug use and (occasionally) violent crime. Once night falls, large groups of individuals descend upon the game tables in Williams-Davis Park, a canopy of large trees lining a large vacant lot directly across from Lake Parc Place, and in the vicinity of a dilapidated pedestrian bridge at 43rd Street. Residents condemn this negative appropriation of space in interviews and frequently spoke out against such behaviours at Chicago Alternative Policing Strategy (CAPS) meetings, the WDPAC, and other community meetings:

> It is a breach of the peace right in my front yard.
>
> (Public housing resident)

> I wouldn't even feel comfortable walking my dog out there when it gets dark and I'm a big guy! Nope, I'm not going over there at night.
>
> (LIHTC renter)

> Until recently, no one felt safe in this neighbourhood no matter what time of day, so the positive activity in the daytime is encouraging. I see mothers outside with their pushchairs when it's light out, but until we see those same women in the evenings when it's dark, something is wrong.
>
> (Market-rate renter)

At these community meetings, residents proposed solutions that would discourage the unwanted appropriation of space and the presence of outsiders – or at the very least move their behaviour elsewhere. Local residents suggested activating the disabled lights located within Williams-Davis Park, removing the trees that disguised the presence of loitering adjacent to Lake Parc Place, and the closure of the 43rd Street pedestrian bridge at nightfall. Two of these requests were realized: the lights were activated in autumn of 2014 after the WDPAC raised the issue of negative activity in the park with the CHA, local elected officials, the Chicago Park District and the Chicago Police Department. The trees were removed following a series of resident complaints about heightened criminal activity. Unfortunately, elite actors would not allow for the closure of the bridge after-hours citing high costs and disagreement about who should bear the financial burden since the bridge spanned land owned by numerous city and state agencies. Each of these resident-driven interventions present natural experiments to test Whyte's (1980) assertion that simple alterations to the built environment could result in transformative change to the lived experience of citizens.

The switch on

Observational data were collected in Williams-Davis Park at two-hour intervals over 12 24-hour periods, including three weekdays and three weekend days both before and after the lights were activated. These observations recorded the number of users in the park by gender and age group, their approximate location, and the range of activities they appeared to be participating in. Figures 9.4, 9.5, 9.6 and 9.7 present observations taken at 4 pm and 2 am on two weekends three weeks apart before and after the lights were activated. The maps are representative of the average use, both in number of users and variety of activities, across all observational periods at these times.

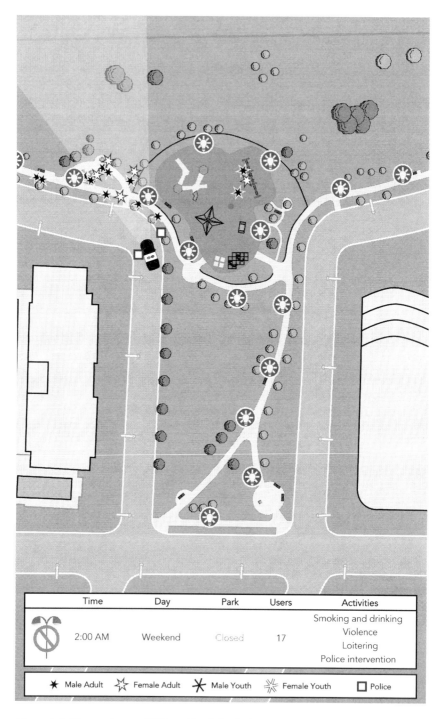

Time	Day	Park	Users	Activities
2:00 AM	Weekend	Closed	17	Smoking and drinking Violence Loitering Police intervention

★ Male Adult   ☆ Female Adult   ✳ Male Youth   ⚹ Female Youth   ☐ Police

Figure 9.4 Observations at Williams-Davis Park (2 am, lights disabled).

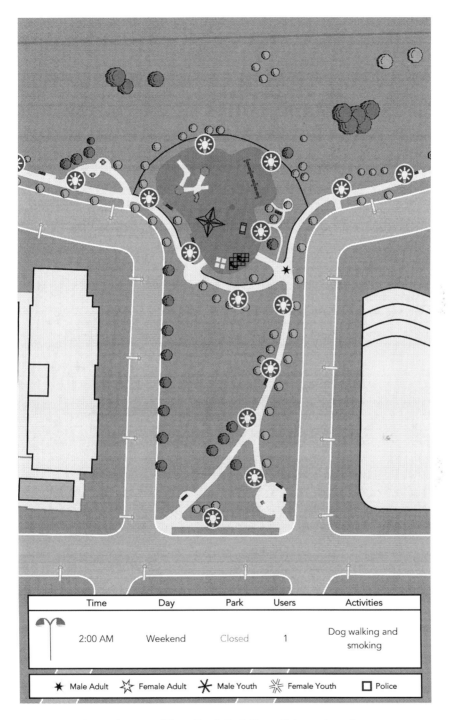

Time	Day	Park	Users	Activities
2:00 AM	Weekend	Closed	1	Dog walking and smoking

✹ Male Adult   ✪ Female Adult   ✳ Male Youth   ⁂ Female Youth   ☐ Police

Figure 9.5 Observations at Williams-Davis Park (2 am, lights activated).

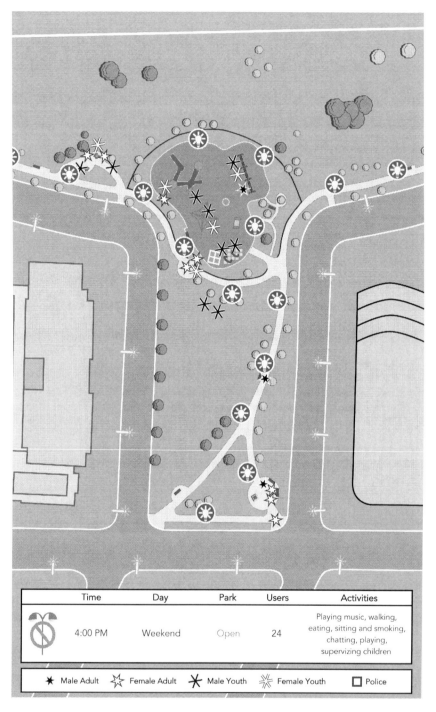

Time	Day	Park	Users	Activities
4:00 PM	Weekend	Open	24	Playing music, walking, eating, sitting and smoking, chatting, playing, supervizing children

★ Male Adult ☆ Female Adult ✳ Male Youth ✳ Female Youth ☐ Police

Figure 9.6 Observations at Williams-Davis Park (4 pm, lights disabled).

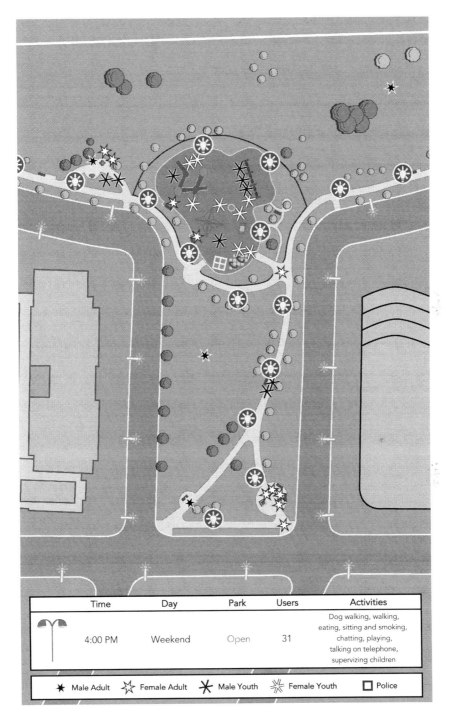

	Time	Day	Park	Users	Activities
	4:00 PM	Weekend	Open	31	Dog walking, walking, eating, sitting and smoking, chatting, playing, talking on telephone, supervizing children

★ Male Adult   ☆ Female Adult   ✳ Male Youth   ⁕ Female Youth   ☐ Police

Figure 9.7 Observations at Williams-Davis Park (4 pm, lights activated).

Park use differed very slightly between weekday and weekend observations. Most obviously, children made use of the park earlier in the day on weekends when they were not in school. The park was well-used by adults on both week-days and weekend observations during daylight hours, though adults were present with slightly higher frequency on weekends, presumably because many adults held jobs on weekdays. Police attended to late-night park activity during five of the six observational periods (three weekend and two weekday) before the lights were activated. Police did not actively intervene in activity in the park following the activation of lights, but their presence was occasionally recorded in the sur-rounding streets during their routine patrols. Ultimately, with the desired aesthetic of place restored to the park, daytime activity following the intervention slightly increased which aligned with intercept survey results that revealed that park users felt safer with the lights activated and felt more comfortable with their children using the playground area after dusk.

From snow cones to chainsaws

Directly across from Lake Parc Place on the west side of Lake Park Avenue sits a privately owned vacant lot fenced off from the street, save for a cutaway (no more than 30 metres in length) around a line of large trees. This cutaway provided a haven for loitering where groups would congregate around parked vehicles. During the warmer months, these individuals would often pose as street vendors offering snow cones for sale in an apparent effort to disguise drug transactions, according to several residents. The trees provided shelter and camouflage to these individuals whose presence rendered the western pavement effectively unusable. Theft and harassment were commonly reported by residents who expressed fear and reluctance about using the street:

> We try and avoid it whenever we can – it's just not worth the risk. We don't feel safe, and we will roll up our windows and lock our doors. It's especially unsafe once it gets dark and they hang out under those trees.
>
> (Homeowner)

A local teenager was shot from a passing car at this location in the summer of 2014. This act sparked an increase in complaints from residents about the heightened criminal activity and its impact on safety and the area was officially designated a problem area at a CAPS meeting. Several homeowners at this meeting were particularly vocal about how crime threatens their property values. This was a complaint well-received from the elite actors in attendance. Following these com-plaints, the trees were removed by City of Chicago contractors and illicit activity dissipated overnight.

Observational data were collected along the 3900–4000 block of Lake Park Avenue both before and after the city removed the trees. Observations were taken at two-hour intervals over eight 24-hour periods, including two weekdays and two weekend days before and after the removal. Figures 9.8 and 9.9 show representative observations from two weekends, one before the trees were removed and the other afterwards at 4 pm and 2 am. The number of individuals present at 2 am reduced from 32 to four following the removal of trees. An intercept survey conducted at the adjacent bus stops confirmed that residents felt safer and more comfortable walking the street after nightfall.

This alteration to the built environment transformed the way in which the street was used by local residents. While elite actors had already attempted to make plain that illicit behaviour would not be tolerated by installing security cameras

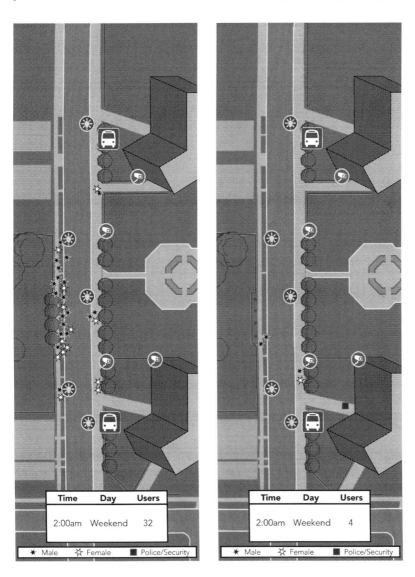

Figure 9.8 Observations at 3900–4000 block of Lake Park Avenue (2 am).

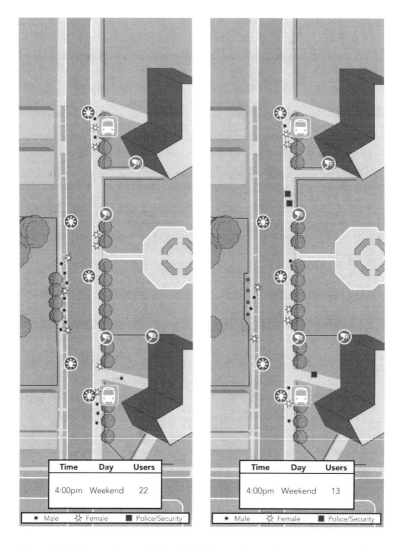

Figure 9.9 Observations at 3900–4000 block of Lake Park Avenue (4 pm).

and stationing police and security officers in the immediate area in response to persistent complaints from residents, this simple alteration, made possible only by the influence of higher-income residents over elite actors, afforded residents the ability to reclaim the streetscape to conform to their desired aesthetic.

Restoring the neighbourhood aesthetic

When an external threat bleeds into the everyday life of a mixed-income neighbour-hood, higher-income residents are privileged to secure and reclaim neighbourhood space to conform to their desired aesthetic in concert with distance elites. In Oakland, higher-income residents and distance elites successfully re-appropriated the neighbourhood through these simple alterations to impose their own ideological aesthetic of how space ought to be represented to the wider community.

In poverty-stricken neighbourhoods, these threats often continue precisely because those opposing them lack the agency to effect change. As a result of this socio-political environment favouring those with greater means, low-income residents are seldom able to command the attention of policymakers. Affluent newcomers have proven themselves more adept at this task, even in smaller numbers. To restore the built environment in a narrow, controlled aesthetic of place, the wealthy rely on their own privilege and influence. Although sometimes their opinions run counter to public housing residents and other low-income renters, their influence could be key to establishing and maintaining a higher quality of life in mixed-income neighbourhoods. However, the question remains: if the aesthetic of a vibrant mixed-income neighbourhood is controlled by the input of wealthy elites, does it truly reflect the community who wish to call it home?

The uneven geographies of housing wealth

The rationale for the appeal of mixed-income neighbourhoods among policymaking circles is perhaps better articulated in the negative than in the positive. It is certainly easier for policymakers to point to all that is wrong with socioeconomic segregation than to convincingly affirm that socioeconomic integration puts things right. Despite sustained efforts to implement mixed-income policies, policymakers have achieved little more than the spatial integration of socioeconomic classes. But the spatial integration actually achieved is quite apart from social integration that mixed-income policies claim to accomplish. Being in close proximity neither guarantees nor even necessarily encourages social interaction across tenure lines, and even if it does, this variety of interaction may produce nothing more than destructive class conflict (Spinner-Halev, 2012). While segregation is undeniably a barrier to social justice, it does not necessarily follow that integration alone is the solution. Even accounting for the benefits laid out in the political economy of place narratives, little is done, and it may very well be its undoing by creating mixed-income neighbourhoods that privilege higher-income residents and fail to address the wider social cleavages or ameliorate the life chances and opportunities to exercise citizenship entitlements for the poor.

In a class-based society driven by private property, geographical conflicts are best understood to be over the legitimacy of various uses of space, and thus of various strategies for asserting the right to exercise entitlements by those who are disenfranchised as a result of the nature of private property rights and the support of elite actors these rights bring forth. To overcome the geography of exclusion, we must seek out alternative mechanisms. Alternatives are perhaps best achieved through financial innovation in the housing market that neutralize the significance of tenure and housing wealth in mixed-income neighbourhoods and afford equal rights and entitlements to residents of all incomes and socioeconomic classes.

Struggles for the right to the city and its spaces must establish a new kind of social order that neutralizes the significance of private property rights. Rather than being constructed around the wishes and claims of higher-income residents and their influence over elite actors, this new order ought to be constructed so as to fulfil the needs of all citizens instead of merely acting in response to the fears of higher-income residents to preserve a particular neighbourhood aesthetic.

Instead, planners of spaces like Williams-Davis Park assert that control-led diversity is more profitable in terms of framing the vision of idealized urban life than the promotion of the difference actually inscribed in mixed-income neighbourhoods. Even as marginalized groups claim the right to inhabit the city and assert their right to exercise their entitlements of citizenship, the homogenization of 'the public' continues to exclude low-income residents from full participation in society. The particular diversity encouraged in mixed-income neighbourhoods is one engineered to unify and homogenize individuals towards commodification of space. But if citizens are unwilling to adhere to this narrow 'consumption' of specified activities they become marginalized from the public and their claims to exercise citizenship entitlements are disregarded.

This attempt to homogenize the public has forged landscapes in which social interactions are carefully planned (Zukin, 1991; Sorkin, 1992; Wilson, 1992) in accordance with the idealized vision of urban life dictated by higher-income residents. These representations of place have come to dominate the discourse driving the construction of new public spaces in mixed-income neighbourhoods (Lefebvre, 1991; Zukin, 1991; Crilley, 1993). According to Amin (2008), public spaces that afford freedom of use produce new rhythms of life and possibility. But the designed and contrived diversity sought after in the planning of mixed-income neighbourhoods has created marketable landscapes that appeal to the affluent and the propertied attracted to a narrowly defined aesthetic of place. Ultimately, the particular vision of urban life held by low-income residents is cast aside, alienating them from their own neighbourhood. The possibilities of unscripted social interactions are lost to the increasing control of the dominant social class over the production and use of space in mixed-income neighbourhoods.

Concluding remarks: overcoming the geographies of exclusion

It is clear that the rights of low-income residents under the current configuration of mixed-income neighbourhoods are severely constrained. By controlling individuals' engagement with space, policymakers are failing miserably to embrace the difference actually inscribed in space and expand opportunities to exercise citizenship entitlements for all. The uneven geographies of housing wealth fashion public spaces that run contrary to the core tenets of mixed-income neighbourhoods. The public spaces actually existing in mixed-income neighbourhoods are spaces of exclusion because the range of spatial engagement is so frighteningly narrow. In an effort to extend the right to the city and its public spaces to low-income residents, Vidler (2002, p.85, emphasis added) calls for 'alternatives that retain the dense and vital mix of uses critical to urban life, rethinking the exclusions stemming from out-dated zoning, real estate values and *private ownership*'. If we are to believe that securing the entitlements of citizenship for all is the intent of mixed-income housing policies, then we must explore mechanisms that mitigate the significance of tenure to overcome the power that affluence, property ownership and housing wealth command over the rhythms of everyday life in mixed-income neighbourhoods.

For mixed-income neighbourhoods to achieve their aims, we might look to smooth the uneven geographies of housing wealth that disenfranchise low-income residents through innovation in the housing market and wealth accumulation policies. These policies might include shared-equity housing strategies including community land trusts, deed-restricted housing and limited-equity co-operatives. 'Care-full' financial innovation (Smith, 2005) in the housing market would further serve to mediate the destructive geographies of exclusion that mark lower-income residents as inherently 'worth-less' following the tacit presumption that they have less to offer than those able to make greater economic investment in the making of a neighbourhood. By engaging in these innovative approaches to the housing market, new opportunities might be forged wherein socioeconomic mixing presents real, tangible opportunities for lower-income citizens to produce neighbourhood spaces and exercise their own citizenship entitlements rather than relying on the benevolence of their more privileged neighbours.

To achieve these ends, we might consider financial instruments that decouple decisions about housing consumption from wealth management behaviours (Smith, 2015). Affording households the opportunity to choose what proportion of any investment returns on their property they wish to buy into will neutralize the significance of housing wealth and smooth the power differentials between residents of mixed-income neighbourhoods. Such innovation presents myriad options for households to part-buy, part-rent, part-share and part-steward in housing systems and might solve not only the crisis of residential capitalism but also facilitate the exercising of citizenship entitlements for all.

Williamson (2010) maintains that democracy commands at least a tacit acceptance of a shared fate and future within society, irrespective of one's socioeconomic class. If mixed-income policies are to have a role in making our urban environment more just, residents must be in proximity on their own terms. Moreover, those terms must command some level of equivalence instead of deepening the geography of exclusion. Undeniably, financial innovation will not necessarily reduce conflicts around ideological aesthetics of place because the sensibilities and attitudes of wealthy residents will not change. However, neutralizing the significance of the tenure divide by expanding the rights of low-income residents may influence the perceptions of the next wealthy newcomers vying to move to these transforming neighbourhoods. If low-income residents can access the benefits codified in housing wealth, more affluent residents will recognize that other residents too have a right to shape neighbourhood aesthetics. At that point, higher-income households can decide whether to accept that aesthetic, or leave it, rather than presume that they can assert control over neighbourhood space.

By default, public spaces represent the desires and sensibilities of propertied, wealthy community members. The struggles that manifest themselves in the function of public space are clashes of class that have been compressed geographically in mixed-income neighbourhoods. If the right to the city experienced in public spaces is to be extended to its marginalized citizens, geographically-oriented integrationist efforts alone are not the answer. Through innovation in the housing market we can bestow the privileges usually only extended to the wealthy, overcoming geographies of exclusion to afford every citizen the opportunity to find that there is space *for* them.

References

Amin, A. (2008). Collective culture and urban public space. *City, 12*, 5–24.

August, M. (2008). Social mix and Canadian public housing redevelopment: Experiences in Toronto. *Canadian Journal of Urban Research, 17*, 82–100.

BauerLatoza Studio. (2004a). Park #532 – Community Meeting #1 (8 September). PowerPoint presentation and slide notes, meeting in Chicago, IL.

BauerLatoza Studio. (2004b). Park #532 – Community Meeting #2 (29 September). PowerPoint presentation and slide notes, meeting in Chicago, IL.

BauerLatoza Studio. (2004c). Park #532 – Community Meeting #3 (3 November). PowerPoint presentation and slide notes, meeting in Chicago, IL.

BauerLatoza Studio. (2015). Chicago Park District Park 532. Retrieved from www.bauerlatozastudio.com/portfolio/site-desig/chicago-park-district-park-532/.

Blomley, N. (2007). The borrowed view: Privacy, propriety, and the entanglements of property. *Law & Social Inquiry, 30*, 617–661.

Blomley, N., & Sturgeon, J. C. (2009). Property as abstraction. *International Journal of Urban and Regional Research, 33*, 564–566.

Bourdieu, P. (1986). The forms of capital. In J. G. Richardson (Ed.), *Handbook of theory and research for the sociology of education* (pp. 241–258). New York: Greenwood Press.

Boyer, C. (1992). Cities for sale: Merchandising history at South Street Seaport. In M. Sorkin (Ed.), *Variations on a theme park: The new American city and the end of public space* (pp. 181–204). New York: Hill and Wang.

Brophy, P. C., & Smith, R. N. (1997). Mixed-income housing: Factors for success. *Cityscape, 3*, 3–31.

Castells, M. (1996). *The rise of the network society*. Oxford: Blackwell.

Chaskin, R. J. & Joseph, M. L. (2013). 'Positive' gentrification, social control and the 'right to the city' in mixed-income communities: Uses and expectations of space and place. *International Journal of Urban and Regional Research, 37*, 480–502.

Chaskin, R. J., & Joseph, M. L. (2015). *Integrating the inner city: The promise and perils of mixed-income public housing transformation*. Chicago, IL: University of Chicago Press.

Chicago Housing Authority. (2000). *Chicago Housing Authority: Plan for transformation*. Chicago, IL.

Chicago Housing Authority. (2013). *Plan forward: Communities that work*. Chicago, IL: Chicago Housing Authority.

Chicago Park District. (2015). Williams-Davis Park. Retrieved from www.chicagoparkdistrict.com/parks/williams---davis-park/.

Clarke, P. (2013). *Chicago park names recognize influential Black Americans, but why not more?* Medill Reports Chicago. Retrieved from http://newsarchive.medill.northwestern.edu/chicago/news-215285.html.

Crawford, M. (1992). The world in a shopping mall. In M. Sorkin (Ed.), *Variations on a theme park: The new American city and the end of public space* (pp. 3–30). New York: Hill and Wang.

Crilley, D. (1993). Megastructures and urban change: Aesthetics, ideology and design. In P. L. Knox (Ed.), *The restless urban landscape* (pp. 127–164). Englewood Cliffs, NJ: Prentice Hall.

Davis, M. (1990). *City of quartz: Excavating the future in Los Angeles.* London: Verso.

DeFilippis, J., & Fraser, J. C. (2010). Why do we want mixed-income housing and neighborhoods? In J. S. Davies & D. L. Imbroscio (Eds.), *Critical urban studies: New directions* (pp. 135–146). Albany: State University of New York Press.

Dekeseredy, W. S., Shahid, A., Schwartz, M. D., & Tomazzewski, A. (2003). *Under siege: Poverty and crime in a public housing community.* Lanham, MD: Lexington Books.

Dennis, R. (2008). *Cities in modernity: Representations and productions of metropolitan space, 1840–1930.* Cambridge: Cambridge University Press.

Draper, Kramer & The Community Builders. (1999). *Lakefront site redevelopment proposal.* Chicago, IL.

Duke, J. (2009). Mixed income housing policy and public housing residents' 'right to the city'. *Critical Social Policy, 29,* 100–120.

Elwood, S., Lawson, V., & Nowak, S. (2014). Middle-class poverty politics: Making place, making people. *Annals of the Association of American Geographers, 105,* 123–143.

Fraser, N. (1990). Rethinking the public sphere: A contribution to the critique of actually existing democracy. *Social Text, 26,* 56–80.

Garreau, J. (1991). *Edge city: Life on the new frontier.* New York: Doubleday.

Goss, J. (1993). The 'magic of the mall': An analysis of form, function, and meaning in the contemporary retail built environment. *Annals of the Association of American Geographers, 83,* 18–47.

Habermas, J. (1989). *The structural transformation of the public sphere. An inquiry into a category of bourgeois society* (trans. T. Burger & F. Lawrence). Cambridge, MA: MIT Press.

Hartley, J. (1992). *The politics of pictures: The creation of the public in the age of popular media.* London: Routledge.

Harvey, D. (1989). *The condition of postmodernity: An enquiry into the origins of social change.* Oxford: Basil Blackwell.

Hunt, D. B. (2009). *Blueprint for disaster: The unravelling of Chicago public housing.* Chicago, IL: University of Chicago Press.

Joseph, M. L., Chaskin, R. J., & Webber, H. S. (2007). The theoretical basis for addressing poverty through mixed-income development. *Urban Affairs Review, 42*(3), 369–409.

Kelling, G. (1987). A taste for order: Community and police. *Crime and Delinquency, 33*(1), 90–102.

Kelling, G., & Coles, C. (1996). *Fixing broken windows: Restoring order and reducing crime in our communities.* New York: Free Press.

Lefebvre, H. (1991). *The production of space.* Oxford: Blackwell.

Lefebvre, H. (1996). *Writings on cities* (selection of writings, Eds. E. Kofman & E. Lebas). Oxford: Blackwell.

Lewis, O. (1975). *Five families: Mexican case studies in the culture of poverty.* New York: Basic Books.

Marston, S. A. (1990). Who are "the people"? Gender, citizenship, and the making of the American nation. *Environment and Planning D: Society and Space, 8,* 449–458.

Mitchell, D. (1995). The end of public space? People's park, definitions of the public, and democracy. *Annals of the Association of American Geographers, 85,* 108–133.

Mitchell, D. (2003). *The right to the city: Social justice and the fight for public space*. New York: Guilford Press.

Mitchell, D., & Van Deusan, R. (2002). Downsview Park: A missed opportunity for a truly public space? In J. Czerniak (Ed.), *CASE: Downsview Park* (pp. 102–113). Cambridge, MA: Harvard School of Design/Prestel Publishers.

Morgan, E. (1988). *Inventing the people: The rise of popular sovereignty in England and America*. New York: W. W. Norton.

Ostrom, E., & Hess, C. (2008). Private and common property rights. In *Encyclopedia of law & economics*. Northampton, MA: Edward Elgar.

Paisner, S. (1994). Compassion, politics and the problems lying on our sidewalks: A legislative approach for cities to address homelessness. *Temple Law Review, 67*, 1259–1306.

Putnam, R. (2000). *Bowling alone: The collapse and revival of American community*. London: Simon & Schuster.

Schwartz, A., & Tajbakhsh, K. (1997). Mixed-income housing: Unanswered questions. *Cityscape, 3*, 71–92.

Sennett, R. (1994). *Flesh and stone: The body and the city in Western civilization*. London: Faber and Faber.

Smith, S. J. (2005). States, markets and an ethic of care. *Political Geography, 24*, 1–20.

Smith, S. J. (2015). Owner occupation: At home in a spatial, financial paradox. *International Journal of Housing Policy, 15*, 61–83.

Sorkin, M. (1992). *Variations on a theme park. The new American city and the end of public space*. New York: Hill and Wang.

Spinner-Halev, J. (2012). *Enduring injustice*. Cambridge: Cambridge University Press.

Tier, R. (1998). Restoring order in urban public spaces. *Texas Review of Law and Politics, 2*, 211–291.

Vale, L. J., & Graves, E. (2010). The Chicago Housing Authority's plan for transformation: What does the research show so far? Chicago, IL: John D. and Catherine T. MacArthur Foundation.

Vidler, A. (2002). A city transformed: Designing 'defensible space'. *Grey Room, 7*, 82–85.

Whyte, W. H. (1980). *The social life of small urban spaces*. New York: Project for Public Spaces.

Williams-Davis Park Advisory Council. (2014). *WDPAC Bylaws*. Chicago, IL.

Williamson, T. (2010). *Sprawl, justice and citizenship: The civic costs of the American way of life*. New York: Oxford University Press.

Wilson, A. (1992). *The culture of nature: North American landscape from Disney to the Exxon Valdez*. Oxford: Basil Blackwell.

Wilson, W. J. (1987). *The truly disadvantaged: The inner city, the underclass, and public policy*. Chicago, IL: University of Chicago Press.

Wortley, R., & Mazerolle, L. (2013). *Environmental criminology and crime analysis*. London: Routledge.

Young, I. (1990). *Justice and the politics of difference*. Princeton, NJ: Princeton University Press.

Zukin, S. (1991). *Landscapes of power: From Detroit to Disney World*. Berkeley: University of California Press.

Zukin, S. (1995). *The culture of cities*. Cambridge, MA: Blackwell.

10 Examining the transformation of Regent Park, Toronto

Prioritizing hard and soft infrastructure

Shauna Brail, Ekaterina Mizrokhi and
Sonia Ralston

Introduction

Regent Park, a neighbourhood in the centre of Toronto, is the site of the largest public housing development in Canada. In 2005, a $1 billion (all monetary figures in this chapter are in Canadian dollars) transformation of the neighbourhood was initiated in an effort to improve the quality of housing and quality of life for the area's residents. The redevelopment process, focused on creating a mixed-income neighbourhood with both non-market and market housing, has been underway for just over a decade and is approximately half complete. The neighbourhood already demonstrates signs of significant transformation in the form of new residential buildings with market and non-market units, a variety of community facilities, commercial activity and street grid extensions that now connect the previously inaccessible neighbourhood to its surroundings. Regent Park, once a neighbourhood stigmatized by dilapidated, concentrated public housing and disinvestment, is becoming a vibrant and desirable residential and recreational part of the city, while continuing to be home to a large number of low-income residents (Micallef, 2013).

The redevelopment process, first initiated in the 1990s and ultimately approved by Toronto City Council in 2005, stemmed initially from resident requests for neighbourhood change (interview, former resident, 6 March 2014). The dramatic transformation plans were developed alongside significant community consultation (Gladki, 2013). Regent Park's ultimate revitalization is the result of a partnership between the Toronto Community Housing Corporation (TCH), the City of Toronto, the Daniels Corporation (a private developer) and Regent Park community leaders. The redevelopment is grounded in an attempt to create a socially inclusive neighbourhood. It is relatively unique among public housing redevelopment initiatives in that full replacement of the 2,083 non-market housing units that existed on the site prior to redevelopment is a key tenet of the plan. An additional 5,400 market units are being built on the site as well, over a five-phase process that is currently in phase 3 and in the twelfth year of the process.

Constructed in the post-Second World War era, the neighbourhood of Regent Park in Toronto was built according to the Garden City model. Crime, sub-standard housing and poverty plagued the housing project (see August, 2014).

Our analysis of publicly accessible documentation from the City of Toronto, TCH and the Daniels Corporation, together with interview materials, allows for an evaluation of the strategies, intentions and outcomes of the relevant parties' efforts. Our findings are based on 32 interviews with residents, community leaders, organization representatives, planners, politicians and others engaged and involved in decision-making processes in Regent Park.

This chapter explores the shifting emphasis on the building of both physical infrastructure, including buildings, roads and community facilities, and 'softer' forms of infrastructure, for example, social networks, and their dual roles in promoting community-building in Regent Park. Soft infrastructure, a term sometimes used interchangeably with social infrastructure, refers to support for human and social capital, including institutions that facilitate the integral community-building necessary for a satisfactory quality of life for residents (Evans, 2007). Soft infrastructure is increasingly understood as being vital alongside the physical process of building community in a transforming environment, though not always sufficiently supported. This is evidenced not only in the literature (Bradford, 2007; Evans, 2007; Oakley et al., 2015), but also in policy focused documentation highlighting that 'while traditionally infrastructure includes physical construction like buildings, roads, railways and utilities, cities increasingly recognize that natural systems and social constructs are core infrastructure for successful cities' (Canadian Urban Institute, 2015). Evans (2007) suggests that soft infrastructure, including affordable housing, presents both economic and social benefits for cities.

By analysing the process of large-scale neighbourhood redevelopment, whereby a low-income community undergoes substantial transformation to a mixed-income community, this chapter highlights the ways in which prioritizing different forms of infrastructure can contribute to the development and redevelopment of a community. These processes of wide-scale change are examined in the context of government devolution of responsibility for social housing, as well as associated principles of governance related to the role of public housing provision. The focus throughout is on the emerging role of 'soft' infrastructure development in the transformation of Regent Park. This chapter assesses the means by which a large-scale redevelopment project can address not only physical redevelopment of a declining building stock, but also the continued building of social relationships and opportunities. Soft infrastructure focused on building social strengths is characteristic of, and necessary for, the potential to create meaningful and sustained community building initiatives.

The remainder of this chapter is organized as follows: first, we highlight the literature associated with understanding the role of supporting, building and incorporating soft infrastructure as a key element of community development priorities, particularly in mixed-income communities; we then draw from documentary analysis, interviews and observations based on our case study of Regent Park to analyse the interactions between developing hard and soft infrastructure as well as community planning implications as a result of these interactions. Following this, we discuss the appropriateness and importance of emphasizing the role of soft infrastructure, and how prioritizing soft infrastructure development may enhance outcomes associated with mixed-income redevelopment initiatives. The chapter concludes with suggestions on how to encourage successful community development and community-building initiatives within the context of government support and with an emphasis on the role that soft infrastructure can play.

Public housing and redevelopment

Our work in Regent Park is situated amidst literature that examines the physical redevelopment of public housing, and particularly the trend in North American cities where post-Second World War public housing is razed in favour of either dispersal of residents or the creation of mixed-income neighbourhoods (see Chaskin & Joseph, 2010; Clampet-Lundquist, 2010; Smith, 2013). Recognizing that the nature and quality of community inputs and the 'soft' forms of infrastructure that strengthen and support neighbourhood development is critical to preparing for transforming neighbourhoods. This is particularly significant in light of the more recent transition of government-led public housing policy, particularly as it relates to processes of devolution of authority and disinvestment in government provision of affordable housing in cities. Recent research identifies the necessary role that the provision of supportive and mutually beneficial community investment plays (Evans, 2007; Oakley et al., 2015). To date, scholarly exploration of Regent Park's transformation has emphasized the significance of both the physical form and housing mix of the redevelopment, as well as critical evaluation of the redevelopment process and impact on residents (Johnson, 2010; Dunn, 2012; August, 2014).

Housing and poverty deconcentration policies in the United States have emphasized the redevelopment of public housing sites as mixed-income neighbourhoods. Only a small proportion of public housing is being replaced on site in many cases, promoting the dispersal of public housing residents and housing rather than on-site renewal (Lucio et al., 2014). While seemingly disregarded in the demolition of older public housing buildings, especially high-rises, the critical role of interpersonal networks and community support to individuals residing in large-scale, concentrated public housing projects such as Pruitt-Igoe in St Louis, and Cabrini-Green in Chicago, has been made clear through retrospective narratives (Austen, 2012) and films such as *The Pruitt-Igoe Myth* (Freidrichs, 2011) and *Voices of Cabrini* (Bezalel & Ferrera, 1999), respectively. Such narratives highlight the significant role of social interaction and informal community support structures in what have been otherwise been described as 'ungovernable inner-city horrors' (Austen, 2012, p. 42).

Clampet-Lundquist (2010) studies the forced relocation of public housing residents in Philadelphia. A key finding from this study is that in the event of resident relocation from high poverty to lower poverty neighbourhoods, strong social ties and networks are frequently disrupted (Clampet-Lundquist, 2010). While Clampet-Lundquist (2010) does not overtly identify disruptions to residents' social networks as a social infrastructure issue, this research emphasizes the policy implications of promoting both improved physical environment alongside support for the social infrastructure within a community. Respondents suggested that it was their strong social ties that protected them, particularly from violence, within their neighbourhood. Clampet-Lundquist (2010, p. 97) notes:

> Combining the stories of the informal warning system with these comments made about feeling as if 'people had your back' or feeling protected by being 'known' by so many people in the neighbourhood illustrates how local social capital affects safety and perception of vulnerability.

It is clear from our present-day understanding of daily life in Pruitt-Igoe (Freidrichs, 2011) and in Cabrini-Green (Bezalel & Ferrera, 1999; Miller, 2008; Austen, 2012) that a strong sense of community, belonging and shared values is of significant importance for improving quality of life. Traditional narratives about decaying physical infrastructure and influences on social form and disarray do not do justice to the reality of what life was like for many residents of physically deteriorating public housing neighbourhoods. Narratives that focus on physical features and physical determinism often neglect to acknowledge the role that collective support plays in a community. A sense of community might be reflected through the sharing of food or childcare, or through the sharing of information intended to ensure the safety of friends, family and community members (Clampet-Lundquist, 2010; Graves, 2010; Austen, 2012).

In Toronto, and across Canada, the redevelopment of public housing sites has not been planned in concert with plans for dispersal of public housing residents. However, policy mechanisms and funds to support social and affordable housing initiatives across Canada at the federal, provincial and municipal levels have substantially waned or disappeared completely over the past few decades. Federal support for new social housing essentially ended in 1993, followed in quick succession by the devolution of responsibility from the Province of Ontario to municipalities between 1996 and 1998 (Suttor, 2014). The creation of TCH in 2002 signalled the city's response to the devolution of responsibility for affordable housing and represented the transfer of the bulk of the city's affordable housing stock to this city corporation. As of 2016, TCH, the largest housing provider in Canada and second largest in North America, owns and operates a portfolio of homes valued at $9 billion, with 58,000 units in 2,200 buildings across the City of Toronto (Mayor's Task Force on Toronto Community Housing, 2016).

Physical infrastructures alone do not and cannot create a community sociologically; however, it is the physical infrastructures and associated costs that are featured most prominently in debates about public housing and its provision. Inclusion of a social development plan, at the outset of redevelopment efforts, developed alongside the plans for physical redevelopment of Regent Park signalled the priority of maintaining and building strong community ties in the neighbourhood. Social development plans also acknowledge the significance of supporting soft infrastructure as part of the redevelopment.

Evidence suggests that, in order to create successful socially mixed communities and positive outcomes for all residents, investment in housing redevelopment should be coupled with investment in other forms of soft infrastructure, such as employment, education and social services (Joseph, 2006). Curley (2010) finds that specific neighbourhood resources, including libraries, recreation facilities, parks, grocery stores and social services contribute more to building strong social networks than strictly the provision of new mixed-income building forms. In a study of a community and social support (CSS) programme for residents of HOPE IV redevelopments in the US, Oakley et al. (2015, p. 728) found that the intention of CSS programmes stress income and labour market improvements for residents – and an emphasis on 'people-based goals'. Their study highlights the connection between physical and social infrastructure in contributing to the building of neighbourhood social capital and sense of community. Unfortunately, the lack of acknowledgement and support for the possibility that low-income residents may never achieve formal sector economic success, and the concomitant lack of support for those who require significant levels of assistance in areas beyond labour market participation, contribute to a substantively flawed system (Oakley et al., 2015).

Much debate has centred on the notion of creating and re-creating a sense of 'community' in mixed-income redevelopments. Research has pointed to the importance of community empowerment and civic engagement, in particular, privileging the role of low-income tenants (Fraser & Nelson, 2008; Chaskin & Joseph, 2010, 2011; Lucio et al., 2014). These findings contrast with redevelopment projects where the philosophy behind creating mixed-income environments is focused on the perceived benefits that low-income residents derive through living in close proximity to residents paying market rent and their subsequent, expected modelling of middle-class family, employment and social norms. Clampet-Lundquist (2010) emphasizes the distinctions created between market and non-market housing residents in mixed-income developments. For example, the application of differential expectations, rules and treatment disproportionately disadvantaged low-income residents and led to the continued building of social barriers. In place of a rationale which implicitly suggests that low-income residents are the primary beneficiaries of social mix, DeFilippis and Fraser (2010) emphasize the need for mixed-income communities to follow a development framework in which a mixed-income neighbourhood is recognized as being mutually beneficial for all residents, regardless of income level. Suggestions that benefits of mixed-income neighbourhoods are exclusive to low-income residents by virtue of living in closer proximity and with the potential of building relationships with higher-income residents are problematic. The perspective that in mixed-income neighbourhoods it is only low-income residents that benefit is not conducive to community-building and ultimately does not support the development of social capital and softer forms of infrastructure that are needed for overall community development.

Regent Park's history and current revitalization has been explored from both theoretical and historical perspectives. Scholars have situated the redevelopment of Regent Park within the wider scope of transitions in the Canadian welfare model in the late 1980s and early 1990s. During those decades, federal government devolution for social housing responsibility was assumed first by provincial governments and shortly after by municipal-level governments (Purdy, 2004; Kipfer & Petrunia, 2009; James, 2010; Dunn, 2012; Kelly, 2013; August, 2014). The general consensus is that, prior to Regent Park's redevelopment, residents experienced a high degree of social cohesion (Johnson & Schippling, 2007; Thompson et al., 2013; August, 2014). The relocation process disrupted existing social networks and created a sense of isolation for those who have been relocated as well as those who remain in Regent Park (Johnson & Schipping, 2007; Thompson et al., 2013 [AQ]). It is within this framework, focused on physical and social renewal, that the experience of Regent Park is telling as a site of large-scale urban transformation.

Shifting focus: from hard infrastructure to soft infrastructure

In Toronto, redevelopment plans for public housing sites stand out as being qualitatively different than the redevelopment that has taken place in cities in the United States. The focus of public housing re-building in the United States has been on the deconcentration and dispersal of public housing supply and residents (Smith, 2013). The current redevelopment of three large public housing sites in Toronto demonstrates an approach that prioritizes poverty deconcentration within the broader plan of creating mixed-income housing with full replacement of the existing public housing stock on-site. In part, this may be a result of learning based on the United States experience, and a specific intent to manage rebuilding with a focus on ameliorating poverty in addition to alleviating poor housing conditions. As one of our interviewees noted:

> It's not through anybody's fault, despite all of our concerted efforts [. . .] none of us significantly moved the needle on poverty and social outcomes in that neighbourhood. And you have got to think maybe it's time to think differently about what you're doing.
>
> (Former housing leader)

Given the above point, the following examination touches on three key elements of Regent Park's redevelopment. First, we provide a brief overview of the history of Regent Park's development beginning in the late 1940s, and the events that precipitated the redevelopment in 2005. Second, we focus on the transition in the orientation of documentation and investment related to the redevelopment. We highlight the process of redevelopment phases thus far, by indicating the manner in which redevelopment has proceeded and the initial emphasis on preparing for and building the hard infrastructure of the neighbourhood. This is followed by the introduction of and attention to developing Regent Park's supporting, socially oriented, soft infrastructure. As the process of redevelopment unfolds, more attention is given to the role of the social environment – specifically the ways in which social interaction takes place and what opportunities for interaction exist. We also consider the contribution of community leaders towards the development of their transforming community. Third, we identify the significance and role of policy in framing the environment and manner of the revitalization and redevelopment process to date.

A brief history of Regent Park

Before the mid-1940s, modern-day Regent Park was a neighbourhood of dilapidated tenement housing with poor sanitation and decaying homes. The Federal government's post-war emphasis on a social welfare model was the impetus for Regent Park's initial development as the first and largest public housing project in Canada (Purdy, 2004). Originally designed and built starting in the late 1940s Regent Park's construction followed a Garden City model based on modernist planning principles. Lorinc (2013, p. 46) describes Regent Park as 'new apartments, geared at low-income working families, were situated in a park-like setting with plenty of open space, ventilation and sunlight'. The neighbourhood was characterized by two general areas referred to as Regent Park North and Regent Park South. The development was divided by Dundas Street, a main east–west thoroughfare. The northern section of Regent Park was dotted with low-rise three-storey walk-up apartments set among grassy areas and sidewalks. Residences in South Regent Park comprised townhomes and five apartment towers (each 14 stories tall) designed by architect Peter Dickinson. The street grid did not extend through the neighbourhood and isolated Regent Park from surrounding areas. A common planning refrain heard during the redevelopment process was that the street network needed to be reintegrated to allow police and emergency vehicles and delivery services better access to the neighbourhood.

The physical design of Regent Park was problematic, as one interviewee remarks:

> The Garden City planning approach from the 1940s that came out of the United Kingdom [. . .] was a dream, [. . .] an idealistic approach to community planning, which, over a very short period of time on the ground, became very clear was not a healthy place for people to be.
>
> (Organization leader)

As a direct result of the devolution of funds for affordable housing across Canada (Suttor, 2014), combined with increasing socio-economic polarization of Regent Park residents in comparison with the rest of the City of Toronto (Purdy, 2003), social and economic prospects for residents were curtailed. In 1949, when the first tenants began to move into Regent Park, tenants were predominantly white, low-income working-class families. Shifts in immigration policy, and the subsequent expansion of immigrant source countries, led to major changes in the racial makeup of Regent Park residents. In 2006, the 7,500 residents of Regent Park spoke more than 50 languages and nearly 60 per cent of residents were immigrants to Canada from one of 56 countries (City of Toronto Social Policy & Analysis Unit, 2013). More recent decades saw a shift in the socio-economic makeup of residents. By 2006 most of Regent Park's residents were on social assistance rather than 'working poor' (Gladki, 2013). As the social and racial makeup of Regent Park changed over the decades it became clear that 'what initially appeared to be a successful approach to social housing gradually morphed into a poverty trap for generations of low-income Torontonians' (Lorinc, 2013, p. 46).

From physical to social infrastructure

Discussions about the need for large-scale physical change in Regent Park took root in the mid-1990s. Led initially by residents who worked with a changing slate of provincial and municipal leaders and the local housing authority, early regeneration discussions focused on the redevelopment of a small portion of the site. Ultimately, the group determined that there was limited feasibility in redeveloping only a small number of the more than 2,000 housing units and therefore the initiative shifted focus to a wholesale rebuilding of the neighbourhood. In 2002, TCH released a call for proposals seeking a comprehensive master plan that would raze and rebuild Regent Park entirely (Gladki, 2013). Failed attempts were linked to long periods of devolution of government responsibility for housing provision and changes in Regent Park housing ownership from federal to provincial to municipal government.

In the summer of 2002, a process of public consultation was initiated and work on planning documents, focusing on street grids, building scale and materials, open spaces and community spaces began in earnest. Of note, there were no public funds available to support the rebuilding of the neighbourhood. This necessitated that the winning redevelopment proposal had to be self-sustaining. As described by an interviewee: 'the whole principle was that the revitalization was supposed to pay for itself – pay for the replacement of all the social housing units on site' (Development leader). Hence, the selected development partner devised a plan in which the building and sale of new market units in Regent Park covered the building costs associated with replacing all of the non-market units. Community input was a key feature throughout the consultation and planning process. Meetings and workshops were held in the neighbourhood with community animators and translators present to provide assistance and information. Following extensive community consultation and engagement, a series of principles to guide the redevelopment were established. A committee comprising community agency leaders, municipal civil servants and Toronto Community Housing staff created a social development strategy for Regent Park, intended to be implemented alongside the physical plans for the neighbourhood (Gladki, 2013). In 2005, the City of Toronto approved the revitalization plans and necessary rezoning to build a mixed-income neighbourhood in Regent Park.

Based on a review of documents from both the City of Toronto and TCH, our research suggests that, despite the co-presence of both such a physical plan and a social development strategy, efforts at the outset were heavily focused on the financial viability of rebuilding. This emphasis extends to the focus on physical site infrastructure, including details related to road widths, sewers and accessibility for emergency services (Toronto Community Housing, 2004).

Our assessment of City of Toronto and TCH documents shows a progression over time. The focus shifted from fiscal restraints and associated hard infrastructure to the concerns and needs of individuals and the community as a whole. Documents particularly from 2007 and later place more emphasis on environmental and social sustainability, whereas their predecessors were concerned with political expediency and finances. The shift in focus from physical planning to social planning suggests that in a revitalization process, a stable financial and political basis is needed before work focusing on individual and community needs can begin. It is also important to note that the progression in focus from hard to soft infrastructure is not an indication that soft infrastructure was intentionally neglected in the early years. In fact, social cohesion, equality and engagement are themes that consistently emerged from the outset.

Representations of soft infrastructure in early documents needed careful evaluation. For example, TCH's 2003 Annual Review and consultation profiled Regent Park's resident activities. The annual review highlights that Regent Park's Revitalization Plan received the Canadian Institute of Planners Award for Planning Excellence by 'taking into account social aspects of community building' (Toronto Community Housing, 2003, p. 10). Despite this praise, the redevelopment process was still in the conceptual, planning stage.

One year after the redevelopment began TCH released a Regent Park Redevelopment Status Update regarding the 10-acre site of Phase 1 (see Ballantyne, 2006). In this early stage of the project, the status update concentrated on the various elements of hard infrastructure. For example, the status update document details planning approvals for the building sites, details on the demolition process, the allocation of site services like sanitary and storm sewers and 'campus-style' electrical distribution (Ballantyne, 2006). The status update document also discusses the physical building design of social housing, market housing and commercial units, without any significant mention of soft infrastructure. Relating to Wise and Perić's study (Chapter 12 in this volume), their work also outlines a number of social conditions to guide the research with local residents. In the case of Regent Park, this omission is extremely important as the lack of attention to the social impacts on temporarily uprooted residents led to the most contested and difficult aspect of the Regent Park revitalization: the relocation process. The imbalance of attention to soft infrastructure in the earliest years of redevelopment resulted in a lack of responsiveness to resident needs during temporary relocation. Residents' greatest source of dissatisfaction with the redevelopment related to the manner in which the relocation process affected individuals and families who were forced to vacate their homes so that rebuilding could take place. Families with school-aged children found the transition to both a new neighbourhood and a new school to be extremely challenging, particularly when moves took place during the school year. Furthermore, all those who were provided with temporary housing that was distant from social networks, employment or services, were challenged to maintain the friendships, networks and support systems that they relied on. Ultimately, TCH responded by making adjustments to the relocation process that were more considerate of residents and provided greater support for relocation in the form of additional staff assistance. This shift in focus is borne out in later documents, which dedicate attention to transparency and other soft infrastructure themes like communication strategies and information sessions (Toronto Community Housing, 2013b).

Table 10.1 presents a timeline of the redevelopment from 2005 to 2015. In the early stages, the City of Toronto documents indicate concerns over creating a framework of by-laws to convince the City Council and critics of the viability of comprehensive redevelopment. The 2005 application to amend the City of Toronto Official Plan and the Community Facilities Strategy are illustrative of documents from this period. The amendment application focused on elucidating the logistics of the proportion of social housing units to be replaced onsite, which ranged from 65 to 85 per cent, as well as the location of proposed offsite replacement housing. This information is no doubt important in showing the degree to which the plan is attainable (City of Toronto, 2005, p. 93). The only notable mention of community in this early period was limited to the Community Facilities Strategy (2005), which established in general terms what the community required in terms of physical spaces for recreation, childcare, services and agencies, and how these facilities would be accessible during construction. One organization leader further explained that a great deal of political manoeuvring and reassurance of the viability of the project was required to establish financial support, an assertion that is no doubt supported by the degree of documentation related to the approval and building of hard infrastructure from 2005 (Political leader). Also emphasized was the notion that, at this stage, the object in question was not the project's larger, social goal to ameliorate the lives of Regent Park residents, but to create a viable policy and political framework (Political leader).

Beginning in 2007, City of Toronto documents began to shift focus from hard infrastructure towards developing tactics and strategies to facilitate social cohesion and opportunities for residents. The TCH Social Development Plan (2007a, 2007b) addressed the issues of social interaction and cohesion between market and non-market residents, how to encourage the development of community governance structures, and how to prioritize space for community organizations. The Social Development Plan was created in conjunction with the Employment Plan for Regent Park (City of Toronto, 2007). The Employment Plan focused on providing diverse employment services for residents and the creation of a platform for local business owners to employ residents. Central to the plan is a physical employment services hub that is easily accessible to local residents and employers. The time lag difference between plans for infrastructure and finance, versus plans for soft infrastructure, suggests that solid legal and financial backing helped enable TCH and the City of Toronto to move forward with developing a social transformation framework.

The early redevelopment plans established guidelines for provision of physical facilities and targeted a social mix of 50 per cent market and 50 per cent non-market housing, were adjusted over the course of the revitalization to respond to new needs that arose. The new aquatic centre, originally planned to be built as part of a neighbourhood school, was considered important for residents to access; its location was therefore moved and the pool was then built adjacent to the centrally located park. Furthermore, while the school-based plan would have required residents to pay a user fee, the Regent Park Aquatic Centre is now included as part of a programme in which some City of Toronto recreational and community facilities do not charge a user fee. The Regent Park Athletic Grounds are another example that demonstrates how a hard infrastructural framework was adapted to accommodate ongoing changes and community needs that were not met. Originally not included in the redevelopment plan, a space was created in the master plan for an artificial turf field next to a preserved outdoor ice hockey rink, in order to meet residents' desires that were expressed during consultation.

The middle phases of revitalization saw planning documents that balance hard and soft infrastructure. Later documents begin to mention actual implementation of niche social programmes and initiatives rather than noting community engagement initiatives in an abstract way. In the 2011 TCH Annual Report, there is a first mention of TCH hiring staff with specialized training in working with residents with mental health issues (Toronto Community Housing, 2011). The report also reveals the establishment of a multilingual programme to welcome new residents into the neighbourhood, demonstrating some understanding of institutional barriers immigrants face (Toronto Community Housing, 2011). Similarly, the 2013 Annual Report announced a $1.4 million investment in the Year of Youth programme (Toronto Community Housing, 2013a). The programme focuses on confidence-building and skills resources for young residents of TCH neighbourhoods.

A further change took place in 2013 when the original 50–50 mix between non-market and market housing was adjusted to a 25–75 mix (Toronto Community Housing, 2013b). This market housing adjustment was initiated by the private developer, instituted by Toronto Community Housing, and approved by the City of Toronto. The readjustment was deemed necessary due to an accounting of the actual costs related to the construction of new facilities and the requirement that the sale of market housing fund the cost of construction to replace all non-market housing. The most obvious impact of the shift to a 1:3 ratio of non-market to market housing mix moved Regent Park to a situation in which market housing would predominate in the neighbourhood. There was, however, no reduction in the absolute number of non-market units to be built, rather the total number of market units was increased. Community members, TCH and the City of Toronto disagreed with the changes; however, without alternative funding options the proposed change stood.

We observed a shift from hard to soft infrastructure in TCH public documents. This shift must be viewed in light of the staggered five-phase structure of redevelopment. At the start of each new planning phase, there is greater focus on the hard infrastructural concerns which are most salient. For instance, the TCH 2013 Annual Review highlights hard infrastructure such as the opening of a new 10-storey rental building (Toronto Community Housing, 2013a) and new construction, referring to Phase 2 areas that were still fairly early in their execution stages. Soft infrastructure also includes that which is intended to support the community as a whole. At times, these initiatives cross-pollinate and deepen the layer of soft infrastructure at Regent Park. The Centre for Community Learning and Development (CCLD), a non-profit organization, has been training recent immigrant women to work as community advocates for many years through the Immigrant Women's Integration Program (IWIP). In 2010, an adult learning centre opened in Regent Park, and a graduate from IWIP was hired as a full-time community engagement worker at the learning centre. Others who were trained, either formally or informally, through neighbourhood advocacy networks are also involved with the centre. These individuals have now gone on to provide continued support to community members and residents, in the form of innovative training programmes designed to facilitate communication and information sharing between youth and their parents, and in terms of continued advocacy for the use of existing spaces and resources. One such advocate, a long-time Regent Park, won a prestigious city-building award in 2015 in recognition of her contributions to supporting positive change within the neighbourhood. Advocacy training can ultimately increase the resilience of the community and lead to the development of new, transferable skills that can also be key in struggles against social inequality.

Table 10.1 Timeline of key Regent Park redevelopment processes

2005	• Application to amend Official Plan brought to Toronto City Council, with particular emphasis on changing the social mix and the development of a Community Facilities Strategy
	• Phase I of construction and demolition begins
2006	• Development partner selected after public Request for Proposal (RFP) proposal and series of negotiations
2007	• Toronto City Council passes Social Development Plan and Employment Services Plan, developed with residents
2009	• Phase II of construction and demolition begins
2012	• Phase I completed
2013	• Report discusses the changes to the social mix, moving from a 50:50 split to a mix of 75% market housing and 25% social housing
2014	• Toronto City Council adopts plans for Phases 3–5 and other related reports, including the 75% market to 25% social housing mix
	• Phase 3 construction begins
2017	• Phase 2 complete (estimate)
2019	• Phase 3 complete (estimate)
2022	• All five phases complete (estimate)

A discussion of policy implications

It would be impossible to carry out a project of this magnitude without adequate funding and support of city by-laws/regulations. Based on the scope and scale of Regent Park's transformation, an emphasis on zoning changes, street system planning, building footprints and phasing in early documents is reflective of the need to first establish a workable physical environment in the neighbourhood in order to facilitate the wholesale redevelopment of the site. As such, only after the physical and financial foundations of the project were prepared could later documents shift to focus on prioritizing and implementing soft infrastructure. This included the development of supportive community structures and amenities focused on meeting community needs and desires. Therefore, the thematic shift of documentation from hard to soft revitalization seems to be characteristic of a logical development project: first the physical neighbourhood plan is implemented and then its uses and social needs are addressed.

Emphasizing and supporting the development and maintenance of soft infrastructure as part of the model for community redevelopment is what distinguishes the Regent Park redevelopment from other North American examples. In Regent Park, the rebuilding of physical infrastructure and the strengthening of social engagement brought about new, unforeseen opportunities for building additional social supports. For instance, the construction of an aquatic centre with an indoor pool, in combination with advocacy by community leaders, led to a number of positive, community-focused outcomes. Resident advocacy led to the creation of women's-only swim times, which helped to accommodate religious groups in the neighbourhood seeking an opportunity to swim while maintaining modesty. Furthermore, resident disappointment with the citywide system governing public swim lesson enrolment, resulted in a successful campaign that increased overall accessibility to the pool and created reserved swim class spaces specifically for Regent Park residents. Similarly, the increase in physical space in the community, in combination with local advocacy, led to a group yoga class being held in a cultural space, free of charge for residents. These types of initiatives are possible only as a result of the combined strengthening and support of both physical and social infrastructure, and as a result of nurturing relationships and promoting advocacy among community members.

Regent Park's redevelopment, as seen from a wide variety of perspectives on city building, is witnessed by city and other government officials, local residents and other observers as a predominantly positive outcome. The transformation of Regent Park has led to the rebuilding of dilapidated non-market housing through a substantial mixed-income redevelopment initiative and has helped to provide high-quality housing opportunities for low-income households. Given the nearly absolute lack of government funding at any level to support affordable housing development in Canada at the time of planning and implementation, it is a model of redevelopment that leverages government relationships, partnership with a private developer, and works only because of high central city land values and a growing demand for housing in the core of Toronto. Scholarly criticism is particularly focused on the decline of Canada's social welfare policy and questions about whether a mixed-income community can indeed be developed as the neighbourhood changes from one of exclusively low-income households to a neighbourhood in which market housing predominates. Nevertheless, the Regent Park model has been lauded broadly at an international scale and attracts the regular attention of governments seeking to redevelop their own stocks of affordable housing.

Although two key goals of the redevelopment were to create neighbourhood cohesion and pursue the vision of the original residents, ultimately, the decision concerning the social mix was determined by financial needs. It is unclear, however, what an ideal mix of market to non-market housing would be, or whether there can be such a thing as an ideal mix. As the redevelopment of Regent Park moves into the final two phases, it is clear that the transformation has already succeeded in reintegrating the neighbourhood with the rest of the city, and that any attempts to replicate the mixed-income housing model developed in Regent Park clearly need to consider investments in both physical and social infrastructure.

Conclusion

Our research suggests that support for affordable or social housing must be understood in relation to concurrent consideration of systems of governance. In neighbourhoods undergoing radical transformation, it is through government priorities that funding mechanisms can be created which provide support for low-income housing and have the potential to empower and bring communities closer to an equitable existence. Investment in both hard and soft infrastructure is critical in this regard. The history of Regent Park has been one of recurring disinvestment, decay, poverty and isolation, but also reinvestment, reintegration and reimagination of the possibilities for socio-economic and urban change. Investment in, and emphasis on, soft infrastructure is materially significant in understanding the present-day environment of transition that is taking place in Toronto's Regent Park neighbourhood. Signs of further hope are on the horizon.

In October 2015, a majority Liberal government was elected and took over the leadership of the Canadian federal government following 10 years of Conservative-led rule. The transition to a new government in Canada has also marked the transition to a new type of leadership. The new government is emphasizing consultation, consensus-building and, most notably, an interest in investing in cities' physical and social fabric. Though the federal government has no formal responsibility for engaging with an urban agenda, the Liberal government has signalled its interest in working with cities across the country on key challenges. One such challenge is infrastructure support and spending; the Liberal Party campaigned on a promise of increasing federal government support for infrastructure by $60 billion over a 10-year period (The Liberal Party of Canada, 2015). In his January 2016 speech to the Toronto Region Board of Trade, Sohi (2016), Minister of Infrastructure and Communities, identified three infrastructure spending priorities, including affordable housing and what is described as 'social infrastructure'. Sohi (2016) used the example of Regent Park as a model where future investments of up to $20 billion could 'make projects like Regent Park possible in cities across the country'. Furthermore, in acknowledging that repairs and maintenance are critical to infrastructure, new federal infrastructure spending commitments will be targeted to both the creation of new infrastructure as well as to recapitalization and repairs. This is significant in the case of social housing, where in Toronto alone the repair backlog has been estimated to be in the range of $2.6 billion over the next 10 years (Toronto Community Housing, 2014).

As urban infrastructure investments, such as the provision and repair of affordable housing stocks, rise in significance, the importance of understanding the role of both physical and social infrastructure in the development of communities becomes increasingly relevant within national and urban contexts. It remains to be seen how and whether new urban investment will result from these policy shifts at the national level, but our ongoing research will follow social trends and changes in policy. Nevertheless, the promise of renewed attention and commitment to leveraging infrastructure investments as a way of developing physical and social change within the scope of affordable urban housing stock launches the promise of urban and community renewal in areas that need it most.

Acknowledgements

This work was supported by the Neighbourhood Change Research Partnership funded through the Social Sciences and Humanities Research Council of Canada.

References

August, M. (2014). Challenging the rhetoric of stigmatization: The benefits of concentrated poverty in Toronto's Regent Park. *Environment and Planning A, 46*, 1317–1333.
Austen, B. (2012). The last tower: The decline and fall of public housing. *Harper's Magazine*. Retrieved from http://harpers.org/archive/2012/05/the-last-tower/.
Ballantyne, D. (2006). Regent Park redevelopment status update. *Toronto Community Housing*. Retrieved from http://www.torontohousing.ca/webfm_send/796/1?#
Bezalel, R., & Ferrera, A. (Directors). (1999). *Voices of Cabrini: Remaking Chicago's public housing*. Motion picture, USA.
Bradford, N. (2007). Placing social policy? Reflections on Canada's new deal for cities and communities. *Canadian Journal of Urban Research, 16*, 1–26.
Canadian Urban Institute. (2015). The Inve$table city: Canadian Urban Forum 2015. Retrieved from http://static1.squarespace.com/static/546bbd2ae4b077803c592197/t/5693d7fc1c1210fdda4175ff/1452529664159/CanadianUrbanForum2015Outcomes-ForPublish.pdf.
Chaskin, R., & Joseph, M. (2010). Building 'community' in mixed-income developments: Assumptions, approaches and early experiences. *Urban Affairs Review, 45*, 299–335.

Chaskin, R., & Joseph, M. (2011). Social interaction in mixed-income developments: Relational expectations and emerging reality. *Journal of Urban Affairs, 33,* 209–237.

City of Toronto Social Policy & Analysis Unit. (2013). *Regent Park (72) social profile #2: Languages.* Toronto: City of Toronto Neighbourhood Planning Area Profiles.

City of Toronto. (2005). *Final Report – Application to amend the Official Plan and zoning By-law – Regent Park revitalization – Toronto Community Housing Corporation (Toronto Centre-Rosedale, Ward 28).* Retrieved from www.toronto.ca/legdocs/2005/agendas/council/cc050201/te1rpt/cl004.pdf.

City of Toronto. (2007). *Employment plan for Regent Park.* Retrieved from www1.toronto.ca/city_of_toronto/employment_and_social_services/telmi/research_and_data/strategic_plans_economic_development_initiatives/files/pdf/regent_park.pdf.

Clampet-Lundquist, S. (2010). 'Everyone had your back': Social ties, perceived safety, and public housing relocation. *City & Community, 9,* 87–108.

Curley, A. (2010). Relocating the poor: Social capital and neighbourhood resources. *Journal of Urban Affairs, 32,* 79–103.

DeFilippis, J., & Fraser, J. (2010). Why do we want mixed-income housing and neighbourhoods? In J. Davies & D. Imbroscio (Eds.), *Critical urban studies: New directions* (pp. 135–147). Albany: SUNY Press.

Dunn, J, (2012). 'Socially mixed' public housing redevelopment as a destigmatization strategy in Toronto's Regent Park: A theoretical approach and a research agenda. *DuBois Review, 1,* 87–105.

Evans, L. (2007). *Moving towards sustainability: City-regions and their infrastructure.* Canadian Policy Research Networks. Retrieved from http://cprn.org/documents/49099_FR.pdf.

Fraser, J., & Nelson, M. (2008). Can mixed-income housing ameliorate concentrated poverty? The significance of a geographically informed sense of community. *Geography Compass, 2,* 2127–2144.

Freidrichs, C. (Director). (2011). *The Pruitt-Igoe Myth.* Motion picture, USA.

Gladki, J. (2013). Inclusive planning: A case study of Regent Park revitalization, Toronto. In Ministry of Housing & Urban Poverty Alleviation, Government of India (Ed.), *Inclusive planning: State of the urban poor report 2013.* Oxford: Oxford University Press.

Graves, E. (2010). The structuring of urban life in a mixed-income housing 'community'. *City & Community, 9,* 109–131.

James, R. (2010). From 'slum clearance' to 'revitalisation': Planning, expertise and moral regulation in Toronto's Regent Park. *Planning Perspectives, 25,* 69–86.

Johnson, L., & Schippling, R. (2009). *Regent Park revitalization: Young people's experience of relocation from public housing redevelopment.* Report for the Canadian Mortgage and Housing Corporation. Catalogue number: NH18-1-2/50-2009E. Government of Canada.

Johnson, L. (2010). Exercising a legal right of return: A Canadian experience in redeveloping public housing. International Conference on Neighbourhood Restructuring & Resident Location: Context, Choice & Consequence, Delft University of Technology, OTB Research Institute for the Built Environment, Delft, The Netherlands, 1–16.

Joseph, M. (2006). Is mixed-income development an antidote to urban poverty? *Housing Policy Debate, 17,* 209–234.

Kelly, S. (2013). The new normal: The figure of the condo owner in Toronto's Regent Park. *City & Society, 25*(2), 173–194.

Kipfer, S., & Petrunia, J. (2009). 'Recolonization' and public housing: A Toronto case study. *Studies in Political Economy, 83*, 111–139.

Lorinc, J. (2013). The New Regent Park. *University of Toronto Magazine.* Retrieved from http://magazine.utoronto.ca/feature/new-regent-park-toronto-community-housing-john-lorinc/.

Lucio, J., Hand, L., & Marsiglia, F. (2014). Designing hope: Rationales of mixed-income housing policy. *Journal of Urban Affairs, 36*, 891–904.

Mayor's Task Force on Toronto Community Housing. (2016). *Transformative change for the TCHC.* Retrieved from www1.toronto.ca/City%20Of%20Toronto/Strategic%20Communications/Mayor's%20Task%20Force%20on%20Toronto%20Community%20Housing/Article/TCH-Task-Force-Final-Report-Jan25-2016.pdf.

Micallef, S. (2013). *Regent Park: A story of collective impact.* Toronto: Metcalf Foundation. Retrieved from http://metcalffoundation.com/wp-content/uploads/2013/03/Regent-Park.pdf.

Miller, B. J. (2008). The struggle over redevelopment at Cabrini-Green, 1989–2004. *Journal of Urban History, 34*, 944–960.

Oakley, D., Fraser, J., & Bazuin, J. (2015). The imagined self-sufficient communities of HOPE VI: Examining the community and social support component. *Urban Affairs Review, 51*, 726–746.

Purdy, S. (2003). 'Ripped off' by the system: Housing policy, poverty and territorial stigmatization in Regent Park Housing Project, 1951–1991. *Labour, 52*, 45–108.

Purdy, S. (2004). By the people, for the people: Tenant organizing in Toronto's Regent Park housing project in the 1960s and 1970s. *Journal of Urban History, 30*, 519–548.

Smith, J. L. (2013). The end of US public housing as we knew it. *Urban Research & Practice, 6*, 276–296.

Sohi, The Honourable Amarjeet, Minister of Infrastructure and Communities. (2016). Speech to the Toronto Region Board of Trade. Retrieved from http://news.gc.ca/web/article-en.do?nid=1028939.

Suttor, G. (2014). *Canadian social housing: Policy evolution and impacts on the housing system and urban space.* PhD thesis, University of Toronto.

The Liberal Party of Canada. (2015). Real Change: An historical investment plan to strengthen the middle class, create jobs and grow our economy. Retrieved from www.liberal.ca/files/2015/08/An-historic-investment-plan.pdf.

Thompson, S. K., Bucerius, S. M., & Luguya, M. (2013). Unintended consequences of neighbourhood restructuring: Uncertainty, disrupted social networks and increased fear of violent victimization among young adults. *British Journal of Criminology, 53*(5), 924–941.

Toronto Community Housing. (2003). Investment in communities. *Annual Review 2003.* Retrieved from www.torontohousing.ca/webfm_send/69/1?#.

Toronto Community Housing. (2004). Partners in communities. *Annual Review 2004.* Retrieved from www.torontohousing.ca/webfm_send/70/1?#www.torontohousing.ca/webfm_send/70/1?#.

Toronto Community Housing. (2007a). *Regent Park social development plan.* Retrieved from www.torontohousing.ca/webfm_send/4213/1.

Toronto Community Housing. (2007b). *Social development plan for Regent Park executive summary.* Retrieved from www.toronto.ca/legdocs/mmis/2007/ex/bgrd/background-file-7300.pdf

Toronto Community Housing. (2011). The road to excellence: Shaping the future of social housing in our city one resident at a time. *2011 Annual Report*. Retrieved from www.torontohousing.ca/webfm_send/8838.

Toronto Community Housing. (2013a). Building community in the city we call home. *Annual Report 2013*. Retrieved from www.torontohousing.ca/webfm_send/10549.

Toronto Community Housing. (2013b). *Regent Park housing issues report*. Retrieved from www1.toronto.ca/City%20Of%20Toronto/City%20Planning/Community%20Planning/Files/pdf/R/Regent_housing_issues_report.pdf

Toronto Community Housing. (2014). Toronto Community Housing invests $3.53 million in home repairs for 9 communities. 12 November. Retrieved from www.torontohousing.ca/news/20141112/toronto_community_housing_invests_3_53m_home_repairs_nine_communities.

11 Theorizing neighbourhood inequality

The things we do with theory, the things it does to us

Amie Thurber

Introduction

> Social change arises from politics, not philosophy. Ideals are a crucial step in emancipatory politics, however, because they dislodge our assumption that what is given is necessary.
>
> (Young, 1990, p. 256)

This is not a chapter about the problems faced by residents of deeply marginalized, stigmatized and racialized neighbourhoods, or about the problem of how to transform sites of inequality and disparity into sites of equity and opportunity. Instead, it is about the problem of 'us', referring to students, scholars and practitioners engaging with these neighbourhoods. In particular, it is a chapter about what we in geography and urban studies do with theory, what theory does to us, and what it does to the people and places with whom we engage. To explore these questions, I offer my experience working alongside residents of a public housing project slated for demolition, while simultaneously working through theories of neighbourhood inequality as a doctoral student in my first two years of study.

In the summer of 2013, I moved to Nashville, Tennessee to begin doctoral study. In the months before my first semester, I received an email about a talk on community-building at a local neighbourhood centre. Intrigued, I rode my bike the couple miles from my home to James Cayce Homes, a 64-acre neighbourhood of barracks-style public housing. It was late June and school was out for the year. The narrow greenways separating the 96 long, rectangular two-storey brick buildings were full of children playing, clothes drying on lines and stray cats peering from beneath porches. Adults were gathered on sidewalks and stoops, working on cars, swapping stories, bringing in groceries and taking out trash.

That day, I learned that the local housing authority, the Metropolitan Development and Housing Agency (MDHA), had recently announced plans to demolish the neighbourhood and replace it with mixed-income housing. I also learned that a group of residents had formed Cayce United, a tenant-organizing effort to mobilize resident voices and interests in the redevelopment process. A few days later, I started volunteering. Over the next two years, I spent between five and 20 hours a week participating in all levels of Cayce United's organizing activities.

My roles were varied, acting in turn as scribe, babysitter, consultant, transporter, co-researcher, door-knocker, facilitator, literacy coach, observer and advocate.

I felt compelled to work with Cayce United as a neighbour, a scholar and a student, three different though not mutually exclusive roles. As a new resident of a rapidly gentrifying city and a neighbour of Cayce Homes, I was eager to learn about my context, and lend whatever resources I could to advancing justice in the place I now live. As a scholar, I was interested in studying the processes of urban redevelopment in and through Cayce Homes, as well as documenting residents' change efforts. It was critical to me to approach and research in partnership with Cayce Homes residents, given the legacy of research and policymaking that has rearranged the lives of poor people with little to no say from residents about where they live, what their neighbourhoods looks and feel like, who their neighbours are, and what they want and need in a community (Bennett, 2000; Duke, 2009; Chaskin et al., 2012; Silver, 2013). As a student studying community development, I was trying to make sense of all I was learning in the classroom as it played out on the ground in my community. Indeed, while working with Cayce United, I was entrenched in my doctoral study coursework and inundated with academic theory. I had daily encounters with scholars writing about places much like Cayce Homes, explicating how these neighbourhoods came to exist, the problems experienced in them, and what ought to be done to improve outcomes for the residents.

As I considered these various theoretical perspectives, it became increasingly clear how theory both reveals and obscures understandings, creates and constrains possibilities, writes some people and alternatives into the future, and leaves others out. What follows is a study of one neighbour/scholar/student wrestling with theory in a particular setting (for a case study of Cayce United, see Thurber & Fraser, 2016). I trace my intellectual engagement through three theoretical perspectives – structural, social-process and post-structural – tracing how with each approach informed my actual engagement in Cayce Homes. I focus here on distinctions between these approaches, though there are clearly points of overlap, as well as heterogeneity and debate within each. My intention to make evident what I was able to do with these theories; what they did to, for and with me; and what they might do to, with, and for the people and place of Cayce Homes.

To ground this inquiry, I draw from a longitudinal constructivist study of the redevelopment of Cayce Homes and the efforts of Cayce United. Data collected between June 2013 and June 2015 include field notes generated from 750 hours of participant observation, semi-structured interviews, informal conversations with Cayce United leaders and other residents, and artifacts related to the redevelopment, including newspaper articles and organizational documents. Conducting extended fieldwork allowed me to build rapport, trust and friendship with residents. As an adult woman and mother of children in the same school district as residents, I share some important aspects of identity and experience with the Cayce United leaders, most of whom are mothers and grandmothers. At the same time, as a white, middle-class professional with a high level of formal education living outside Cayce Homes I was, and remain, an outsider in this predominantly African American, low-income neighbourhood. My understanding of the context is necessarily partial and incomplete. This is all the more reason it has felt increasingly urgent that I – and all of us hoping to positively intervene in sites of neighbourhood inequality – get more honest about the assumptions we carry into places, which are often bolstered by academic theory, and to consider what we might carry otherwise.

Theorizing neighbourhood inequality

> How we represent space and time in theory matters, because it affects how we and others interpret and then act with respect to the world.
>
> (Harvey, 1989, p. 205)

Given chronic problems with mould, mice, overcrowding and under-maintained buildings, most residents of Cayce Homes were in favour of the redevelopment. Yet, many were concerned with how the redevelopment would impact their families, and whether they in fact were the intended beneficiaries. One resident, Ms Audrey mentions: 'the plan they got is good. But is it for us? That's the main thing.' Another resident adds: 'Or is it just for them?'' Observed during the course of this study, a core group of six to eight Cayce United residents organized around three primary goals related to the redevelopment: 1) no resident displacement, 2) the creation of job opportunities and 3) the integration of needed social supports.

As Cayce United worked to mobilize their neighbours, educate the community, shape the public narrative of the redevelopment and win resident goals, resident organizers – and those who worked alongside them (myself included) – were often stymied by the same questions that challenge many scholars of neighbourhood inequality. What will produce more equitable outcomes in urban communities? How can positive social change occur? Who can (and ought to) be involved in transforming urban neighbourhoods? These are theoretical questions, and the answers vary based upon the theoretical perspectives used.

Structuralism 101: the root problem of is structural

Most well-developed theories of urban inequality draw on macro-level economics to explain neighbourhood-level change. Structuralists argue that neighbourhoods – whether poor, middle class or wealthy, or racially homogenous, segregated or integrated – do not spontaneously take shape. Rather, they are constructed through processes of *uneven development*, wherein some places (neighbourhoods, cities or countries) are systematically less developed, enabling other places to become increasingly valued and valuable (Brenner & Theodore, 2002). Uneven development differentially marks neighbourhoods by design: areas of concentrated poverty and concentrated wealth are produced through historic and ongoing policies and practices. The resulting inequalities allow the accumulation of wealth for economic elites through the exploitation of particular people and places, a process Harvey (2005) coined as *accumulation by dispossession*.

As race scholars have made evident, geographic processes are highly racialized (Pulido, 2000; Lipsitz, 2007; Neely & Samura, 2011). In North America, the uneven development of land and accumulation by dispossession can be traced to colonization, as settlers manufactured racially 'pure' spaces through extermination and forced removal of indigenous people (Harris, 1993). Since these beginnings, geographic concentrations of risks and opportunities have tilted the scales of health and well-being in favour of affluent residents, who are predominantly white, while concentrated risks pool in areas that are disproportionately home to poorer residents and people of colour (Pulido, 2000; Lipsitz, 2007). Opportunity-rich areas are marked by access to superior resources and amenities, while opportunity-poor areas are provided inferior schools, health care, food and transit access (Lipsitz, 2007; Austin, 2013; Davis & Welcher, 2013). Furthermore, these same opportunity-poor areas bear increased environmental risks, such as racial disparities in the siting of hazardous waste, which creates heightened occupational health risks born by communities of colour (United Church of Christ, 1987; Pulido, 2000). Unsurprisingly, people living in opportunity-poor areas experience disproportionately deleterious outcomes in dimensions such as academic achievement, exposure to violence, physical health and employment (see Reece et al., 2013).

Structural theorists posit that the present deepening of neighbourhood inequality was exacerbated by the turn to neoliberalism in the 1970s (Brenner & Theodore 2002; Harvey, 2005; DeFilippis, 2008; Wacquant, 2008). Condemned as a 'political project to re-establish the conditions for material accumulation and to restore the powers of economic elites' (Harvey, 2005, p. 19), neoliberal economic policies are characterized by the simultaneous *roll back* of government mandated social supports for the majority of citizens (e.g. labour protections and subsidized housing) and the *roll out* of mechanisms that favour free market economics and wealth production for the few (e.g. privatized water, prisons and education services; reduced taxes for the wealthy and corporations; and the ability of multinational corporations to operate outside of national regulation) (Peck & Tickell, 2002). Critics argue that these practices have dramatically increased economic inequality, which has resulted in increasingly economically stratified neighbourhoods (DeFilippis, 2008). During the 1970s and 1980s, this stratification took a particular spatial form: poor people and people of colour lived in higher concentrations in urban centres and more affluent people lived in opportunity-rich outer ring suburbs. Yet the nature of uneven development requires that the finite spaces in the city be made and remade again in order to provide new opportunities for wealth production. This remaking is evident in today's *back to the city* movement: a return of the middle and professional classes to the urban core. This return produces gentrification – the displacement of poor and working-class residents – and the suburbanization of poverty, as formerly urban residents are pushed to the (once desirable) outer rings of cities (Hyra, 2014).

Structural theory applied

Studying foundational texts of Structuralism 101 shaped my understanding of the history and context of public housing, in general, and Cayce Homes, in particular.

Conceived during the Great Depression (when a quarter of the workforce was unemployed), the first housing projects in the United States were designed with a dual purpose: to remove slums blighting the urban core and to stimulate a devastated economy (Friedman, 1966). By simultaneously tearing down housing deemed substandard and constructing new housing, the intervention stimulated demand for the very product it brought to the market. However, it was never intended to provide housing to the destitute (Friedman, 1966). Accordingly, public housing policy was arguably a tool of uneven development from its inception: it exploited both the *needs* and the *labour* of the poor to stimulate the economy, without actually serving those with the greatest needs (Friedman, 1966; Stolloff, n.d.).

When James Cayce Homes were built in 1941, it was for white people only, tucked into one of East Nashville's few racially integrated neighbourhoods (Houston, 2012). In what was a nationwide pattern, Urban Renewal projects of the 1950s annexed the Cayce Homes neighbourhood, while drawing middle-class white families (along with their property taxes and political capital) to the suburbs. Discriminatory Federal Housing Acts (of 1934 and 1968) skewed opportunities for upward mobility in favour of white residents (Massey & Denton, 1993). By the early 1970s, Cayce Homes was no longer only for white people, but there were now few opportunities for black families to move *out of* the projects. Thereafter, the area surrounding Cayce Homes experienced years of disinvestment, and its residents became increasingly black and poor (Houston, 2012).

As federal funding failed to keep up with maintenance needs, much public housing across the country fell into disrepair, and residents endured mould, lead, insect infestations and other environmental hazards (Schwartz, 2010). Concurrently, the loss of industrial jobs and the roll back of social welfare that began in the 1970s deepened poverty and inequality, particularly in urban areas. These losses were profoundly felt in public housing projects and surrounding neighbourhoods. Yet, rather than generating widespread societal scrutiny of the policies producing rampant inequities, the projects and the people who lived in these environments became the subjects of 'territorial stigmatization' (Wacquant, 2008) that marked both the place of public housing and the people that lived there as deviant and dangerous (Henderson, 1995; O'Connor, 2001).

Such has been the case in Cayce Homes, where many residents are negatively affected by the intersecting conditions of material poverty, experiences of violence and neighbourhood stigmatization. Today, Cayce Homes is the largest remaining public housing project in Nashville. The 2,000 people who live at Cayce Homes (half of those children) are predominantly African American (87%) and very low-income; 60 per cent are unemployed and the average family lives on less than $5,500 a year (MDHA, 2013). Already racially and economically marked, the neighbourhood has been deeply stigmatized as a site of danger and deviance. Whether because of increased policing or increased incidents, violence remains elevated in Cayce Homes. Residents experience significantly higher rates of domestic violence and assault than city-wide averages, and rates of murder and non-negligent manslaughter, though infrequent, are almost five times greater in Cayce Homes than the citywide average (Speer, 2014). In a recent survey, most residents reported feeling unsafe in their neighbourhood at night and having very low feelings of community trust and social cohesion (MDHA, 2013). Thus, despite the stigma attached to the Cayce Homes, given East Nashville's proximal location to downtown, the surrounding neighbourhood is now dramatically and rapidly changing (Lloyd, 2011). As predominantly white, middle and upper-income residents now encircle Cayce Homes, the 64 acres of land beneath the projects is rapidly increasing in value. In March 2013, MDHA announced 'Envision Cayce' – a year-long community planning process aimed at the complete demolition of James Cayce Homes. While MDHA suggested the planning process was to gather community input on the redevelopment design, it announced early on a plan to build a mixed-income housing development, tripling the population density and adding three market-rate rental units for every two public housing or low-income units (EJP Consulting, 2013). Naturally, this created not unfounded displacement concerns among the current residents: MDHA's four previous public housing redevelopments significantly cut the number of subsidized units available (Fraser et al., 2012), consistent with a national trend that has displaced thousands of families (Popkin, 2004).

As an emerging scholar, a structural analysis provided me insight into why the Cayce Homes neighbourhood is changing, the timing of that change, and who are the intended beneficiaries. East Nashville has been made and re-made over time, a once-vibrant neighbourhood, marginalized by intentional disinvestment, and now revitalized and reconstituted as a location for wealth production. Yet, as I carried a structural frame into weekly meetings with Cayce United leaders, there was not much I could *do with* the theory to help us move a local, neighbourhood-level change effort forward. Harvey (2005, p. 187) calls for broad-base national and transnational movement building, targeting neoliberalism by 'reversing the withdrawal of the state from social provision' and 'confronting the overwhelming powers of finance capital'. Although I could see the scholarly clout of Harvey's revolutionary calls, the tasks were well beyond the scope of what six public housing resident organizers and their allies might undertake in Cayce Homes. Other scholars offer more localized suggestions, such as the creation of worker-owned cooperatives (DeFillipis, 2008). But, as none of the Cayce United organizers own a computer, and some were still learning to read, even this recommendation seemed daunting.

While the lack of a clear, local direction for change was concerning, more troubling to me was the degree to which some structuralists seemed to render poor people powerless to affect change. Consider Harvey's (2005, p. 185) perspective on those people, like many Cayce residents, outside the market system:

> Their only hope is to somehow scramble aboard the market system either as petty commodity producers, as informal vendors (of things or labour power), as petty predators to beg, steal, or violently secure crumbs from the rich man's table, or as participants in the vast illegal trade of trafficking in drugs, guns, women, or anything else illegal for which there is a demand.

Wacquant's (2008, p. 242) treatment of people living in poverty similarly excises agency, claiming that public housing neighbourhoods are 'no longer a shared resource that African Americans can mobilize and deploy to shelter themselves from white domination and where they hope to find collective support for their strategies of mobility'. These structuralist views reflect few possibilities for resident-led change, as virtually no human strength is rendered visible, and whatever actually existing resistance to oppression – individual or collective – underway at Cayce Homes is seemingly ignored or rendered inconsequential.

Each of the Cayce United organizers I worked with have been shut out of the labour market in significant ways, and yet these mothers and grandmothers did not accept the fate proscribed by these scholars, and their lives and efforts were in fact a testament to the resources that *do exist* in their community. While providing important historic and contextual accounts of the problems residents face in Cayce Homes, by the end of the course I could no longer carry a theory into the neighbourhood that so thoroughly dismissed and diminished my com-rades' efforts to improve their community. Further, I felt uneasy about what such theorizing did *to me.* To adopt a structuralist accounting would suggest that it is a waste of time to struggle alongside Cayce residents, and that my scholarly and studious battles would be more efficiently fought on some other register of lived experience, one at a greater distance from Cayce Homes. It was time for a new class. I left Structuralism 101 and headed to Social Process Theory 101: Social Movements.

Social Process Theory 101: social movements can (sometimes) effect social change

Social process theorists focus on the many ways that lived experience is both shaped by and shapes macro-forces (Giddens, 1984). As explained in Giddens's (1984) theory of structuration, all structure constrains and enables human agency. The institutions, rules, practices that govern society are created, maintained and changed recursively through human actions, and human actions are always embedded in structures. Giddens suggests that the longer-standing the structures (such as capitalism and white supremacy), the more deeply they are embedded, and the more resistant they are to immediate change – but they can and do change. Social process theorists are interested in the *processes* through which this repro-duction and/or transformation takes place.

While there are several social process approaches to understanding urban change, one particularly applicable to Cayce United focuses on the role of social movements and community organizing in addressing conditions of inequal-ity. Social movement scholars agree with structuralists that political power and wealth are concentrated in the hands of the few, and that systemic racial, gen-der and other inequalities shape life chances in profound and measurable ways (McAdam, 1999; Mitchell, 2003). At the same time, those who study social movements recognize that under certain conditions, marginalized people can and have achieved important victories, as demonstrated by the labour, suffrage and Civil Rights movements.

Movement scholars work to explicate the conditions under which such efforts succeed and fail. Having studied a number of such movements, McAdam (1999) contends that three factors facilitate successful social movements: political opportunity, organizational strength and cognitive liberation. *Political opportunity* arises from instability in the current political moment – resulting from an unpopular policy, significant demographic changes to the electorate, or growing economic inequality – that renders the status quo vulnerable to change. Additionally, social movements require the *organizational strength* to connect and organize members (this capacity is often found in pre-existing organizations, such as churches or unions). Finally, social movements necessitate *cognitive liberation*, a critical mass of members who recognize that current conditions are not just, believe that these conditions can be changed, and see themselves as having the potential to affect that change (McAdam, 1999). Although this model of movement emergence was developed to account for national and transnational scale movements, McAdam (1999) contends that these elements are also applicable at local community level.

Social process theory applied

I was eager to carry social movement theory into my work with Cayce Homes. I found an impressive history of resident-led organizing efforts to achieve positive outcomes in public housing projects. Throughout the 1960s, public housing residents in cities across the United States organized rent strikes, resulting in improved housing and services (Fossum, 1965; Karp, 2014). Some of these efforts had wide-ranging effects. For example, the 1969 St Louis rent strike led to increases in federal funding to public housing nationally (Karp, 2014). In recent history, community organizing continues to improve local and national housing policy (Speer et al., 2003; Speer & Christens, 2012).

These successes provide a vital source of inspiration to groups like Cayce United, and a network of experienced organizers who can help resident groups develop specific community-based campaigns. At the same time, if McAdam (1999) is right, Cayce United must contend with three critical factors: 1) is the political moment right for change?; 2) does Cayce United have the infrastructure needed to mobilize their neighbours?; 3) does it have or can it build a critical mass of residents who believe change is needed and possible? Answering these questions was neither simple nor straightforward.

By the end of their first year, the core team of Cayce United leaders organized a small base of resident members, and had a number of significant accomplishments. They mobilized residents to get involved, walking the neighbourhood daily and encouraging people to get involved. As Ms Mae explained: 'We're here to let everybody know [. . .] you have a voice, if you don't like the redevelopment plans, say so. If you do like it, say so. But let's have a voice.' This outreach resulted in increased resident attendance at MDHA board meetings and forums about the redevelopment. At their peak, Cayce United turned out over 80 residents to attend a single public meeting with MDHA, where residents asked pointed questions about how the plans would affect their lives.

Between meetings, residents and those working with them, researched the plans, funding proposals and federal regulations to understand how the redevelopment could help and/or harm their neighbourhood. Given high rates of resident unemployment, the strong desire for work among residents, and knowledge that the redevelopment would likely create hundreds of new jobs, Cayce United demanded that MDHA create employment opportunities for residents. However, MDHA staff were frequently dismissive about the number of skilled people in the neighbourhood who might be interested in future employment. In response, Cayce United conducted independent action research of the workforce capacity of their neighbourhood, concluding that in addition to their being a density of people determined to work, there were also a density of skills in the neighbourhood (Thurber, 2014). After months of sustained pressure, organizers secured two important verbal commitments from MDHA: first, MDHA committed to one-to-one replacement of public housing units, and second, that MDHA would provide targeted job training and hiring of residents. Notably, MDHA is actually required to provide the latter under the United States Department of Housing and Urban Development (HUD) regulation Section 3, which calls for targeted training and hiring of residents in HUD-funded development projects taking place in public housing (hud.gov). However, HUD has not enforced this provision and MDHA has long operated without implementing it. It was not until Cayce United's public and persistent instance that MDHA acknowledged their obligation to train and hire residents. With this accomplishment, it appeared that Cayce United might have the political momentum, capacity and base to achieve their goals.

However, Cayce United's efforts were not without challenges, including multiple institutional barriers created by MDHA. For example, MDHA frequently changed public meeting locations at the last minute, making it difficult for residents to attend. When residents asked questions at meetings, the answers were often inconsistent, leading Ms Constance to conclude:

> Something doesn't seem right about this, it just doesn't seem right [. . .] I feel like we are rats in a maze, just scrambling around trying to figure all this out. And they're just waiting for the first big mistake and they're gonna snatch it all away.

Perhaps the biggest obstacle was MDHA's refusal to recognize or even meet with Cayce United. Ironically, MDHA justified this refusal with a federal regulation intended to provide for resident participation in decision-making. The regulation requires that MDHA negotiate with, and only with, 'a duly elected resident council' (964.18). However, MDHA has failed to maintain a resident council in Cayce Homes, and it was in response to this lack of representation that residents first formed Cayce United. Nonetheless, MDHA executives contended they can only legally negotiate with a civic organization that does not exist. In doing so, they buffered the agency from having to engage with residents who are organized, mobilized and have built a base of power.

In addition to, and perhaps exacerbated by, these constraints from MDHA, after its first year organizing Cayce United had difficulty sustaining resident involvement. Just as it began to win important verbal commitments, which would have undoubtedly required pressure to bring to fruition, organizing efforts began to falter. The seasoned organizer who helped found Cayce United moved out of state, and with the transition to a less-experienced organizer, the weekly leadership team dwindled to two or three members, and then ceased. Some residents accepted that displacement was inevitable. Within a few short months, it no longer appeared as though Cayce United had political opening, capacity or base, to leverage social change. All of this left me wondering: if the three conditions requisite for effective movement building are not met, what then? Is it still possible for residents to affect the course of the redevelopment of their community? Did Cayce United's efforts matter?

Social movement models recognize the latent power of residents, and point in the direction of a concrete strategy that organizers can implement. The degree to which structure and agency work in concert with one another was clearly evident in the ways in which Cayce United simultaneously challenged, and was constrained by, MDHA. But, as with structuralist approaches, the theory privileges structural constraints over enabling potentiality, offering a restricted model of change. After such a promising start to the semester, at the end, I was unsure what I could do as an individual or in unison with Cayce United with what I had learned. What the theory seemed to do *to me* was provide yet another reason for me to redirect my energy away from Cayce Homes, something I was not yet ready to do. It was time for me to go back to the classroom.

Post-structuralism 101: inequality and transformation

Structuralist and social process theories assume, to varying degrees, that social inequality and social transformation can be captured in a single explanatory theory. Following Foucault et al. (2003, p. 80), who warn against the 'the inhibiting effect of global, totalitarian theories', post-structural theorists suggest that such models are inherently incomplete and reductionist, and argue that life cannot be modelled or diagrammed, or derived from a single root cause (Deleuze & Guattari, 1988). For some scholars, at issue is not whether there is any empirical accuracy to claims regarding the exploitative effects of capitalism, the destructive power of systemic racism, or the devastating consequences of poverty, but rather the ways that structuralist narratives do not tell the whole story, and the damaging effects of this omission (Gibson-Graham, 2006; Tuck, 2009).

Feminist, queer and critical race scholars contend that oversimplified accounts of social inequality re-inscribe some people and groups as *only and always* victims (Gibson-Graham, 2006; Tuck, 2009). Gibson-Graham (2006) warns against (re)telling victim/perpetrator stories where only certain racially, spatially and gendered bodies can play certain roles, such that white, Western and/or male-dominated systems are cast as holding complete power to dominate and control, while people of colour, non-Western, women are cast as powerless. Doing so empowers the continuation of these relationships of inequality by rendering them natural, inevitable and impermeable to change. Further, hegemonic representations of oppression ignore existing complexity in 'the experiences of people who, at different points in a single day, reproduce, resist, are complicit in, rage against, celebrate, throw up hands/fists/towels, and withdraw and participate in uneven social structures' (Tuck, 2009, p. 420). Indeed, where a structural analysis foregrounds only the most probabilistic outcomes of social inequality, post-structuralists seek moments where these trends are being contested, undone and reimagined – no matter how seemingly small or insignificant – and considers ways to amplify, extend and enlarge these efforts.

In place of traditional attempts at modelling social phenomenon (often in terms of dependent and independent variables), Deleuze and Guattari (1988) offer the metaphor of a rhizome, a living organism with multiple (if not infinite) entry and exit points, and new lines of flight constantly being created. Relatedly, Tuck (2009, p. 416) suggests embracing a desire-based framework for scholarship, one that makes evident 'complexity, contradiction, and the self-determination of lived lives'. Examples of desire-based research include the work of Gibson-Graham et al. (2013, p. 11) who reject renderings of ghettos as places without markets and instead point to what they call the 'iceberg economy' – the broad, diverse and interrelated types of market activities always at work just below the waterline of capitalist wage labour. This iceberg includes: work done in families, schools, churches and between friends; moonlighting, unpaid and illegal work; barter, cooperatives and informal lending. These scholars conclude, 'Once we include what is hidden below the waterline – and possibly keeping us afloat as a society – we expand our prospects for taking back the economy' (Gibson-Graham et al., 2013, p. 11). And these are just the economic possibilities of attending to already-existing multiplicity. Lipsitz (2011, p. 19) writes of alternative geographies imagined and created by enslaved Africans (and later, their descendants) who focus on scopes of space and stakes of space, in their capacity to 'turn segregation into congregation, to transform divisiveness into solidarity, to change dehumanization into rehumanization'. Moreover, Lipsitz (2011, p. 17) sees 'tools for building a more decent, humane, and just society, not just for black people but for everyone'. In other words, these are lines of flight worth following.

Post-structuralism theory applied

Reading about multiplicity, rhizomes and desire was at times thoroughly confusing and yet deeply compelling. I had been given a new set of tools that I was not quite sure how to work with, but I was eager to try. I started simply by considering both gentrification and Cayce United's organizing efforts as rhizomatic rather than driven by a single actor or set of preconditions. This produced shifts in what I noticed, valued and how I engaged in the community. I began attending more to the desires of Cayce United members, which included but were not limited to their specific organizing goals. Finally, it compelled me to follow the lines of flight

Cayce United travelled in the two years of work together, and how those lines continued in spite of the group no longer formally organizing.

As discussed previously (Thurber & Fraser, 2016), Cayce United made some important, though modest, gains toward their original organizing goals; much harder to map are the gains that continued even when the organizational structure fell away. Some of these were individual – such as developing literacy, confidence and fellowship – and may shape residents' futures in unforeseen ways. I remember sitting with Ms Constance, together researching HUD policy for a letter to the editor, as she also learned to use a mouse and computer for the first time. Struck by the efficiency of our work – in stark contrast to her experience trying to access clear and accurate information through MDHA – she exclaimed, 'I need to get me one of these. You can get a lot done on that! You can find out all kinds of things!' Ms Ella, a founding member of Cayce United, reflects that organizing in her community, 'made me see that I can do things that I didn't know I could do, I never thought I could get up in front of people and speak, I never thought I could do any of those things it has impacted me to show me that, hey – you can do this! Just do it!' While it was not always evident how these individual gains enabled future actions, sometimes it was.

Several months into Cayce United's door to door organizing, Ms Mae became concerned about the needs of teenagers in Cayce Homes:

> What really got me thinking was this young man, he told me his mom was always coming home with bags of clothes for his baby sister, and doesn't have nothing for him, and he was fixin' to start selling weed so he could get himself some clothes. You know, a lot of people think young people today are only interested in technology – I think a lot of these kids would be really happy to have like a new school uniform. So that's what I'm going to do. I'm talking to folks around here, and I'm going to do some research with teens to ask them what they want.

Just two weeks later, Ms Mae excitedly updated fellow Cayce United leaders about her first focus group with eight teenagers. 'It was just awesome, I'm really excited, my thing is that I just love to give back. I asked them what would you like to learn about? They came up with a big list – mentoring, career, financial planning, how to get into college.' In response to the needs identified by these young people, and drawing on many of the connections she made through Cayce United, she launched a volunteer-run girls' empowerment programme called Positive Attitudes. With 15 young women attending weekly, Ms Mae's programme is now the post-popular teen programme available in Cayce Homes, and has been running consistently for over a year.

Other seeds of activism planted within Cayce United have even shot up across the city, among other public housing residents. Six months after the last formal Cayce United meeting, residents from another project slated for redevelopment reached out to Cayce United leaders, seeking materials – including flyers and the previously mentioned letter to the editor co-authored by Miss Constance – as tools for educating residents about their rights. These are examples of Cayce

United's lines of flight, ways that the change efforts imagined by residents branch out, burrow in or build up (Lipstiz, 2011).

Granted, the post-structuralists make no guarantees, and they offer no template to follow, other than the map of our own desire. An obvious critique of post-structuralism is that on the other side of the possibility inherent in multiplicity, desire and the imaginary is the painful probability, made evident in incarceration rates and police killings and employment barriers, that black and brown lives don't matter, no matter how branched, burrowed or built up their lines of flight. Nonetheless, a post-structural approach did something to, with, and for the residents of Cayce Homes that other theories did not, and did something to, with, and for me as a student, scholar and a neighbour. It encouraged me to stay in and with Cayce residents after formal organizational efforts appeared to dissolve; to take seriously their visions, hopes and desires; to account for rather than dismiss or ignore their actions.

What we do with theory, and what it does to us

> I found a place of sanctuary in 'theorising,' in making sense out of what was happening. I found a place where I could imagine possible futures, a place where life could be lived differently.
>
> (hooks, 1994, p. 63)

Laying theory on the ground of a particular place is much like bringing a quilt from the workshop to the bedroom; it is only in use that the fits and misfits are revealed, that it becomes obvious what parts of social life have been accounted for, and whether any toes are left hanging in the cold. Working alongside Cayce United organizers while grappling with social theory provided a unique opportunity to wrestle with these fits and misfits. Structuralism explains the forces driving gentrification, yet bracketed out the potential of those most harmed to affect change. Social process models suggested specific strategies to mobilize for change, yet the requisite preconditions (the trifecta of political opportunity, organizational strength and cognitive liberation in the social movement model) undercut its potential utility for emergent community organizing efforts in sub-optimal conditions. Post-structuralism succeeded in capturing indigenous knowledge, strength and potential, but offered no specific instructions on what groups ought to do with that strength to achieve their goals.

Thankfully, as neighbours, students and scholars concerned with neighbourhood inequality, we need not be restricted to drawing from only one theoretical orientation. We can draw insights across scholars, fields and perspectives, asking ourselves, as suggested by Massumi, in the translators' foreword to Deleuze and Guattari's (1988, p. xv) text, 'not: is it true? But: does it work? What new thoughts does it make it possible to think? What new emotions does it make it possible to feel? What new sensations and perceptions does it open in the body?' We can consider, in the tradition of feminist scholar Lather, the perspective's catalytic validity, 'the degree to which the research process re-orients, focuses, and energises participants toward knowing reality in order to transform it' (1986, p. 68). For those working in solidarity with communities experiencing inequality, these questions can easily be applied to our theoretical perspectives. What do our theories do to us, and what can we do with them? Do they open up new thoughts and feelings; do they *energize* us towards transformation?

Theorizing is generative. What we think we know shapes what we imagine to be possible and the actions we take. There are many problems faced by residents of deeply marginalized, stigmatized and racialized neighbourhoods. When we – the students, scholars and practitioners engaging in these spaces – don't account for the fullness of their lives and experiences, *we* become a problem, writing off people and places and possibilities. In tracing the kinds of understanding and actions different theoretical approaches generated in me, it is my hope that this inquiry might engage others intervening in spaces of neighbourhood inequality to critically reflect on our theorizing, so that we might re-enter such neighbourhoods equipped with a broader set of conceptual tools for building just communities. Perhaps we would do best to heed Stewart's (2008, p. 72) call for 'weak theory in an unfinished world', remembering there are possibilities and potentialities, within and around us, that we cannot yet see or measure. Given the unfinished-ness of the world, and incompleteness of our own understandings, our theorizing must be always living, always draft, always contextual, and never quite right. Ending my first two years of doctoral study, I drew greater comfort from philosophy than social theory. As Rorty (1999, p. 82) cautions:

> You cannot aim at 'doing what is right,' because you will never know whether you have hit the mark. Long after you are dead, better-informed and more sophisticated people may judge your action to have been a tragic mistake [. . .] But you *can* aim at ever more sensitivity to pain, and ever greater satisfaction of ever more various needs [. . .] of taking the needs and interests and views of more and more diverse human beings into account.

It is not required that our theory be right, only that it aim toward justice. Weak theory compels us to keep noticing, to keep thinking and to keep taking the most just actions possible given what we now know.

References

Austin, A. (2013). *The unfinished march: An overview*. Economic Policy Institute. Retrieved from www.epi.org/unfinished-march/.

Bennett, S. (2000). Possibility of a beloved place: Residents and placemaking in public housing communities. *Saint Louis University Public Library Review, 19*, 259–307.

Brenner, N., & Theodore, N. (2002). Cities and the geographies of 'actually existing neo-liberalism'. *Antipode, 34*, 349–379.

Chaskin, R., Khare, A., & Joseph, M. (2012). Participation, deliberation, and decision making: The dynamics of inclusion and exclusion in mixed-income developments. *Urban Affairs Review, 48*, 863–906.

Davis, T. M., & Welcher, A. N. (2013). School quality and the vulnerability of the black middle class: The continuing significance of race as a predictor of disparate schooling environments. *Sociological Perspectives, 56*, 467–493.

DeFilippis, J. (2008). Paradoxes of community-building: Community control in the global economy. *International Social Science Journal, 59*, 223–234.

Deleuze, G., & Guattari, F. (1988). *A thousand plateaus: Capitalism and schizophrenia.* London: Bloomsbury Publishing.

Duke, J. (2009). Mixed income housing policy and public housing residents' 'right to the city'. *Critical Social Policy, 29*, 100–120.

EJP Consulting. (2013). Envision Cayce Community Meeting #1 Minutes.

Fossum, J. C. (1965). Rent withholding and the improvement of substandard housing. *California Law Review, 53*, 304–336.

Foucault, M., Bertani, M., Fontana, A., Ewald, F., & Macey, D. (2003). *'Society must be defended': Lectures at the Collège de France, 1975–1976* (Vol. 1). London: Macmillan.

Fraser, J., DeFilippis, J., & Bazuin, J. (2012). HOPE VI: Calling for modesty in its claims. In G. Bridge, T. Butler, & L. Lees (Eds.), *Mixed communities: Gentrification by stealth* (pp. 209–229). Chicago, IL: Policy Press.

Friedman, L. M. (1966). Public housing and the poor: An overview. *California Law Review, 54*, 642–669.

Gibson-Graham, J. K. (2006). *'The' end of capitalism (as we knew it): A feminist critique of political economy.* Minneapolis: University of Minnesota Press.

Gibson-Graham, J. K., Cameron, J., & Healy, S. (2013). *Take back the economy: An ethical guide for transforming our communities.* Minneapolis: University of Minnesota Press.

Giddens, A. (1984). *The constitution of society: Outline of the theory of structuration.* Berkeley: University of California Press.

Harris, C. I. (1993). Whiteness as property. *Harvard Law Review, 106*, 1707–1791.

Harvey, D. (1989). *The condition of postmodernity an enquiry into the origins of cultural change.* Oxford: Blackwell.

Harvey, D. (2005). *A brief history of neoliberalism.* Oxford: Oxford University Press.

Henderson, A. S. (1995). 'Tarred with the exceptional image': Public housing and popular discourse, 1950–1990. *American Studies, 36*, 31–52.

hooks, b. (1994). *Teaching to transgress: Education as the practice of freedom.* London: Routledge.

Houston, B. (2012). *The Nashville way: Racial etiquette and the struggle for social justice in a Southern city.* Athens: University of Georgia Press.

Hyra, D. (2013). Mixed-income housing: Where have we been and where do we go from here? *Cityscape, 15*, 123–134.

Karp, M. (2014). The St. Louis rent strike of 1969: Transforming black activism and American low-income housing. *Journal of Urban History, 40*, 648–670.

Lather, P. (1986). Issues of validity in openly ideological research: Between a rock and a soft place. *Interchange, 17*, 63–84.

Lipsitz, G. (2007). The racialization of space and the spatialization of race: Theorizing the hidden architecture of landscape. *Landscape Journal, 26*, 10–23.

Lipsitz, G. (2011). *How racism takes place.* Philadelphia, PA: Temple University Press.

Lloyd, R. (2011). East Nashville skyline. *Ethnography, 12*, 114–145.

Massey, D. S., & Denton, N. A. (1993). *American apartheid: Segregation and the making of the underclass.* Cambridge, MA: Harvard University Press.

McAdam, D. (1999). *Political process and the development of Black insurgency, 1930–1970.* Chicago, IL: University of Chicago Press.

MDHA. (2013). Resident needs assessment highlights, June. Metropolitan Development and Housing Agency, Nashville, TN.

Mitchell, D. (2003). *The right to the city: Social justice and the fight for public space.* New York: Guilford Press.

O'Connor, A. (2009). *Poverty knowledge: Social science, social policy, and the poor in twentieth-century US history*. Princeton, NJ: Princeton University Press.

Neely, B., & Samura, M. (2011). Social geographies of race: Connecting race and space. *Ethnic and Racial Studies, 34*, 1933–1952.

Peck, J., & Tickell, A. (2002). Neoliberalizing space. *Antipode, 34*, 380–404.

Popkin, S. J., Katz, B., Cunningham, M. K., Brown, K. D., Gustafson, J., & Turner, M. A. (2004). A decade of HOPE VI: Research findings and policy challenges. The Urban Institute.

Pulido, L. (2000). Rethinking environmental racism: White privilege and urban development in Southern California. *Annals of the Association of American Geographers, 90*, 12–40.

Reece, J., Norris, D., Olinger, J., Holley, K., & Martin, M. (2013). Place matters: Using mapping to plan for opportunity, equity, and sustainability. Kirwan Institute for the Study of Race and Ethnicity.

Rorty, R. (1999). *Philosophy and social hope*. London: Penguin.

Schwartz, A. F. (2010). *Housing policy in the United States* (2nd ed.). New York: Routledge.

Silver, H. (2013). Mixing policies: Expectations and achievements. *Cities, 15*, 73–82.

Stewart, K. (2008). Weak theory in an unfinished world. *Journal of Folklore Research, 45*, 71–82.

Speer, P. (2014). Report for Nashville Force for Good Steering Committee. Unpublished document.

Speer, P. W., Ontkush, M., Schmitt, B., Raman, P., Jackson, C., Rengert, K. M., & Peterson, N. A. (2003). The intentional exercise of power: Community organizing in Camden, New Jersey. *Journal of Community & Applied Social Psychology, 13*, 399–408.

Speer, P. W., & Christens, B. D. (2012). Local community organizing and change: Altering policy in the housing and community development system in Kansas City. *Journal of Community & Applied Social Psychology, 22*, 414–427.

Stewart, K. (2008). Weak theory in an unfinished world. *Journal of Folklore Research, 45*(1), 71–82.

Stolloff, J. A. (n.d.). A brief history of public housing. Report. US Department of Housing and Urban Development. Washington, DC.

Thurber, A. (2014). Cayce Homes: Working Neighborhood Assessment. Prepared for Cayce United.

Thurber, A., & Fraser, J. (2016). Disrupting the order of things: Public housing tenant organizing for material, political and epistemological justice. *Cities, 57*, 55–61.

Tuck, E. (2009). Suspending damage: A letter to communities. *Harvard Educational Review, 79*, 409–428.

United Church of Christ Commission for Racial Justice. (1987). Toxic wastes and race in the United States: A national report on the racial and socio-economic characteristics of communities with hazardous waste sites. Public Data Access.

Wacquant, L. (2008). *Urban outcasts: A comparative sociology of advanced marginality*. Cambridge: Polity.

Young, I. M. (1990). *Justice and the politics of difference*. Princeton, NJ: Princeton University Press.

12 Developing a research agenda to assess local social impacts of sports tourism regeneration in Medulin, Croatia

Nicholas Wise and Marko Perić

Introduction

From a social geographical perspective, sports tourism-led transformation and creative change can result in both inclusion and exclusion. New facilities, venues or amenities are invested in and built to attract visitors and encourage spending. Local interests are therefore not always adequately considered and research notes that locals feel excluded as a result of renewal (Spirou, 2010). Questions that pertain to local interests (that relate to inclusion) revolve around how change and new developments will benefit or impact the local community and its residents. More work by geographers and social scientists is needed to address and assess local social impacts. Such a broad-reaching question attempts to understand how local residents perceive and experience ongoing change around them (referring to sports tourism-led regeneration in this case). Conducting case-specific research in local communities will contribute further insight into the intangible outcomes of regeneration and transformation. Such research is also an opportunity for local residents to voice their wants and needs and to describe to what extent (if any) regeneration has benefitted them or transformed their lives. This chapter proposes a research agenda in an area where sports tourism redevelopment is ongoing: in Medulin, Croatia on the Istrian Peninsula. The purpose of this chapter is to address methodological development and research design in our future research. Below we will discuss a number of social conditions and conceptualizations concerning social impacts and sports tourism-led regeneration.

By outlining a research agenda to assess the social impacts of sports tourism regeneration in Medulin, Croatia, this chapter follows the direction of a longitudinal study in a place that has recently upgraded its sporting infrastructures. It is important in contemporary research that we consider the reach of impact. Chalip (2006) and Wise (2016) argue that too much work focuses solely on measuring economic impacts through consideration of financial gains, incentives and benefits. Scholars are also interested in environmental impacts and the effects that industries such as tourism have on the environment. While economic and environmental issues are important, they often overshadow social impacts. It can be difficult for us as researchers to complete case studies without the assistance of local people who inform us by speaking about their everyday experiences and challenges (Ehn et al., 2016). We focus on regeneration all too often as a term that broadly implies tangible change. Local people, tourists, event attendees and researchers can all see physical and infrastructural change. What we do not always see, or recognize, are social and intangible impacts. This is why we as researchers need to design research in a manner that seeks to uncover social impacts of regeneration alongside the people who can insightfully inform our understanding. This way, through our findings we uncover local knowledge that can better inform local and regional policies to improve the lives of those immediately affected by regeneration.

Regenerating towns and cities significantly impacts local populations. Although sport and tourism are important and relate to creative change, this chapter is not interested in tourist perceptions or the wider impacts of sports tourism. Instead we are interested in social impacts and local opportunities gained from sports-led regeneration. We have published some initial papers looking at sports tourism in Istria (see Perić & Wise, 2015; Wise & Perić, 2017; Wise et al., 2017). To extend our research, we outline in this chapter an approach that focuses on longitudinal data collection. Specifically, we want to find out how locals take advantage of new enterprise or entrepreneurial opportunities and how new facilities, amenities and infrastructures are used by locals to increase well-being, overall sense of community and pride in place. By developing and outlining an approach that involves working with local residents and researching intangible impacts, we intend to provide valuable insight into the social impacts of change, renewal and regeneration. It is important to note that private companies are often key generators of (i.e. investors in) sports tourism-led regeneration. Therefore, a long-term focus is required at both the organizational and socioeconomic levels (Stubbs & Cocklin, 2008). Companies should also adopt a systemic approach that seeks to address the dimension of social sustainability to generate shared value creation for all stakeholders, especially the community and residents (Bocken et al., 2015). While companies are concerned about finances and returns on their investments, academics can assist in informing social understandings that support value creation for all stakeholders.

Research impact and social conditions

Sport and tourism regeneration scholarship has seen increased interest in the last several decades (Chalkley & Essex, 1999; Evans, 2001; Gratton & Henry, 2001; Matheson, 2010; Spirou, 2010; Smith, 2012; Edgell & Swanson, 2013; Wise & Whittam, 2015). Many cities undergo regeneration and utilize sport and events to promote and increase tourism by investing in new facilities, infrastructures and venues (Getz, 2003; Smith, 2012; Weed, 2007). From the economic perspective, sports tourism regeneration promotes a range of new enterprise and entrepreneurial opportunities in the creative and cultural industries (Hall, 2006; Preuss, 2007; Waitt & Gibson, 2009; Smith, 2009; Zhao et al., 2011). Enterprise opportunities are especially important because they also represent a social benefit, where local people are able to gain by starting new businesses that will support the aforementioned growing industry. However, critically, it is important that local residents are able to get involved. In many cases, existing companies absorb the economic benefits, and if profits leave, the only money retained locally is in the form of the payment local employees receive. It is important that training programmes are initiated, local skills are assessed and sought out and involvement among local residents in the immediate and surrounding community is promoted and encouraged. This is how local financial impacts are dependably maintained. Critical scholars have noted that regeneration can lead to further exclusion if local people are not involved, and if social policies and legacy initiatives are not in place to protect local residents (García, 2005; Smith, 2012).

When we consider social issues alongside regeneration strategies (local perceptions will help us gain knowledge specific to each locale) academic critique and conceptualizations are not found to be generalized (Richards et al., 2013; Smith, 2012). Although regeneration efforts may seem comparable across a number of different places, they are inherently different because places vary in terms of culture, skills and overall well-being. As academics, it is our job to conduct research that will help to inform social and cultural policy, and this means looking for new ways to measure impact specific to a place and group of people. There are also increased pressures for us as academics to focus more on social conditions, social impacts and change within the community (Deery et al., 2012; Kim et al., 2013; Edwards, 2015; Altinay et al., 2016; Clark et al., 2016). Alongside such policy implications, more research has been dedicated to critically assessing local perceptions of tourism, social tourism and local development in communities (Dwyer, 2005; Higgins-Desbiolles, 2011; Deery et al., 2012; Smith, 2012; Richards et al., 2013; Wise & Whittam, 2015). This initiative focuses on improving the lives and well-being of local residents alongside planning for sport, tourism and subsequent leisure opportunities and experiences (see Clark & Kearns, 2015; Perić & Wise, 2015). In terms of impacts on people and communities, positive socio-cultural benefits are based on education, local experiences, improvements to residential facilities, maintaining local cultural traditions and how change increases civic pride and sense of place (see Harrill, 2004; Yen & Kerstetter, 2009; Smith, 2012; Wise, 2015). Beyond these conceptual approaches often assessed by academics, we need to develop research that engages local residents so our results reflect local opinions, reactions, concerns and trends (see Higgins-Desbiolles, 2011; Naidoo & Sharpley, 2016). In places that have seen sports tourism-led regeneration, similarly we need to understand how local residents become involved and engaged by considering what we see as important social conditions, outlined below. Chalip (2006) noted that too much focus is placed on economic impacts, and more work needs to be done to address the social value of sports, events and tourism activities.

Since this book focuses on urban renewal and creative change, and because cities, towns and regions are continually transformed, the people who live in close proximity to areas undergoing transformation are either included or excluded. As noted above, we visually assess transformations such as aesthetic enhancements to landscapes or improved venues or facilities at face value. We habitually notice changes based on tangible transformations because they leave lasting images of places. When we understand how social transformation results from renewal agendas, then we start to understand how new opportunities are founded, but these local understandings are not so widely publicized, again because a new stadium or attraction will more likely become synonymous with a place. For instance, training and education programmes are necessary to ensure local residents and young adults gain the necessary skills required to gain employment in the new industries created. What sort of enterprise or entrepreneurial opportunities can result from new skills and knowledge acquired by locals? Investments in leisure and tourism require a range of services. Informing locals of opportunities is a form of social and research impact. By gaining an understanding of local wants and needs, we need to then transfer this knowledge to inform social policy, as opposed to merely critiquing social policy.

There is a range of social impacts, and their measurement demands close consideration. To understand how locals benefit from sports tourism regeneration, transformation and creative change, we will consider the following 14 social conditions in our research:

(1) Clear policies on social benefits for local residents.
(2) Mutual understanding and tolerance between planners, businesses and locals.
(3) Local population is involved and supports sports tourism initiatives.
(4) Local population benefits from new sporting opportunities and experiences.
(5) Mentorship and educational programmes exist to train and involve locals.
(6) Encouragement of local enterprise opportunities.
(7) Establishment of volunteer programmes.
(8) Inclusion and exclusion plans to assist people from underprivileged communities.
(9) New opportunities for young people, students, elderly and disabled.
(10) Pride in place and satisfaction.
(11) Sense of community and identity.
(12) Venues and facilities are co-managed to support local resident use.
(13) Legacy training and participation incentives for locals.
(14) Local population is aware of legacy agendas and benefits.

The above conditions result from a review of work outlined by Laurence Chalip (2006), Andrew Smith (2012) and Donald Getz (2013). We use these 14 points as a framework to assess social impacts. Each condition will be further discussed below when talking about each phase of the research; the conditions are organized in such a manner that the research progresses each year to expand the focus of the research. It must also be noted that these 14 social conditions are intended as guidance to begin the research, and we do anticipate this list will change: new conditions could be added, or specifics may become further defined during the research process. Social change is about altering people's outlook and attitudes, gaining support and encouraging cohesion and involvement among community members. Impacts are an evaluation of the results that need to be assessed from a range of perspectives. Geographically and sociologically, we need to consider individual and social capital (Atherley, 2006; Zhao et al., 2011). In terms of management, creative capital and entrepreneurial opportunities also need to be considered in order to understand whether training programmes are in place to educate and encourage people to create new enterprises. We are referring here to individual and social capital, which involves the formation of networks, norms and trusts that enable people to work together to pursue and achieve a number of set shared objectives across the community (Quinn & Wilks, 2013). To achieve pride in place, or even a better sense of community, bonding capital is necessary to help forge community ties to create a better sense of belonging (Putnam, 2000; Wise, 2015).

Sports tourism in Medulin

Medulin is located to the south of the city of Pula (the largest city in Istria County), positioned in the south of the Istrian Peninsula on the Adriatic Coast (which is the westernmost part of Croatia). This region of Croatia has long attracted visitors from countries in Central Europe, specifically Germany and Austria. While the Istria region already has an abundance of well-developed existing tourism infra-structures, we are concerned with destinations that are the focus of regeneration and transformation strategies to upgrade facilities further developing the sports tourism industry. While the region seeks to create more tourism opportunities to maintain its competitive advantage, we need to consider how locals and regional residents gain from the regeneration and availability of new facilities, and ulti-mately what opportunities exist for them. For the sports tourist, the moderate climate and range of sporting amenities enables year-round sports activity. One of the challenges in Croatia is a lack of tourists during the winter months. This may seem unremarkable in most 'sun and sea' destinations, but it translates as a burden on local people due to lack of employment opportunities during the slow months. With the development of new sporting facilities and infrastructures, now, ideally, locals will also have the opportunity to take advantage of year-round activity. This research will address this in terms of employment and enterprise activities, in addition to considering people's own personal recreational interests and over-all well-being. This research will be conducted in Medulin because it is an area where extensive physical regeneration has taken place to grow the sports tourism industry. In the light of this recent regeneration, we seek to gain perspectives from people in Medulin and across the greater Pula area to understand access, usage and opportunity among people who reside in the area year-round.

Sports tourism training facilities in Medulin have existed since the 1970s, and in 2014 Medulin's sports tourism infrastructures were updated. For example, football training in this area is attractive to clubs based in Central and Northern Europe. Another example of existing sports tourism in Istria is tennis camps and events in destinations such as Pula and Umag (see Perić & Wise, 2015). There has also been a focus on further developing biking, hiking and running trails for subsequent leisure and recreational purposes. Upgraded biking, hiking and running trails are ideal for local residents as well because they are maintained for tourists and locals can use them year-round. New sports facilities in Medulin include six upgraded FIFA-sized football pitches, managed and maintained by the hotels (football fields are based on Fédération Internationale de Football Association's (FIFA) regulation pitch size). For the professional and amateur sports clubs Medulin plans to attract, it offers changing facilities alongside the new pitches, as well as storage space for equipment, fitness/weightlifting facilities, and nutritionists who work with sports clubs to ensure dietary regimes are optimal. These additional facilities and amenities are located in the hotel premises and are private, so that teams can focus on training with few distractions. There are also new conference/meeting rooms for strategic planning.

In terms of organizations and investments, sports development is organized by Arenaturist; the Park Plaza Belvedere maintains facilities and rents the spaces. Arenaturist provides tourism, hospitality and catering services and sells its capacities (and existing sporting infrastructures) to tourist agencies (see Perić & Wise, 2015). The intention here is these sports tourism investments will create opportunities to sustain tourism in the off-season and assist with off-season unemployment/underemployment, as noted above. The challenge and what requires attention is how private investments will benefit local residents. Beyond the perceived economic benefits, there is the potential for locals to benefit in terms of improving their well-being by making use of the new facilities to encourage active, healthy lifestyles. Some of the facilities (football pitches and tennis courts) will have limited access, but the improved biking, hiking and running trails are more accessible. What this research seeks to further understand is how sports tourism investments will impact locals, because the purpose for these (private) investments are aimed at promoting year-round tourism in this region.

Research approach

Research focusing on intangible regeneration and transformation cannot be generalized, as mentioned above. Bottom-up approaches conducted through fieldwork and engagement in communities will allow new knowledge and understanding specific to a particular case study to emerge. We need to understand how locals view change, in addition to how they embrace or disregard change, which can offer insights into inclusion and exclusion. As noted, the intention of this chapter is to outline our research by discussing how our research design focuses on social impacts looking at sports tourism regeneration in Medulin. While the present book includes a range of cases and research results, this chapter differs because it puts forward a research approach. Similarly, our research is linked to Amie Thurber's chapter (11) and Shauna Brail, Ekaterina Mizrokhi and Sonia Ralston's chapter (10) in this collection because we will gain direct insight from local community leaders and residents. We will also link this work to our teaching, and we will involve students in the research process. The content covered in the classroom will put emphasis on the significance of social impact and each year students will practically engage with data collection. The students in the class will change each year, so the teaching emphasis will be updated accordingly to link with the focus and approach emphasized in each phase of the research. Teaching will examine the social impacts of sports tourism using the social conditions outlined above as guidance, although only a small number of social conditions will direct the focus of the research in each phase.

This research will be linked to a project in a module entitled 'Sports Management in Tourism', taught at the University of Rijeka in Croatia. Third-year undergraduate students will assist the research process in an attempt to stress the value of social impacts in teaching and research. Each year, a class on sports management in tourism is led by Marko Perić, and Nicholas Wise lectures on the class for one week each academic year. The authors of this chapter will lead the research and build on the content outlined in each phase of this research (see Table 12.1). The authors have begun conducting research with urban and regional planners and tourism business managers; these results are currently being collated and will appear in forthcoming publications. We will conduct research with industry stakeholders alongside community residents, but in this chapter we will address the above-noted social conditions and focus of each phase of the longitudinal research. Each student in the class will maintain contact with research participants to collect data at different stages during the February to July semester each academic year. Results will be analysed each year to look for consistencies and differences among the communities impacted by sports tourism related regeneration. A number of social conditions will be considered in each phase.

The aim of conducting longitudinal research is to build on observations each year. Below we outline the first four phases of this research (each phase progresses the research each year). These four phases put emphasis on different social conditions and ask participants to reflect on points and offer observations. We intend to extend this research further to address social impacts over an extended period of time to assess legacy initiatives, but given the timely regeneration, this phase of the research is being planned to coincide with it. Addressing opportunities and how people have benefited from tangible investments, we need to transfer these understandings from perceptions and perspectives over an extended period of time if we want to evaluate social meanings and intangible outcomes. By focusing part of the sports management in tourism class content upon social conditions and the intangible outcomes of regeneration, we will involve students who will assist with interviewing research participants each year. The researchers will conduct periodic focus groups with community participants each year and maintain regular contact with industry representatives, government officials and planners to gain regular updates on social policy and community planning initiatives. The methodological approach involves the use of several qualitative research methods to collect data inductively, as discussed below. The following subsections discuss the approach taken in each year and focus on social conditions. Table 12.1 outlines each phase of this study.

Table 12.1 Outlining the focus, method and social conditions covered in each phase of research

Phase	Focus	Method	Conditions
1	Initial perceptions	Focus groups, journals	1, 2, 3
2	Experiences, opportunities & involvement	Interviews, journals	4, 5, 6, 7
3	New opportunities, place & community	Interviews/spatial mapping, journals	8, 9, 10, 11
4	Legacy and comprehensive summative social impact assessment	Survey, journals, focus groups	12, 13, 14

Phase 1

The first phase involves recruiting participants, group interviews and focus groups. We will first meet with community representatives in Medulin to discuss our study. It is vital that a relationship of trust with community residents is established, and that the purpose of the research is clear to them. We will ask those willing to participate in the study to provide regular updates through each phase of the research. Our research will initially focus on residents in Medulin, but we do intend to reach out to other towns across the greater Pula region to assess the geographical distribution of perceptions and local social impacts as the study develops. Each case will be specific in order to avoid the pitfall of making generalizations.

For the foundation stages of this study we are most concerned with the first three social conditions: 1) clear policies on social benefits for local residents; 2) mutual understanding and tolerance between planners, businesses and locals; and 3) local population is involved and supports sports tourism initiatives. We have recently conducted a survey with sports tourism stakeholders in Medulin to get a sense of community involvement and legacy planning (this work is not yet published but is prepared for publication). We also need to consider how local residents understand policies and what opportunities they feel they will gain, or not gain, from sports tourism in Medulin. Tourism is an industry that requires mutual understanding and mutual relationships between business stakeholders (public and private), planners and developers, and the local community. Because the destination will attract people from the outside, this will alter perceptions and behaviours of local residents. Communities across Croatia are accustomed to tourism since the industry is part of the country's economic base, but a niche type of tourism (such as sports tourism) offers different benefits and potential for both visitors and locals alike. We need to conduct some conceptual grounding with research participants first (in accordance to social conditions 1 and 2), and from that point we can explore how members of the community and locals may intend to become involved and support sports tourism (social condition 3).

To attract research participants in Medulin, we will first meet with community representatives to help us recruit research participants. We will send out and post calls for local residents to participant in focus groups. Semi-structured focus groups will focus on each of the first three social conditions to get a sense of residents' attitudes and perceptions. Data from the focus groups will help guide our data collection in future phases of study. We will strive to recruit between eight and ten participants for each focus group, and we will conduct focus groups periodically over the first three months. Once we reach the point where sufficient numbers of focus groups satisfy this initial data collection process (or the point of data saturation), we will reach out to participants to take part in future study phases. We will include students who will help conduct regular interviews with participants and we will ask residents to keep a journal to record their experiences, opportunities and involvement in sport and sports tourism. More specifically, participants will be asked to keep a journal and record their perceptions and attitudes based on current events, noting especially when they feel they are impacted by the local sports tourism industry: how they are involved, engaged or make use of new facilities. Participants will be supplied with a journal to keep a regular record. We will ask participants to discuss how they engage with new facilities and amenities, to keep track of their thoughts, involvement, opportunities and well-being. We are also interested in if local residents feel they have limited access to new facilities and amenities. We will ask research participants to record their thoughts and experiences in the journal every two to three months. This approach has been used in studies to gather regular recordings of people's perceptions over extended periods of time (see Mooney et al., 2015; Ortlipp, 2008).

In this first phase, we are seeking to understand local residents' perceptions and interpretations of change and sports tourism policies. We also want to get a sense of how people are getting involved – for instance, whether the new facilities increase and encourage well-being, or whether residents are finding new employment or enterprise opportunities. We will involve students in this first phase by putting those involved in the class in groups to work with us to facilitate the focus groups and assess social policy documents. We need to develop a series of materials and guiding questions as we prepare content to cover in the focus groups. Because part of this stage requires a review of policy documents and conceptual insights, students will help prepare this initial stage by critically reviewing social policy and planning documents linked to sports tourism regeneration in Medulin.

Phase 2

After gaining a comprehensive foundation of policies, local understandings and what support exists, the next step is to focus more on experiences, opportunities and involvement. The next four social conditions will be articulated in this section: 4) local population benefits from new sporting opportunities and experiences; 5) mentorship and educational programmes exist to train and involve locals; 6) encouragement of local enterprise opportunities; and 7) establishment of volunteer programmes. Social impacts cannot be fully understood until we obtain a sense of how people take advantage of opportunities and what experiences they gain. Notions of inclusion and exclusion are also important here and we anticipate problematic issues may arise – these are explored in more depth in the next phase of this research. When we consider economic contexts, Wise (2016, p. 32) notes: 'government authorities try to provide business support and start-up funding for small and medium size enterprises to encourage entrepreneurial activity in the service sector'. In reality, there is much reliance on the private sector to invest in local tourism industries, but profits gained are not always retained locally (see McLennan et al., 2012). That is also why we need sustainable business approaches that incorporate a triple bottom-line approach (Bocken et al., 2015). However, wider public support is needed, and local tourism industries need local businesses and local involvement to ensure growth is sustained over the long term (Wise, 2016).

Given the conditions used to guide data collection and focus in Phase 2, we need to evaluate the existence of education or training programmes. Such programmes are essential because they get local people involved and motivate them to seek opportunities such as embarking upon a new business venture. This is especially important for younger generations. As observed elsewhere in the former Yugoslavia, a lack of opportunities (or a lack of exposed opportunities) results in declining populations. Research has noted places need to maintain their level of opportunities to keep people employed, so this will help create a competitive advantage locally (see Hall, 2006; Mulec & Wise, 2013). All of the conditions outlined in this section are interrelated to the extent that experiences promote opportunities. Education, training and volunteer programmes motivate opportunities, and enterprise and entrepreneurial opportunities help sustain local involvement to support the growth of a new, existing or growing industry.

Students will assist by conducting in-depth interviews with research participants in this second stage. Students will work in groups to obtain interview data from all research participants. Structured interview questions specific to each case and how the research has developed from the first stage will be developed. For the purpose of research planning, in this second phase, questions will be based on the above-mentioned social conditions. As will be discussed in each phase, we will refer to observations from the participants' journals so that we continue to build on observed data each year.

Phase 3

Chalip (2006) wrote about social interactions and the involvement of people at events. He focused on attendee experiences, but we argue here more work is needed to conduct similar assessments with local community residents outside the actual activity, as relevant to our work on sports tourism. Inclusion and exclusion was noted in Phase 2. To be critical of opportunities and involvement, regeneration in the form of new infrastructures can be exclusively for those who can afford to use facilities or amenities. New infrastructures, especially those that make significant alterations to the sporting landscapes, can offer much in terms of benefits for locals. For instance, upgraded training facilities and parks are beneficial to locals for everyday leisure activity and well-being. Other facilities such as football pitches or tennis facilities may not be accessible because they are located on private space or are used only for team training (because of the terms of renting the space), and thus have no effective local use.

Four social conditions come into focus in this phase of the study: 8) inclusion and exclusion, plans to assist people from underprivileged communities; 9) new opportunities for young people, students, elderly and disabled; 10) pride in place and satisfaction; and 11) sense of community and identity. We bring these conditions into the mid-point of the study to give participants time to elaborate on policy and opportunities first, before introducing more sociologically informed conditions. We are also interested in opportunities in this phase – especially those which focus on people from underprivileged communities – and what opportunities exist for people not considered part of the productive-aged working population cohorts. By continuing the assessment of opportunities across a wider range, we then begin to see how sociological and social-psychological understandings linked to place and community arise. People continually strive for a sense of community, but depending on opportunities this can either positively or negatively influence people's pride in place, their connections and comradeship. Satisfaction and pride in place can link well depending on the direction of industries, people's attainment and influence. Sense of place and sense of community are also important. Sense of community refers to membership, influence, shared emotional connections and involvement (see McMillan & Chavis, 1986; Wise, 2015), whereas sense of place 'is the phrase used by many geographers when they want to emphasize that places are significant because they are the focus of personal feelings' (Rose, 1995, p. 88).

We will involve students in the same manner as Phase 2, but interviews will focus more on place and community using spatial mapping techniques. Interviews will be conducted using aerial photographs accessible in Google Earth and Google Maps (see Wise, 2015). During interviews, people will be asked to locate places that engage in recreational and leisure activity: in this way, it is possible to develop a sense of how people are using new facilities or amenities. Wise (2015) used this technique to address place-making to understand how we can spatially reference a sense of community and socialization patterns. We will also use Chalip's (2006) conceptualizations in detail as a guidance to understand social leveraging, which will aid comprehension of community involvement and pride in place. The focus on experience, opportunities and involvement, to be assessed in Phase 2, will be approached differently to put more emphasis on place, with more emphasis on sociability, comradeship and liminality.

Phase 4

Phase 4 addresses social legacy. The final three social conditions are considered in this part of the study: 12) venues and facilities are co-managed to support use by local residents; 13) legacy training and participation incentives for locals; and 14) local population is aware of legacy agendas and benefits. Smith (2012) and Getz (2013) outlined legacy initiatives. Legacy is difficult to measure because legacies are proposed. Impacts and results of legacies are especially difficult to measure and need to be periodically examined in years following the event or development activity. The notion of legacy involves understanding what plans or policies exist to inform and train locals to better understand the benefits and impacts of current or ongoing regeneration projects. For a destination to plan for a socially sustainable future, it is important that local residents need to be not only informed, but also involved in plans, decisions and future outcomes.

For the purpose of our work looking at sports tourism-led regeneration, numerous scholars have looked at major and mega-events (e.g. Agha et al., 2012; Richards et al., 2013; Pappalepore & Duignan, 2016). A key point discussed is if the regeneration is going to be successful, then local people need to be aware, informed and involved (see also Getz, 2013). However, legacy is very difficult to measure because we, as researchers, cannot truly measure if legacy initiatives are successful until five, sometimes ten, years after the event (Smith, 2012). Retrospective studies will determine if an event was successful, but in such early stages, we want to understand if local residents are aware of plans, and what part residents play in the ongoing transformation of their community. In some destinations (for instance, the United Kingdom and Germany), event and tourism planners put a lot of emphasis on legacy and include intended legacy when speaking to the general public. However, in Croatia, the situation is different, and we want to understand to what extent the local community is involved in future planning and strategy.

This phase will complete the first part of this longitudinal study. We do intend to extend the research beyond four years because legacy studies require a continuation of data collection. We anticipate changes in the literature, so after this stage of the research we will reassess changes in the literature, and implement accordingly to wider knowledge and directions observed in this study. Phases 2 and 3 focused on certain social conditions, and this final phase will rely on an open-ended survey and make a summative assessment of the conditions across the duration of this research with participants. Again, students will be involved in a similar manner as Phases 2 and 3, but the focus will be directed more towards legacy and they will assist with collection open-ended survey data. The survey will be developed based on themes that emerged throughout the research process. We are looking for further points of discussions to lead into another series of focus groups. For the focus groups, they will be conducted in a similar manner to Phase 1. We intend to refer back to social policy to understand how residents perceived or experienced any changes in policy, opportunities and involvement. The final two points of data collection will look across the data collected from the research participants' journal entries and summative open-ended survey. The focus groups will bring together any final queries that we left unexplored or open for interpretation in the findings.

Concluding remarks

The research approach outlined in this chapter goes beyond a critique of policy and economic impact assessment as covered in many of the studies discussed and referenced above. This project is concerned with community perspectives and will measure social impacts locally by conducting longitudinal research in situ. Conducting research over a period of time will allow us to pinpoint if and when communities achieve benefits from regeneration initiatives to grow tourism in the region. This research will include researchers and students working with local residents and communities to collect data. Our results aim to inform social policy and public sector planning techniques. The proposed study will take place over the next four years. Each year will be discussed as a different phase (Phases 1, 2, 3 and 4) to show how we plan to progress the research each year.

Because there has been substantial investment in sports tourism across Istria and the greater Pula region (which includes Medulin), it is important to understand reach across communities. Scoping activity has identified several cases and an assessment of social impacts will be conducted in an initial study over the next four years to understand early impacts following recent developments and new investments completed in the last several years. The goal is to extend the study and update the approach accordingly to shift the focus to mid- to longer-term social impacts after completing this first phase to extend the longitudinal focus of this impact study. As argued by Dwyer (2005), Chalip (2006) and Wise (2016), all too often (sport, event, tourism) impacts are assessed based on economic returns and a destination's income-generation. In response to this shift from short-term financially driven projects to a nascent policy agenda that focuses more on longer-term initiatives, it is increasingly important that we, as researchers, develop research strategies that practically address conditions that look at social impacts and well-being for communities and residents. Increasingly tourism stakeholders, officials and planners are concerned with measuring and managing impacts in an attempt to get local residents involved in tourism products and activities. Measuring and managing social impacts involve outlining and assessing what opportunities exist and locals can benefit.

To conclude, sports tourism is an industry that depends on its own resources, and a focus on transforming spaces for sport creates new opportunities for tourists and locals alike. No other industry's long-term economic success is so closely aligned with the success of local communities, specifically their well-being and involvement. Debates concerning regeneration impacts are ongoing, as budgets are tightened, especially in the public sector. As noted above, since the 1980s' private sector-led development has driven regeneration resulting in capital gains for investors, there is a need to identify wider societal impacts to understand how local people and communities benefit, or do not benefit, from regeneration. As this study develops, we will analyse previous, current and planned regeneration initiatives across the Istria Region of Croatia beyond Medulin.

References

Agha, N., Fairley, S., & Gibson, H. (2012). Considering legacy as a multi-dimensional construct: The legacy of the Olympic Games. *Sport Management Review, 15*, 125–139.

Altinay, L., Sigala, M., & Waligo, V. (2016). Social value creation through tourism enterprise. *Tourism Management, 54*, 404–417.

Atherley, K. (2006). Sport, localism and rural social capital in rural Western Australia. *Geographical Research, 44*, 348–360.

Bocken, N. M. P., Rana, P., & Short, S. (2015). Value mapping for sustainable business thinking. *Journal of Industrial and Production Engineering, 32*, 67–81.

Chalip, L. (2006). Towards social leverage of sport events. *Journal of Sport & Tourism, 11*, 109–127.

Chalkley, B., & Essex, S. (1999). Urban development through hosting international events: A history of the Olympic Games. *Planning Perspectives, 14*, 369–394.

Clark, J., & Kearns, A. (2015). Pathways to a physical activity legacy: Assessing the regeneration potential of multi-sport events using a prospective approach. *Local Economy, 30*, 888–909.

Clark, J., Kearns, A., & Cleland, C. (2016). Spatial scale, time and process in mega-events: The complexity of host community perspectives on neighbourhood change. *Cities, 53*, 87–97.

Deery, M., Jago, L., & Fredline, L. (2012). Rethinking social impacts of tourism research: A new research agenda. *Tourism Management, 33*, 64–73.

Dwyer, L. (2005). Relevance of triple bottom line reporting to achievement of sustainable tourism: A scoping study. *Tourism Review International, 9*, 79–93.

Edgell, D. L., & Swanson, J. R. (2013). *Tourism policy and planning: Yesterday, today and tomorrow*. London: Routledge.

Edwards, M. B. (2015). The role of sport in community capacity building: An examination of sport for development research and practice. *Sport Management Review, 18*, 6–19.

Ehn, B., Löfgren, O., & Wilk, R. (2016). *Exploring everyday life: Strategies for ethnography and cultural analysis*. New York: Rowman & Littlefield.

Evans, G. (2001). *Cultural planning: An urban renaissance*. London: Routledge.

García, B. (2005). Deconstructing the City of Culture: The long-term cultural legacies of Glasgow 1990. *Urban Studies, 42*, 841–868.

Getz, D. (2003). Sport event tourism: Planning, development and marketing. In S. Hudson (Ed.), *Sport and adventure tourism* (pp. 49–85). New York: Haworth Hospitality Press.

Getz, D. (2013). *Event tourism*. Putnam Valley, NY: Cognizant Communication Corporation.

Gratton, C., & Henry, I. (2001). *Sport in the city: The role of sport in economic and social regeneration*. London: Routledge.

Hall, C. M. (2006). Urban entrepreneurship, corporate interests and sports mega-events: The thin policies of competitiveness within the hard outcomes of neoliberalism. *The Sociological Review, 54*, 59–70.

Harrill, R. (2004). Residents' attitudes toward tourism development: A literature review with implications for tourism planning. *Journal of Planning Literature, 18*, 251–266.

Higgins-Desbiolles, F. (2011). Resisting the hegemony of the market: Reclaiming the social capacities of tourism. In S. McCabe, L. Minnaert, & A. Diekmann (Eds.), *Social tourism in Europe: Theory and practice* (pp. 53–68). Bristol: Channel View Publications.

Kim, K., Uysal, M., & Sirgy, M. J. (2013). How does tourism in a community impact the quality of life of community residents? *Tourism Management, 36*, 527–540.

Matheson, C. M. (2010). Legacy planning, regeneration and events: The Glasgow Commonwealth Games. *Local Economy*, 25, 10–23.

McLennan, C. J., Pham, T. D., Ruhanen, L., Ritchie, B. W., & Moyle, B. (2012). Counterfactual scenario planning for long-range sustainable local-level tourism transformation. *Journal of Sustainable Tourism*, *20*, 801–822.

McMillan, D., & Chavis, D. (1986). Sense of community: A definition and theory. *Journal of Community Psychology*, *14*, 6–23.

Mooney, G., McCall, V., & Paton, K. (2015). Exploring the use of large sporting events in the post-crash, post-welfare city: A 'legacy' of increasing insecurity? *Local Economy*, *30*, 910–924.

Mulec, I., & Wise, N. (2013). Indicating the competitiveness of Serbia's Vojvodina Region as an emerging tourism destination. *Tourism Management Perspectives*, *8*, 68–79.

Naidoo, P., & Sharpley, R. (2016). Local perceptions of the relative contributions of enclave tourism and agritourism to community well-being: The case of Mauritius. *Journal of Destination Marketing & Management*, *5*, 16–25.

Ortlipp, M. (2008). Keeping and using reflective journals in the qualitative research process. *The Qualitative Report*, *13*, 695–705.

Pappalepore, I., & Duignan, M. B. (2016). The London 2012 cultural programme: A consideration of Olympic impacts and legacies for small creative organisations in east London. *Tourism Management*, *54*, 344–355.

Perić, M., & Wise, N. (2015). Understanding the delivery of experience: Conceptualising business models and sports tourism, assessing two case studies in Istria, Croatia. *Local Economy*, *30*, 1000–1016.

Preuss, H. (2007). *The impact and evaluation of major sporting events*. London: Routledge.

Putnam, R. (2000). *Bowling alone: The collapse and revival of American community*. New York: Simon & Schuster.

Quinn, B., & Wilks, L. (2013). Festival connections: People, place and social capital. In G. Richards, M. P. de Brito, & L. Wilks (Eds.), *Exploring the social impacts of events* (pp. 15–30). London: Routledge.

Richards, G., de Brito, M. P., & Wilks, L. (Eds.). (2013). *Exploring the social impacts of events*. London: Routledge.

Rose, G. (1995). Place and identity: A sense of place. In D. Massey & P. Jess (Eds.), *A place in the world* (pp. 87–132). Oxford: Oxford University Press.

Smith, A. (2009). Theorising the relationship between major sport events and social sustainability. *Journal of Sport & Tourism*, *14*, 109–120.

Smith, A. (2012). *Events and urban regeneration*. London: Routledge.

Spirou, C. (2010). *Urban tourism and urban change*. London: Routledge.

Stubbs, W., & Cocklin, C. (2008). Conceptualizing a "sustainability business model". *Organization & Environment*, *21*, 103–127.

Waitt, G., & Gibson, C. (2009). Creative small cities: Rethinking the creative economy in place. *Urban Studies*, *46*, 1223–1246.

Weed, M. (2007). Editorial: Event sports tourism. *Journal of Sport & Tourism*, 12, 1–4.

Wise, N. (2015). Placing sense of community. *Journal of Community Psychology*, *43*, 920–929.

Wise, N. (2016). Outlining triple bottom line contexts in urban tourism regeneration. *Cities*, *53*, 30–34.

Wise, N., & Perić, M. (2017). Sports tourism, regeneration and social impacts: New opportunities and directions for research, the case of Medulin, Croatia. In N. Bellini &

C. Pasquinelli (Eds.), *Tourism in the city: Towards and integrative on urban tourism* (pp. 311–320). Berlin: Springer Vieweg.

Wise, N., & Whittam, G. (2015). Editorial: Regeneration, enterprise, sport and tourism. *Local Economy, 30*, 867–870.

Wise, N., Perić, M., & Armenski, T. (2017). The role of sports tourism and events to regenerate and sustain off-season tourism in Istria, Croatia: Addressing perspectives from industry managers and planners. In N. Wise & J. Harris (Eds.), *Sport, events, tourism and regeneration.* London: Routledge.

Yen, I., & Kerstetter, D. (2009). Tourism impacts, attitudes and behavioral intentions. *Tourism Analysis, 13*, 545–564.

Zhao, W., Ritchie, J. R. B., & Echtner, C. M. (2011). Social capital and tourism entrepreneurship. *Annals of Tourism Research, 38*, 1570–1593.

Conclusion

Research directions going forward

Julie Clark and Nicholas Wise

The fundamental achievement of this book is to look beyond the physical aspects of change by focusing upon who is affected by urban transformation agendas, as authors examine how both people and place are changed by policy and planning decisions.

The 12 chapters in the volume have explored a range of perspectives, approaches and cases, addressing different dimensions of process and outcome as urban spaces are reclaimed, reused and recreated. We hope that the collection will be particularly useful to people active in the fields of urban geography, urban studies and regional studies because it challenges scholars, students, planners and policymakers alike to think critically about place, policy and practice in relation to the geographies of urban renewal and creative change.

While the specifics of each case are unique, embedded within distinctive social, economic and political structures, alongside their own cultural and historical context, thematic connections with wide relevance have emerged across the chapters. There are numerous critical perspectives engaging with the concepts of inclusion and exclusion in relation to the planning and practice of urban transformation. Changes to the built environment demonstrate that renewed spaces are frequently orientated towards new uses, created for new people as well as new purposes. The chapters in this collection interrogate the ways in which our understanding of the past can inspire or inhibit our ability to imagine urban futures, urging policymakers to recognize the complexity of the urban world and think about how interventions fit local needs.

Places are often transformed based on ambitions to generate demand from business, consumers and private owners, without thought for inclusive strategies that aim to generate a sense of community among *all* urban residents. Urban renewal can create sheltered islands (Cowan, 2016) that allow access for those with the necessary means to (economically) survive or spend accordingly. The crucial role of governance and planning systems in securing a just distribution of resources is also investigated; even policies intended to mitigate the impacts of deindustrialization can favour economic development over environmental justice, if not carefully designed and monitored. The different scales at which decisions are taken and impacts are experienced form a recurrent theme, highlighting the need for social, political and financial mechanisms to ameliorate inequalities and ensure that all community voices are heard and respected. Creating an environment that supports empowered citizens and is more amenable to democratic participation can result in better long-term decision-making.

Carefully targeted planning interventions can be used to foster liveable and amenity-rich urban environments, which can contribute to community-building and the integration of migrant populations. However, neoliberal 'competitive city' policies represent a destructive force for urban residents who lack power and influence (Fraser, 2004). Operating at regional and city scale, we have also seen how insensitive urban strategic planning and infrastructure development can threaten rather than support place, identity and community. Planning for change, along with decision-making in relation to process, is initiated and undertaken by, necessarily, interested stakeholders. Whether these are politicians, public officials or private investors, it is easier to build a coalition around a new tangible edifice or increased profits and tax revenues than around intangible benefits, such as supporting social cohesion and increasing local social capital. However, renewal projects are targeted towards specific areas or neighbourhoods in cities. Gentrification, new sports and cultural venues or high-end residential complexes do not remedy social problems or cure urban ills. Those residents who are economically displaced by renewal and creative change do not see their problems solved – they see their problems relocated.

This volume also emphasizes the value of a theoretically grounded overview of who and what our urban spaces are for, stressing the importance of local people and diverse voices in the place-making process. Beyond flagship urban projects, authors identify the quality and management of housing and public space at neighbourhood level as no less important or contested territory, where we can mitigate rather than exacerbate inequalities. Where urban interventions are purely market-driven, conforming to the neoliberal hegemony, transformation and renewal produce only particular types of change. Investment in both physical and social infrastructure is needed to achieve *community* renewal and, alongside social mixing initiatives, innovative approaches to housing finance can reduce the tenure divide and support community integration. As critical thinkers in geography have noted (e.g. Agnew, 1987; Lefebvre, 1991; Mitchell, 2003; Soja, 2010; Harvey, 2012), when policies are driven by politics of power and exclusion, what we see at the surface only tells one part of the story. Theory can have a generative function, opening up new possibilities for action. By attending to the plurality of different experiences, planning research agendas that interact with all stakeholders throughout processes of urban change, we can aspire to engage with as well as evaluate policy, advocating inclusive practice.

Geographers will continue to examine and critique the forces that shape our cities, integrating existing epistemological debates into practice, and deploying both traditional and new methodological approaches to understand the world around us. Contributors have engaged with a range of methods, spatial analysis, theoretical reflection and more to identify the hidden effects of urban transformation, suggesting directions for more inclusive social and economic urban policies. The initiatives put forward and carried out by public and private policymakers tell only one part of the renewal narrative, and we can pursue innovative approaches and new technologies to move forward both inductive and deductive research agendas. We need research that tells the story of renewal from the perspectives of those who witness and are impacted by change first hand. This edited collection challenges scholars to continue conducting research that not only works to inform knowledge but also to serve community members who want to tell, and shape, their own stories of urban transformation.

References

Agnew, J. (1987). *Place and politics*. Winchester, MA: Allen and Unwin.

Cowan, A. (2016). *A nice place to visit: Tourism and urban revitalization in the postwar Rustbelt*. Philadelphia, PA: Temple University Press.

Fraser, J. (2004). Beyond gentrification: Mobilizing communities and claiming space. *Urban Geography, 25*, 437–457.

Harvey, D. (2012) *Rebel cities: From the right to the city to the urban revolution*. New York: Verso Books.

Lefebvre, H. (1991). *The production of space*. Oxford: Blackwell.

Mitchell, D. (2003). *The right to the city: Social justice and the fight for public space*. New York: Guilford Press.

Soja, E. (2010). *Seeking spatial justice*. Minneapolis: University of Minnesota Press.

Index

Page numbers in *italics* refer to figures; those in **bold** refer to tables.

Taylor & Francis eBooks

Helping you to choose the right eBooks for your Library

Add Routledge titles to your library's digital collection today. Taylor and Francis ebooks contains over 50,000 titles in the Humanities, Social Sciences, Behavioural Sciences, Built Environment and Law.

Choose from a range of subject packages or create your own!

Benefits for you

>> Free MARC records
>> COUNTER-compliant usage statistics
>> Flexible purchase and pricing options
>> All titles DRM-free.

Benefits for your user

>> Off-site, anytime access via Athens or referring URL
>> Print or copy pages or chapters
>> Full content search
>> Bookmark, highlight and annotate text
>> Access to thousands of pages of quality research at the click of a button.

REQUEST YOUR FREE INSTITUTIONAL TRIAL TODAY

Free Trials Available
We offer free trials to qualifying academic, corporate and government customers.

eCollections – Choose from over 30 subject eCollections, including:

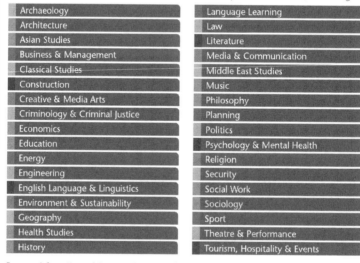

Archaeology	Language Learning
Architecture	Law
Asian Studies	Literature
Business & Management	Media & Communication
Classical Studies	Middle East Studies
Construction	Music
Creative & Media Arts	Philosophy
Criminology & Criminal Justice	Planning
Economics	Politics
Education	Psychology & Mental Health
Energy	Religion
Engineering	Security
English Language & Linguistics	Social Work
Environment & Sustainability	Sociology
Geography	Sport
Health Studies	Theatre & Performance
History	Tourism, Hospitality & Events

For more information, pricing enquiries or to order a free trial, please contact your local sales team: www.tandfebooks.com/page/sales